Christian Unity in Northeast India

Christian Unity in Northeast India

Challenges and Prospects

Bendangtemjen

Christian World Imprints

Edition: 2022

Christian World Imprints
Christian Publishing & Books from India
C-3, Shop No. 14, Ground Floor
Wazirpur Industrial Area, **Delhi-110052**
cwidelhi2017@gmail.com
www.ChristianWorldImprints.com
Phone: +91 11 41526079

ISBN: 978-93-5148-402-8 (HB)
ISBN: 978-93-5148-403-5 (PB)

Printed in India.

Contents

Foreword

The book "Christian Unity in Northeast India: Challenges and Prospects" is a wonderful and unique book, very essential for all the Christians to read and learn history of Christian Unity in Northeast India. The author has done an excellent work by making historical analysis method to carry on the discussion on Christian unity in Northeast churches. The Unity of divided churches has become an important principle in the life of the Christians at this present generation. This historical attempt has been very meaningful and significant in the present context of Northeast India. Because it appears that most of the Christians in the region are still not aware of what is Christian unity. Although, people at the theological circle are well informed about what is Christian unity, but the larger number of people is not yet awakened to what is going on. Therefore, such research work will provide proper education at grass root level so that the people will respond favourably on to it. It will also help in creating new awareness and a wider ecumenical vision to the church leaders as well as local churches about the importance of Christian unity.

The researcher has intensively explored some of the existing church union models, which would be helpful to give a possible Christian unity structure that could be considered by the churches in Northeast. While exploring the possible model, the efforts were made to attempt the challenges to the life and witness of the churches in the region, in which certain common concern projects such as, mission and evangelism, education and literature, and other social activities may be taken up in joint venture.

The important discussions in the book includes general views of the people on church unions in North East India, Baptist Beliefs and the emergence of Christian missions, historical formation and negotiation of church unions in NEI, exploration of the challenges of church union movement to the Baptists in NEI, and how CBCNEI withdrew its decision to the formation of Church of North East India (CNEI) proposal. It also discusses how then CBCNEI is now a full member of the World Council of Churches (WCC) since June 2016. Finally it discusses on the challenges to the life and witness of the churches in North East India.

The author's concern is that, the understanding of Christian unity need to shift from church centeredness to people centered. This means that the kingdom of God could not be limited to the expressions of the Christian community alone. The concerns of Christian unity had to be widening integrally that involved justice, peace and concern of all creation. As such Christian unity is not for its own sake, but for the sake of the world and its integrity for whole creation. This will shape the new ecumenical calling of the Baptist churches in Northeast India.

If one wants to learn more about the importance of ecumenical relations then this is the right book one must read. It is meant for pastors, theological teachers, church leaders and for all Christians. I send my best wishes and appreciation to Rev. Dr Bendangtemjen, for bringing out such a scholarly book.

Rev. Dr Solomon Rongpi
General Secretary
Council of Baptist Churches in North East India (CBCNEI)
Guwahati, Assam

Acknowledgement

In publishing this book, first of all I give thanks to the Almighty God, who has strengthened, inspired and guided me throughout my research work and by whose enduring love I could complete this book.

I extend my heartfelt gratitude and thanks to CSAR (A Collaboration of Scholars Leader International, Theological Book Network and South Asia Institute of Advanced Christian Studies, Bangalore that facilitates Research by Helping Scholars to produce articles, academic books and resources for advance theological education in South Asia) for giving me the opportunity and resources to write this book with a kind scholarship and hospitality. I am indebted to the Senate of Serampore for giving me permission to publish my doctoral dissertation, which is partly published in this book.

I owe my humble gratitude to Rev. Dr Solomon Rongpi, General Secretary, Council of Baptist Churches in North East India (CBCNEI), for writing the foreword of this book. I also want to express my thanks to Dr. Elizabeth Varghese former English Professor at CMS College, Kottayam, and Dr Pearly Jacob, HOD Management Studies & Placement Coordinator at St. Aloysius College, Jabalpur, MP, for their willingness to correct the language in my book. Without which it would not have been possible to bring out into this form.

Also thanks to Prof. O. L Snaitang and Fr Dr T. I. Varghese, for their encouragement, suggestions that shaped my thoughts with their scholarly advice and contributions without which the completion of this book will not be possible. A special note of appreciation to Rev. Luen Jamir, Rev. Dr Moanaro, Rev. Dr Vanlalnghaka Ralte, Mr Toshitemjen Aier, Rev. R. Vanlaltluanga, whose creative suggestions and inputs sharpened my thoughts during the writings of my book. I am grateful to Christian World Imprints for their kind gesture and promptness to publish this book.

I am much indebted and grateful to my children Etenla Jamir, Taienla Jamir, Loren Jamir and my wife Dr Bendanglemla Longkumer, and also all our family members and relatives for their constant prayer, encouragement, correction, understanding and always standing with me. I wish to express sincere thanks to all those who have been the source of inspiration and support behind the completion of this work.

Special thanks and gratitude to the Library staffs of SAIACS, Bangalore; Orthodox Theological Seminary, Kottayam; Mar Thoma Theological Seminary, Kottayam; Kerala United Theological Seminary, Thiruvananthapuram; United Theological College, Bangalore; Eastern Theological College, Jorhat, Assam; CBCNEI Office, Panbazar, Guwahati; NEICC Office, Shillong, Mokokchung Town Ao Baptist Church Library and Clark Theological College Library, Mokokchung, for allowing me to access all the available materials for my work.

Lastly, being the first edition, I welcome suggestions and comments from the readers, that would help me to improve on my further research. It is my humble prayer that the book will be helpful to those who seeks for the unity of the church.

Introduction

The question of Christian unity is a pertinent question in today's situation. It is important to note that whenever we discuss the question of Christian unity we are not simply talking about a sociological convenience. In fact, we are responding to the demands of a theological mandate: the Christian proclamation that God is, God demands that we name the various idolatries that sway us away from our singular commitment to God. Most of our divisions have resulted from distinctiveness to the truths and understandings, and thus a divided church stands under the judgment of God, the God of the whole universe. Thus, the mystery which as Christians we hold dear and precious invites us to mourn sincerely our divisions and seriously seek ways to express our unity which is grounded in our commitment to the Lordship of Jesus Christ.

All these are difficult but important questions; the future of Christian Unity in Northeast India depends on our willingness to face them with utmost seriousness. They show how in the global church we need each other, we teach each other and we learn from each other. This openness makes it possible that we will one day find the unity which is so desirable in region of multi-cultural distinctiveness.

Northeast India's distinctiveness and its beauty lie with its natural components which celebrates the goodness and greatness of the merciful God who cares for His world, His church and His children. When we look around we see, how God unfolds His master plan and intensely care for His people, church and world to live in unity and harmony in the midst of its diversity. With such backdrops when we look at the settings of Northeast region, it is distinctive of being independent in geographical and political unit from the beginning of its existence. Northeast is distinctive feature of being a heterogeneous mass of population representing people of great diversity in terms of ethnic components, linguistic affinity and lifestyle, with many divisive elements based on geographical isolation. This mixed people came into this region from different directions at different times and inhabited the different areas ranging from hills of the Himalayan ranges down to the plains of the Brahmaputra valley. Each of the many small tribes has traditionally lived in isolation from the others. In addition to and owing to their uncommon history of origins, the people's long settlement in the region resulted in the rise and development of autonomous and independent cultural strands even among the homogenous groups.[1] Therefore their culture, religion, tradition, history, philosophy, politics and social living are entirely different from the rest of Indians.

There have been great socio-cultural and political diversities. The people in the plains areas are historically ruled by Rajas, whereas the hills tribals traditionally had a more democratic polity. In many of the hills area each village was a state unto itself, being subject to no other village. Hence, NEI contains many divisive elements based on topographic settings like, tribal identity, language, culture, religion and political system. Christianity was introduced into this region by different denominational missionaries with different historical settings like Roman Catholic, Presbyterian, Baptist, Anglican etc. The general character of the people in the hill is of self-dependence and hence when they embraced Christian religion they did not depend on the missionaries but stood by themselves. Having such Christian background, the development of Christian unity among the existing Christian community happens to be very essential in the region.

The idea of Christian Unity became so evident and many churches began to show interest on the Christian Unity beginning from 1910 missionary conference. The form and structure of Christian Unity, which was carried out by the various organizations and churches are of different forms. Subsequently, such idea of Christian Unity had its impact even on the churches in NEI, particularly among the protestant churches but it could not develop further. The Christian unity in the North East India which was initiated in 1926, turned to be a failure basically because of the particular nature of negative attitude shown towards it from the Baptist Church there. Causes for such attitude are theological and non-theological factors. Hence, an essential change in attitude is required from the part of the Baptist Church, after a thorough and serious consideration of all challenges, which are hindering the progress of the Christian Unity.

The study is important in order to understand the nature and problems that obstruct the formation of Christian Unity in NEI, particularly it will assess the attitude of the Baptist Church towards the Christian Unity. The research is an attempt to look forward to the possible Unity, which should form a viable Christian Unity in future. It will also help in creating new awareness and a wider ecumenical re-visioning to the church leaders as well as common people about the importance of unity.

---

[1] O. L. Snaitang, "Development of the Ecumenical Movement in Northeast India," *Indian Church History Review*, XXXVII/1 (June, 2003): 42.

This study is conducted from a historical methodology of Christian Unity, limiting to the Northeast India Christian Council in Northeast region. The year 1926 marks the beginning of discussions on Church Unity in the region under the banner of ACC/NEICC (Assam Christian Council/North East India Christian Council). Therefore, the period of study is limited to the year since 1926 to the present. Owing to the vastness and the complexity of the subject area undertaken in terms of its geographical location and issue, the study here is limited to the Baptist Church under the Council of Baptist Churches in North East India (CBCNEI), even though references to the Protestant Churches, Roman Catholic and others are vaguely supplemented.

So far, no detail research has been done on this specific problem from the Baptist perspectives. However, there have been studies that have bearing on the subject in microforms. These includes F. S. Dawns, "Tribal Ecumenism in North East India: The Christian Role in Solidarity Movements" in *Good News For North East India: A Theological Reader* (edited by Renthy Keitzar. Panbazar, Guwahati: CLC, 1995); Frederick S. Down, *Church Union: Theological and Non-Theological Factors* (Shillong: The Church Union Committee of the NEICC, 1965); Jyrwa, J. Fortis "Church Union Movement in North East India: A Historical Prespective" in *Church Ministry and Mission: Easy in Honour of K. I. Aier* (edited by Renthy Keitzar. Panbazar, Guwahati: CBCNEI, 1988); O. L. Snaitang, "Development of the Ecumenical Movement in Northeast India" in *India Church History Review* Vol. XXXVII, No. 1 (June 2003), and "Ecumenism and Hill People's Culture in North-East India" in *Journal of Tribal Studies* Vol. II, No. 1 (January-June, 1998); Stafford E. Papers, "A Brief Report of the Church Union Consultation" (Unpublished Manuscript CBCNEI Office, Panbazar, Guwahati, 1971); Vanlalchhuanawma. "An Appraisal of Church Union Movement in Northeast India" in *Presbyterian Review* Vol. IX, No. 33 (January – March, 2003); Aier Toshi, "Church Union Movement in North East India: A Reflection" in *Perspectives: Current Issues in Theological Thinking* (edited by Akheto Sume. Aolijen, Mokokchung: Jongshinokdang Trust, CTC, 2002); T. Likok, *A Picture of an Organic Church Union* (Impur: ABAM, 1975); M. Thongkhosei Haokip, *A History of Ecumenical Movement in North East India* (ISPCK/CCA, 2015). As mentioned above no concrete study has been done on the Baptists attitude towards the Christian Unity in North East India. The available articles in some edited books and journals do not deal with the subject in a serious manner but give descriptions of the church union negotiation in the region.

Sources for this study include primary as well as secondary data. Reliable primary source materials were from the proceedings of the Assam Christian Council, North East India Christian Council and reports and minutes from various Synods and Associations like, Ao Baptist Church Association, South Mizoram Baptist Association and the like in the region are made use of. It also includes sources like American Baptist Mission reports, missionary letters both published and unpublished mostly available at the archives of CBCNEI, Guwahati; Eastern Theological College Library; UTC Library; North East India Christian Council Office, Shillong and Nokten Memorial Library, Impur, Nagaland. The secondary sources include writings on this subject by native scholars as well as Western missionaries. Unpublished papers, Seminar papers, Souvenirs, Periodical and Journals unpublished are made use of as important source of information in this study. Besides, materials are also drawn from personal interviews and enquiries with the local congregation as well as church leaders from different level.

The structure of this research is divided into eight chapters with general introduction and conclusion. It begins with an introduction, which provides a description of the problem to be investigated. It also contains the hypothesis, elaboration of the problem, purpose of study, scope and limitation, and the description of the structural sequence of the study.

Chapter one examines the historicity of the origin and development of the Christian mission in NEI during nineteenth and twentieth centuries. The main focuses in this parts is to deals with the historical analysis of the origins and development of the arrival of Christian mission in North East India. It provides an important overview of how each denomination emerged with its theology and distinctiveness. Chapter two examines the meaning and the various concepts of Ecumenism that was development among the churches in different nations. Chapter three contains the main thrust of the study, which examines the formation and further discussions of the Christian Unity in the Northeast India and to why this church union could not achieve as what they are intended when the council was formed.

Chapter four explores the challenges of Christian Unity before the Baptist Church in Northeast India. The challenges are from both theological and non theological factors. No doubt there are various theological issues which divide the Christian Unity discussion and also there are some area causing hindrances, which does not belong directly to theological differences, but which springs from some other cause like geographical isolation, socio-cultural and linguistic differences etc. will also be examine. Fifth chapter discusses the CBCNEI attitude towards the Christian Unity and then how CBCNEI is now a full member of the World Council of Churches.

Chapters six searches for a viable model of Christian Unity that draws a possible solution against the challenges of Church Union Movement in NEI. This chapter explores some of the existing church union models, to pick up viable model of church unity by doing some survey, which would be a helpful to give a possible church union structure which could be consideration to the churches in NEI. Chapter seven deals with the challenges to the life and witness of the churches in the region, in which certain common concern projects such as, mission and evangelism, education and literature, and other social activities, may be taken up in joint venture. Collaboration in such common projects will enhance a new sense of unity and fellowship to one another while recognizing the cooperation to endeavor a successful church union discussion in Northeast India in future. The basic focus in final chapter is to analyse that our understandings of the nature of the unity we seek have shifted in recent years moving from an emphasis upon structural and institutional unity to one that finds its focus in relationships and cooperation centered in Jesus Christ. Therefore the understanding of Christian Unity needs to shift from church centeredness to people centered. The book ends with a conclusion, appendix and a bibliography.

Chapter 1

Christianity in Northeast India

INTRODUCTION

The coming of good news of Jesus Christ marked a new era in the life and history of the people in Northeast India (NEI). In the retrospective, the people of North Easterner's were rough but Christianity that came as an eyes opener for them. It is fact that Christianity emerged in Europe and America as a great force in the sixteen century or even later. Its impact on mission in India as well as Northeast region as elsewhere began to be felt only from the beginning of eighteen century. By the turn of the nineteenth and twentieth centuries both Protestant and Roman Catholic assumed a significant attempt. Therefore in the history of Christianity in NEI the nineteenth and twentieth centuries witnessed a tremendous growth and expansion of Christian mission. This chapter is an attempt to trace the history of the emergence of Christianity in NEI during nineteenth and twentieth centuries. During these period a number of Christian mission with different historical backgrounds were functioning in the region, which was equally diverse in historical, socio-economic and cultural heritage.

1.1. THE CONTEXT OF NORTHEAST INDIA

1.1.1. PHYSICAL FEATURE

Northeast India, through the ages, has been an integral part of the Indian sub-continent. But, at the same time, NEI is distinctive of being independent geographical and political entity from the beginning. Geographically, it is a sub-country in itself, which can be considered as geopolitical unit. The Northeast region has wide variation in physical, ranging from plains of Brahmaputra Valley to Meghalaya Plateau and the extended Himalayan Mountain ranges. It covers the total area of 2, 55,000 sq. km that has represented about 7.7% of the total geographic area of India. The people are distributed over 200 scheduled tribes.[2] It consists of 'seven sisters' or states,[3] and newly joined states of Sikkim. With the inclusion of Sikkim now it is designated as Northeastern India or Eastern India. It is bound by China and Bhutan in the north, Myanmar in the south east and Bangladesh in the south west.[4] They belong to different ethnic and linguistic backgrounds. However, the majority of the people in Northeast are a distinct ethnical stock of Mongoloid race that migrated to the present compact areas from South-East Asia probably through Myanmar.

A larger part of the population of this region is made up of tribal people. Though the tribal people of NEI differ among themselves in many ways like linguistically, ethnically, culturally, socially and economically. However, all these states come under a political arena known as North Eastern Council (NEC), which came into being by an Act of Parliament in 1971 and started functioning from August 1972.[5] The region has internationally been connected with the rest of the country through a narrow corridor in North Bengal and its border with China and Bhutan in the North, Myanmar to the East and Bangladesh in the west.

1.1.2. SOCIO-CULTURAL BACKGROUND

The socio-cultural life of the people is extremely multifaceted. The people of the region can be roughly divided into two categories on the bases of geographical location. The first groups are plain's people, inhabiting the plains of Assam, Manipur and Tripura and were more or less Sanskritised[6] with the migration of the Aryans from North India.[7] The other groups who inhabited the hill areas are called Tribals. Evidently those groups were Mongoloid in their racial stock.[8] Minorities of these populations follow their traditional religions, whereas the majority of the tribals have followed Christianity.

---

[2] J. Puthenpurakal, *Impact of Christianity on North East India* (Shillong: Vendrame Institute Publications, 1996), xiii.

[3] Arunachal Pradesh, Assam, Nagaland, Meghalaya, Mizoram, Manipur, and Tripura.

[4] Amar Khrishna Paul, *Northeast A-Z General Knowledge* (Panbazar, Guwahati: Good Books Distributors Pub., 2003), 264-265. (Hereafter referred to as Paul, *Northeast A-Z …*).

[5] Amar Khrishna Paul, *Northeast A-Z …*, 265.

[6] K. Thanzauva, *Theology of Community: Tribal Theology in the Making* (Aizawl: Mizo Theological Conference, 1997), 12. (Hereafter referred to as Thanzauva, *Theology of Community…*).

[7] Frederick S. Downs, *Christianity in North East India: Historical Perspectives* (Guwahati: ISPCK, 1983), 5. (Hereafter referred to as Downs, *Christianity in NEI …*).

[8] Panger Imchen, *Ancient Ao Naga Religion and Culture* (New Delhi: Har-Anan Pub. 1993), 13.

The Northeasterners are comprised of people belonging to diverse geographic areas, tribal identity, language, culture and socio-political system, etc. These mixed people came into that region from different direction at different period. From the time of their migration each tribes had its own identifying marks in culture, beliefs, language and area of occupation. However, each tribe prefers to keep their own name like Ao-Naga, Mizo, Khasi, etc., to make themselves distinctive from other. Therefore various ethnic groups of the region have different dialects of their own languages.

Traditionally, the people of NEI have rich cultures, which varied from tribe to tribe. Each tribe has lived more or less in isolation from the others and each has its own distinct history, which is different from that of other tribes. These are not actually differences but rather 'distinctiveness:'[9] that's how each community is distinct in its own way. However the commonality of tribal societies within the region has their customary laws, beliefs and practices, which govern them. The social customs of matrimonial are distinct from each society that ranges from the patriarchal to the matrilineal. The majority of tribes had been practicing the patriarchal pattern, except Garos, Khasi-Jaintias follows matrilineal structure.

The most picturesque ingredients of the tribal social life were its dormitory system; *Zawlbuk* (in Mizoram), *Morung* (in Ao Nagas), *Nokpants* (in Garo), etc.[10] were practiced strictly for both young boys and girls to disciplines and to create a sense of self-sufficiency, fidelity and service to the society. The cultural practice of headhunting had been carried out prominently among the hill tribes. Because of such practice there was no peace, disunity, mistrust and it dominated the whole societies.[11] Such practice had dominated almost all the social life and that carried on from one generation to another. In the socio-cultural life religion played an important role in the life of the people, in their festivals, their agricultural and social celebrations. Some plains tribals group such as the Bodos, Kacharis mostly followed Hinduism, and a large number of tribals retained their religion, referred to as animism in which they worshipped one or more gods and propitiated several malevolent spirits and superstitious beliefs and practices. Such was the background into which Christian missions entered in the Northeast region.

1.1.3. POLITICAL BACKGROUND

The political set up of Northeast India differed from place to place. The hill tribes' administrative structure was ranging from chieftainship to egalitarian democracy,

---

[9] Renthy Keitzar, "A Study of the North-East India Tribal Christian Theology," in *Good News for North East India,* edited by Renthy Keitzar (Panbazar, Guwahati: CLC, 1995), 32.

[10] Renthy Keitzar, "Tribal Cultural Ethos and Christianity in North East India," *ETC Journal,* Vol. II (1988), 48.

[11] Wati Longchar, "Headhunting: A Socio-Religious Factor for Oppression of Women in North East India," in *Good News for the North East India: A Theological Reader,* edited by Renthy Keitzar (Panbazar, Guwahati: CLC, 1995), 198.

whereas the plain areas were ruled by king or rajas. In many tribal areas the village was an autonomous unit, a kind of village state, which was often in conflict with neighboring villages of the same tribe. During early 18th century, the *Ahom*[12] *monarchy was extended to both the plains and hills. But not long after the rule of Ahom* kingdom gradually declined and the Burmese Kings occasionally controlled the land and subsequently it (state) was integrated into British India.[13] Before the British rule came in the Northeast India, the people living in this region were living an independent life. The village council was and is very strong and the whole matters regarding the administration are taken care of by the members of the village council. Anybody, who did not abide by the rules and regulations of the council, required heavy punishment. However, with the coming of civilization and modernization many changes have taken place in the political sphere.

The British appeared as a protector of Assam from the Burmese and reinstated her dynasty. Therefore, the British were called "the saviour of Assam."[14] This invasion led to British intervention and annexation of Assam into British territory, ratified by the Treaty of Yandabo,[15] on 24, Feb. 1826.[16] The one hundred year of British rule not only brought changes in the political and administrative system but also brought entire regions under their control. Some states were allowed to continue to be governed by their own chiefs/Rajas under a system known as indirect administration.

David Scott was put in charge of the British headquarters at Guwahati in 1826. Scott died in 1831 and Captain Francis Jenkins was appointed as commissioner and Agent to the Governor General of Bengal in Assam from 1834-1861.[17] He was the son of an English clergyman and had strong evangelical conviction. It was in response to a direct invitation from him that the first American Baptist missionaries came to Assam.

By 1842, when the British administered the entire tribes of NEI, they brought outsiders from Bengal, Bihar for administrative work. Their (British) venturing into Hill Tribes was not with the intention to colonize but with the sole

---

[12] The *Ahoms* were originally a *Shan* tribe who wandered into Bramaputra valley from Mayanmar. The origin of assimilation may be trace back to the coming of *Ahoms* in about the year AD 1226. And the *Ahoms* kingdom in Assam was a tribal kingdom.

[13] B. B. Goswami, "The Tribes of Assam: A Few Comments on their Social and Cultural Ties with the Non-Tribes," in *Tribal Situations in India*, edited by S. K. Singh (Simla: Indian Institute of Advance Study, 1972), 273.

[14] H. K. Barpujari, *Problems of the Hill Tribes North East Frontier 1822-1844* (Guwahati: Lawyers Book Stall, 1970), 20.

[15] In Treaty of Yandabo, whereby the king of Burma signed and agreed to abstain from further interference in the affairs of Assam and hills region. The conclusion of the war left to British in control almost of Assam.

[16] Frederick S. Downs, *History of Christianity in India: North East India in the Nineteenth and Twentieth Centuries,* Vol. V, part 5 (Bangalore: CHAI, 1992), 16.

[17] Downs, *History of Christianity in India*, vol. V, part 5 ..., 23.

aim of safeguarding their economic interest in Assam. But, slowly they introduced their policy into the traditional culture in hills region and this had greatly affected the life of the people.[18]

In 1912 Assam administrative divisions were recognized and a new system of administration was introduced. The Naga Hills, North Cachar Hills, Garo Hills, Khasi-Jaintia Hills, Lushai Hills and the Mikir Hills formed five ordinary districts of the state, while the Northeast border area of Assam were put under the government of India to be administered by the government of Assam.[19] By 1914 almost all the regions were brought under the British administration. The government of India Act of 1919 did not change the policy of isolation but tried to define and determine the limits and extent of isolation. From this Act arose what were called 'Wholly excluded Areas' and 'Areas of Modified Exclusion'. On Nov. 8, 1927, Simon Commission was set up to examine the problem of further constitutional reform.[20]

Because of the sensitiveness of Northeast India as a border region with Burma, China and Bangladesh, restriction were made during the British regime to entry of outsiders to this region. Till today this is continued by the government of India to protect the borders from foreign intrusion. Often the Central government suspects a foreign hand in any agitation taking place in the North East India. Thus foreigners are very much restricted in this region. There emergence of many political movements in the region are due to various factors.[21] Those movements are Naga National Council (NNC), The Mize National Front (MNF), the Tripper National Volunteers (TNV), the National Socialist Council of Nagaland (NSCN), the Peoples Liberation Army of Manipur (PLAM), the People's Revolutionary Party of Kangleipak of Manipur (PREPAK), the All Assam Student Union (ASSU), the United Liberation Front of Assam (ULFA), All Bodo Students Movement (ABS), Karbi-Anglong Students Association (KSA), the Khasi Students Union (KSU), the North Cachar Barak Valley Students Union (NCVSU). The government of India calls these movements as Insurgent groups

---

[18] S. C. Jamir, "Nagaland - A Society in Transition," *Nagaland Post*, 14 Nov. 1997, 78.

[19] B. C. Chakravorty, *British Relation with the Hills Tribes of Assam Since 1858* (Calcutta: Firma KLM Pvt. Ltd., 1981), 173.

[20] Thanzauva, *Theology of Community* ..., 20.

[21] In the case of the rise Naga National movement, V. Sanyu, give two factors: Firstly, the Nagas are perhaps the first indigenous group in Asia to conceive of an ideology to transform this tribal polity into a modern nation state on par with the concept of sovereignty. Secondly, the Nagas claim that Nagaland was never part of Burma or India and the question of secession does not arise. From the Naga perspective, their national struggle is a war of resistance against invasion not an "insurgency" against a previously established authority. Ref. Visier Sanyu, "The Nagas in the 1st half of the 20th Century" in *From Darkness to Light*, edited by Nagaland Baptist Church Council (Kohima, NBCC, 1997), 153-154.

and mishandles the situation and people of the Northeastern states, which worsen the situations in many cases.[22]

The period of Indian independence was a vital stage of alteration for the NEI. Among the tribal leaders political consciousness was beginning to develop but was suppressed by the administrations. There was a quest for new identity and it was marked by the rise of insurgency, which remains one of the most scorching issues of the country.[23] Political unrest existed in almost the whole area of NEI. Political corruption, insurgency, intertribal feuds and feeling of being excluded created the instability in NEI. This was the milieu of social and political reality of NEI into which Christianity came. Whatever may be the grounds of the issue, this unstable situation was a clear indication for the failure of the political policy as well as the Church Union policy in NEI.

1.1.4. ECONOMIC STRUCTURE

The economic structure of the region centers on its ecological factors. The hills and valleys, the rivers and streams, the marshy and swampy tracts, high rainfall, unwholesome climate, the technological backwardness in the hills, the extension of the artisan and agrarian methods of Eastern India to the valley regions, the availability of the raw materials and adaptability of the craftsmen influenced the occupational patterns. In this region the village had been the backbone of the economic life of the people.[24]

Majority of the total population in the region live in rural areas where they are mainly engaged in agriculture. The rest are engaged in office work, teachings, business industries and the like. Among the hill tribes, however Jhum or shifting cultivation was the prevalent practice. The people were also craftsmen at leisure.[25] The extensive trade between the tribal villages and between the hills and plains in the region as well as with other countries like Bhutan, Tibet, China and Burma enabled the people to exchange their products through the prevalent barter system to balance the deficit of essential consumption. The economic condition of the region was nevertheless believed to be on the whole satisfactory.

1.1.5. RELIGIOUS MILIEU

Even before the advent of Christianity, the religion occupied a central place in the life of the people in Northeast India. The role of the religion in an individual's life is the prototype of the role of religion in the socio-cultural system of a people

---

[22] O. M. Rao, *Baptist Distinctives* (Panbazar, Guwahati: CLC, 1980), 2

[23] H. K. Sarun, *Insurgency in North East India: A Study of the Sino-American Role* (New Delhi: Sterling Pub. Pvt. Ltd., 1980), 5.

[24] S. C. Dutta, *The North East and the Mughals* (1661-1714) (Delhi: D.K. Publication, 1984), 6.

[25] Joseph S. Thong, *Glimpses of Naga Legacy and Culture*, edited by Phanenmo Kath (Kottayam: Spciety for Naga Students Welfare, Kerala, 1997), 165-166.

in general. One's religious philosophy guides and controls one's various activities and decides one's attitude to the political, social and cultural system. Religion in all these areas was and is in some areas, primitive animism or primal religion. Renthy Keitzar points out that "both the term primitive or primal religion do not precisely define the tribal religion and so it is better to call it as traditional religion."[26]

Assam, Manipur and Tripura are predominantly Hindu, some tribes like Khasi-Jaintia, Karbis and Arunachalis came under the influence of Hinduism and some of their people were Hinduised.[27] The traditional religion, be it Khasi, Naga, Mizo or any one of the others has all the basic features of religious beliefs, practices and moral teachings based on oral traditions and customs. Thus, the oral traditions and customs are accepted as authoritative or the faith and practice of the people. These can be carefully preserved and transmitted from one generation to another, even down to this day.[28] Therefore the traditional tribal religion of Northeast India in each case is a distinctive religion, having all the phenomenal aspects of a true religion.

Religious beliefs and concepts are expressed in the form of symbols and rituals that influence the individual and communicate one's attitude towards the world of nature and one's fellow beings. Thus, for most people of Northeast India, belief in Supreme Being or a High God for Ao-Naga called *Lichaba*[29] as distinctive features. He is also understood and believed as the Great Spirit. He is the creator and sustainer of humans and the whole universe, is believed to be loving and benevolent in contrast to the malevolent spirits. Besides their beliefs in Supreme Being, they also believe in many deities and spirits which are, however, secondary. The Supreme Being is worshipped by them and offerings are given to him in thanksgiving for blessings in the family and for great harvests. They trust him for protection and deliverance from evil spirits. Life does not end in death but continues to live on in the next world even after death and so they believe in immortality of the soul. All the religious duties and rites are performed by functionaries like the Lyngdoh (Khasi), Putir (Ao), Puthiam (Mizo), Kamal Nokma (Garo) and so on.[30] Their functions and institutions are regulated by

---

[26] Keitzar, *A Study of the North-East India Tribal Christian Theology* ..., 32.

[27] Keitzar, *A Study of the North-East India Tribal Christian Theology* ..., 33.

[28] Keitzar, *A Study of the North-East India Tribal Christian Theology* ..., 33-34.

[29] Ao-Naga believe in a god above all creature. *Lichaba* is believed to be the creator of the earth and everything therein. He is the lord of earth and he is regarded as having the greatest influence upon the earth and is responsible for natural calamities. He bestows blessings and inflicts punishment according to mans attitude towards him. A major ceremony is observed yearly to offer sacrifices and prays to him. *Lichaba*, the creator of the earth, remains under the earth and is responsible for everything that happens which is connected with the earth. He is considered to hold the earth between his two hands and so he is conscious of all events. Thus Ao-Nagas believed he is the highest or greatest god. Ref. Panger, *Ancient Ao Naga Religion and Culture* ..., 32-33.

[30] Keitzar, *A Study of the North-East India Tribal Christian Theology* ..., 34.

customary forms and formalities which have been preserved and transmitted by oral traditions from time immemorial.

Concept of sin and life after death in the traditional religion is very vague. According to British political agent T. C. Hudson and missionary J. N. D. Anderson, the life of tribal is remarkably free from lying and stealing as a general habit and adultery is a crime punished with a heavy fine according to their custom and law.[31] Traditional believes that Supreme Being is great god, worshipping him the soul may fine peace in heaven. They also believe that those who live a good life in this world will have a good life in another world. Thus, the religious milieu in the Northeast India during pre-Christianity was therefore quite complex, as seen in above brief descriptions.

1.2. THE ADVENT OF CHRISTIAN MISSION IN NORTHEAST INDIA

The genesis of Christianity in India had been argued, since the religion was introduced to the nation in the 1st Century CE. Depending on the available sources relating to the genesis of Christianity in India, western source namely the Acts of Thomas (AD c.180 – 230) which was written in the Syriac language, stated that St Thomas went to the Kingdom of Gudnaphar in North India. Archaeology finding found that the coin that bore the name of the King belong to the 1st Century.[32] On the other hand, an indigenous source namely the Malabar Oral Tradition stated that St Thomas came to India by passing through Socutra and landed in Cranganore in 52 AD. From there he went to preach among the Jews colonies in South India, converted the Brahmin and established seven churches in Kerala. These ancient communities attributed to the preaching of the apostle are at Cranganore, Palayur, Koottamangalam, Niranam, Quilon and Nilackal.[33] As a result, Christians in south India accredited to St. Thomas, who preached the first good news to different people and communities that shaped the life-style and form of liturgical worship of the ancient church in India.

The growth and development of European Empires in India started at the end of the 15th Century, when Vasco Da Gama, a Portuguese navigator discovered a sea route to India and landed at the Port of Calicut (now in Kerela), on the South-West coast of India, in 1498 has been an important feature of world history. Thus marked the colonial era in India that began in 1502, when the Portuguese Empire established the first European trading centre at Kollam, Kerala. In 1505 King Manuel I of Portugal appointed Dom Francisco de Almeida as the first Portuguese viceroy in India, followed in 1509 by Dom Afonso de Albuquerque. Since then, many Europeans powers like Portugal, France, Holland Denmark,

---

[31] Chiru, *American Baptist Mission: Integrating Agent of Nagas into Indian Union …*, 12.

[32] Cyril Bruce Firth, *An Introduction to India Church History* (Madras: The Christian Literature Society, 1961, reprinted 1992),

[33] Xavier Koodapuzha, *Christianity in India* (Kottayam: Oriental Institute of Religious Studies India, 1998), 33.

and Britain extended their imperialism and entered in the tussle of colonialism in consequence to their trade.[34]

1.2.1. EARLY CHRISTIAN CONTACT WITH NORTHEAST INDIA

Since its beginning in the 18th century, the Christian mission began to enjoy an impressive spiral of growth. The Christian mission sought to broaden its vision of spiritual need and quicken its effort in evangelistic outreach it even reached the extreme parts of Northeast India.

When we look at the documentary sources, it is intricate that Christianity entered the North Eastern Region of India even before British Colonization of India. Those missionaries were the two Jesuits, Fr. Stephen Cacella and Fr. John Gabral, who were looking for passages to Tibet, had turned to the Brahmaputra valley as early as 1626.[35] F S Downs, in his essay "*Rangamati: A Christian Community in North-East India during the 17th and 18th Centuries*" remarks that there are pastoral visits by the Augustinian and the Holy Cross priests to several Indo-Portuguese settlements at Rangamati located on the frontier of Bengal with Assam, Bondashill in Cachar and Mariamnagar in Tripura. For example, Bishop Laynes of Mylapore accompanied by Fr. Barbier called on the Rangamati settlers on the easternmost frontier of the Mughal Empire in 1714.[36] These visits however were infrequent and did not establish the Catholic influence in the region apart from their pastoral functions. In the matter of evangelization they had not done any extensive work in this region.

However, there was Christian Community at Rangamati,[37] (presently it is located at Goalpara District of Assam) which was the border of the Mogul territories with the *Ahom*[38] kingdom. They were either Christian soldiers or camp followers of the Mogul armies, who fought against the *Ahom* kingdom in between

[34] Koodapuzha, *Christianity in India* ..., 85-90

[35] Milton S. Sangma and David R. Syiemlieh, eds., *Essay on Christianity in North - East India* (New Delhi: Indus Pub. Co., 1994), 40.

[36] Frederick S. Downs, "Rangamati: A Christian Community in North-East India during the Seventeenth and Eighteenth centuries," *ICHR, Vol. XII, No.2* (Dec. 1978), 88-89.

[37] For a time during the eighteenth century there was a very large Christian community associated with the Moghul garrison at Rangamati in the present Goalpara district Assam. One source, dated 1862 says there were 7000 Christians there and in January 1715 Bishop F. T. Laynez of St. Tome-Mylapore confirmed one thousand persons during a three week visit according to a priest who accompanied him. British source may reference to what might have been the remnants of this garrison community living in Goalpara in the early nineteenth century but it eventually disappeared entirely. Ref. F.S. Downs, "Early Chrisitan contacts with North East India," *Indian Church History Review, Vol. V. No. 1* (June 1971), 70-71; "Rangamati: A Christian Community in North-East India during the Seventeenth and Eighteenth centuries," *ICHR, Vol. XII, No.2* (Dec. 1978), 88-89; C. Baker, *History of the Catholic Mission in North East India 1890-1915*, translated and edited by G. Stadir & S. Karotemprel (19980), 99-118.

[38] The *Ahoms* were originally a *Shan* tribe who wandered into Bramaputra valley from Mayanmar.

1662 and 1669.[39] At Bondashil in the Charchar district of Assam, evidence of a small Portuguese Catholic community, the remnant of Mughal army and a similar community at Mariamnagar in Agratala, all that remains of earlier Christian presence in the region can be found.[40] There is only a little fragmented evidence to prove that Christian community had lived in the region of Rangamati for a short period of time. However from the sudden appearance and disappearance of this community it can be implied that they were outsiders either Europeans or Indians. Whatever opinion we hold to testify, there is no doubt that a Christian community existed in Rangamati. Hence, it can be said that, the Catholics were the first among the Christian missions to have entered the region and they were operating in the region prior to the East India Company foundations of formal empire.

1.2.2. CHRISTIAN MISSION AND COLONIALISM

When expressed the onset of European Colonialism in India, it is strongly linked with the global extension of Christianity and its mission activities from the Western world. Since the dawn of the modern age, Colonialism and Christianity were tag together and became inter-reliant with each other as it these two terms are interrelated and signify the same meaning. Therefore, it so happened that the development of Christianity coincided, if not associated with the European colonialism leading to the argument and disagreement among historians and other social scientist as to the relation between Colonialism and Christianity. However, the focus here will be narrowing down to the British East India Company because it was British Colonizers who opened the way for Christian missionaries to do mission work in Northeast India.

1.2.2.1. THE BRITISH COLONIALISM IN INDIA

The British East India Company joined the fray in establishing their political power in India during the 17th Century and eventually emerged as the most powerful colonial power in India by the middle of 18th Century. By the beginning of the 19th Century, the British domination extended over a large part of the Indian sub-continent. The British East India Company primary concern was trade and commerce rather than religious activities. Naik and Syed stated in their book "*A Student's History of Education in India*" that in 1659 the Board of Directors of the British East India Company resolved that 'it was their earnest desire by all possible means to spread Christianity among the people of India an allowed missionaries to embark on their ships.'[41] In 1698, the British Parliament inserted the famous Missionary clause in the company's charter. This clause

[39] E. Gait, *A History of Assam* (Calcutta: Thacker Spink and Co. Ltd., 1905), 131.

[40] Downs, *History of Christianity* ..., 65.

[41] J. P Naik and Syed Nurullah, *A Student's History of Education in India*, (S.G. Wasani for Macmillan Company of India, 1974.

directed the company to maintain ministers of religion at their factories in India. The company had learnt to use Christian mission activities to its advantage whenever necessary. But, the scenario changed when the company emerged as a political and economic power in India by the end of the 18th Century that lead them to give less importance to the spread of Christianity and declared religious neutrality as their policy.

In 1823, Christian missionaries were given freedom for to work without license by the British parliament in India, yet the officials were indifferent and unreceptive to mission activities. This situation leads to ambivalent attitude in their treatment of Indian Christians, where Indian were excluded from military services, debarred from appointment in Government offices and lost the right to inherit their parent's property on account of their conversion to Christianity. In spite of this harsh prospect of the British East India Company, yet some British officials were extremely helpful to promote missions work, namely *Lord Wellesley* became the patron of the translation project of the William Carey in Bengal, *Lord William Bentinck* stood firmly for the rights of Indian Christians, *Lord Dalhousie* worked for the betterment of the people, *Colonel Munro* and *Colonel Macaulay* helped the Syrian Christians and were involved in bringing the Church Missionary Society mission of help to the Syrian Christians.

Many Christian missionaries enjoyed the protection and support from the British Government. Duncan B. Forrester in his book '*Truthful Action: Exploration in Practical Theology*' stated that 'the missionaries generally understood British's Rule as a providential ordering, a sign of God's care for India rather than simply an opportunity for the making of individual converts.'[42] (*Forrester: 2000*) Thus Christian missionaries provided a religious justification to European Colonialism in India and on the other hand, imperialism influenced their very act of evangelism and the theology of mission. This is represented in terms like campaign, stations, field, enforcement, etc., on which are pure imperialistic terms borrowed from imperialism. The nature of the British East India Colonial power was different from that of the Portuguese and other European Colonialists counterpart. Yet they did support the spread of Christianity in their Empire with much vigilance and judgment.

1.2.2.2. THE BRITISH COLONIALISM IN NORTHEAST INDIA

The British rule (Colonialism) and the Christianity existed in NEI as side by side therefore any research attempt on the beginning of Christian mission in North Eastern region without acknowledging the Colonial involvement, the research and scholarship will be one sided and incomplete and perhaps biased.

[42] Duncan B. Forrester, *Truthful Action: Exploration in Practical Theology*. Edinburgh: T & T, 2000.

The British East India Company had established its commercial connections with Assam in 1771.[43] The British policy was to capture the economic zone in Assam valley, which was under the Burmese possession. Accordingly the British declared war with the Burmese and the first Anglo Burmese war, which was ended with the signing of the Treaty of Yandavo[44] on Feb. 24, 1826.[45] Thus, the whole region was brought for first time into a political link with a major Indian power.[46] Since then the British administration had gradually expanded and started phase-wise annexation of all the self-ruling tribes. Assam was constituted as a separate chief commissioner province in 1874 with its headquarters in Shillong. Shillong served as the capital for the entire North Eastern states till the 1960s.[47]

The British had two opinion regards to deal with the hill tribes of Northeast from its inceptions. Some suggested that the need of educating them, so they plead His Excellency to give a grant for the Mission of civilization, so that they may be able to protect these tribals from raids in the plains and inter tribal wars among them. The other view was that these tribal people should be left entirely alone, except for military proofs to keep them under the control and prevent raids on the plains.[48] However in the initial stage the British officials were in favor of the evangelization in the region. Even some of the pioneer British officials in Northeast area were very committed and evangelical Christians as well.

1.2.2.3. THE BRITISH COLONIAL ADMINISTRATORS

1.2.2.3.1. DAVID SCOTT

Historically point up that at this phase, the British Colonial administrators showed keen interest in evangelizing in the region that they encouraged and supported Christian's missionaries' activities. David Scott was a British administrator in Assam between 1826 and 1861. He was a student of William Carey at Fort William College in Calcutta. Before Scott became the Commissioner of Assam he served as the political agent to the Governor General, North East Frontier at Rangpur (presently Sibsagar). He was also responsible for British interest from Sikkim in

---

[43] M. Ramuny, "Historical and Cultural background of North East India from Ancient Time to the Time of Independence", in *Crisis in North East India*, edited by Adiss Arnold, (Madras: Gurukul Publication, 1981), 21.

[44] In Treaty of Yandabo, whereby the king of Burma signed and agreed to abstain from further interference in the affairs of Assam and hills region. The conclusion of the war left to British in control almost of Assam.

[45] B.B. Goswami, "The Tribes of Assam: A Few Comments on their Social and Cultural Ties with the Non-Tribes," in *Tribal Situations in India,* edited by S.K. Singh (Simla: Indian Institute of Advanced Study, 1972), 273.

[46] H.K. Barpujari, *Problems of the Hill Tribes North East Frontier 1822-1844* (Guwahati: Lawyers Book Stall, 1970), 20.

[47] N. Toshi, *Mission to the Nagas* (Impur: Radha Offset Printers, 1995), 21.

[48] Ramuny, "Historical and Cultural ..., 23.

the North to Cachar and Sylhet in the South, with special duties in relation to Goalpara district and Garo hills.[49] It was said that he used to distribute Bengali New Testament freely to the Garos. In 1819 he requested the Calcutta authorities for permission to invite missionaries to work among the Garos. He also invited the Serampore Mission to come and work in Guahati in 1829. Subsequently the Serampore Mission did establish a school in Guahati, but closed it down due to the lack of funds. On the process of inviting the Christian missionaries, he was killed in the Anglo Khasi war and the scheme could not be implemented, as he desired.[50] In spite of the opposition Scott contributed much in Christian missions activities in North East India.

1.2.2.3.2. FRANCIS JENKINS

British administer, Capt. Francis Jenkins was son of a clergyman and from the early age he had a very strong evangelical conviction. He became the Chief Commissioner of Assam Province in 1834. The neighboring areas of plain Assam were the hill people, who constantly a raid upon the plain people and creating lots of trouble to the British administrators and it was difficult to live peaceably. There was no security for the inhabitant of the plain areas. For which the security reasons as well as to present the gospel and get the people converted the British officials invited the Christian missionaries to Northeast region.

Keeping those objectives in mind, Jenkins began to write to the American Baptist Mission Home Board, to send some Christian missionaries to the region. Jenkins also added that he would contribute Rs.1000/- to help the missionaries who settle themselves in Sadiya, Assam. This invitation and offer seemed to be an opportune moment for the Baptist in America. Just prior to that invitation the American Baptist at the Richmond Convention had decided to enter into every unoccupied field and to extend their operations as widely as possible.[51]

So, when the offer came from Jenkins they thought that a mission at Sadiya would enable them to convert the frontier tribes into Christianity and also open up an entrance into the kingdom of China. With that great joy and expectation they accepted the appeal and invitation of Jenkins. It was in response to a direct invitation from Jenkins that the first American Baptist missionaries came to Upper Assam. On this background the Christian mission emerged in Northeast region.

---

[49] Frederick S. Downs, *History of Christianity in India Vol. V, part 5: NEI in the Nineteenth & Twentieth Centuries* (Bangalore: CHAI, 1992), 16. (Hereafter referred to as Downs, *History of Christianity).*

[50] Toshi, *Mission to…*, 24.

[51] Bronson, "Mission to Assam", *Baptist Missionary Magazine*: Vol. LI, No. 10 (Oct 1871), 375.

1.2.3. THE BAPTIST MISSION

When we evaluate the Baptist mission activities in Northeast India through the years, their works were enormous and immense and that cannot be mentioned all. The early nineteenth century marked a significant history in the life of the Churches in NEI. *Ferdaen A Quarish* rightly mentioned that 'the Missionary interest in Northeast region could be witnessed with the arrival of the Serampore Baptist Mission in 1813.'[52] It is said that when William Carey received a letter from W.N Garrett, judge at Sylhet[53] suggesting that someone be sent to evangelize several Khasi tribesmen in NEI, who had taken up residence in East India Company territory. In response Carey sent Khrishna Chandra Pal, the first Serampore convert to NEI.[54] Khrishna Pal left Serampore in 1813 and took up residence at Pandua, a marketing center of the Cherrapunji Syiemship. During the eight months of his stay in Pandua he remained under military protection, where he baptized seven persons.[55] After working in Pandua for eight months K. C. Pal returned to Serampore due to the tension created by the opposition of the natives.[56] The early Serampore Baptist Mission in NEI was short lived without establishing a regular work, yet one positive result can be seen and it was the decision made by the Serampore to translate the Bible into the Khasi language. Thus the first edition of Khasi New Testament was brought out in 1824.[57]

The next Serampore Mission, which contact with the NEI was made in 1829 at Guwahati. The school was under the charge of a young Scotsman named James Rae. The aim was to reach the Garos and Manipuris as well as Khasis and neighboring people. This work too was discontinued due to the resignation of James Rae.[58]

Afterwards the Guwahati station was opened, the Serampore Mission revived its earlier contacts with the Khasis in NEI by sending a missionary named Alexander B. Lish to Cherrapunji 1832. Cherrapunji was chosen as the place at which to take up where Krishna Pal had left off because the government recently

---

[52] Ferdaen A. Quarish, *Christianity in the North East Hills of South Asia* (Dhaka: The University Press, 1987), 17.

[53] According to Morris, Garrett was the nephew of Robert Rakies, the founder of English Sunday School Movement.

[54] John Hugh Morris, *The History of the Welsh Calvinistic Methodist Foreign Mission to the End of the Year 1904* (Calcutta: KLM Pvt Ltd, 1910), 70.

[55] They were four Sepoy, two natives of Khasi namely U Duwan and U Anna and one Assamese. Indeed this Assemese would be the first known converts from among the people but unfortunately nothing further is heard about him.

[56] O.L. Snaitang, *Christianity and Social Change in North East India* (Shillong: Vendrame Institute, 1993), 66. Also referred in Frederick S Down, *Christianity in NEI* (Delhi: ISPCK, 1983), 88

[57] Down, *Christianity in NEI.., 90.*

[58] Snaitang, *Christianity and Social Change…*, 66.

established a rest station there. A school was opened in three places at Cherrapunji, Mawsmai and Mawmluh. Reading lessons for use in the schools were prepared in both in English and Khasi by using Bengali script.[59] The work was difficult because Lish found it hard to discipline the pupils, who preferred to behave as they pleased. Moreover, language was apparently the main obstacle. Lish considered the use of Roman alphabet instead of the Bengali because he thought it might be easier for the people to learn and better fit the tribals phonic system, but he could not put this into practice because the reorganization of the Serampore Mission in 1838[60] led to the abandonment of the Cherrapunji Mission.[61]

The Serampore Mission of the British Baptist Society (BBS) made an early missionary contact in the plains of Assam as well as in the hills. The work was encouraging but due to the deficiency of missionary in the field, the labor was offered to Baptist Mission Society (BMS). Therefore, the credit of the most successful evangelization among the people in NEI goes to the Baptist Mission Society.

Just as the Serampore Mission wound up, the American Baptist Missionary Union[62] appeared in the region. Of course, the Commissioner of Assam had issued an invitation to this mission. Subsequently, the first permanent Christian communities of the NEI came into existence. Thus, the statement of the *F.S. Downs in 'Christianity in North East India'* is worth mention,

> "The American Baptist and Welsh Presbyterians, who picked up where the Serampore Mission had left off at Cherrapunji, were the major Christian mission in the region throughout the nineteenth century and in the twentieth century were joined by only one other large mission, that of the Roman Catholic Mission. The dominance of these three groups is evident in the fact that in 1971, 89% of the Christian in the region belong to churches originally established by them."

---

[59] Many of the northeastern tribes have a tradition that at one time they had a written language but that they lost it for one reason or another. There are many stories about how their script was lost. In mot of these stories a manuscript with the writing on it was lost through human carelessness. A man lost it while swimming a river or carelessly placed it where it was eaten by a dog, pig or some animal or dropped it in a fire.

[60] Quarish, *Christianity in the North East Hills*....35, Also see in Snaitang, *Christianity and Social Change*..., 67.

[61] With the death of the last of the Serampore Tio, Joshua Marshman in 1838 the work of the Serampore Mission reverted to the Baptist Missionary Society (Northeast India), the parent body from which it had worked separately for some years, which was in no position to maintain the widespread operations, which had been undertaken by Serampore.

[62] The name American Baptist Missionary Union was later changed to American Baptist Foreign Mission Society and more recently to Board of International Ministries, American Baptist Mission.

Hence, the nineteenth and twentieth centuries the history of the Christian movement in the NEI is the basis from this history particularly from the mission and ecclesiastical perspective. The coming of American Baptist ecclesiology in NEI dates back to 1836, with the arrival of two American Missionary couples namely Mr. & Mrs. Nathan Brown and Mr & Mrs. Oliver Cutter, who landed at Sadiya, Assam on 23rd March 1836.[63] Though, at the beginning American Baptist ecclesiology stations in NEI was not established for the purpose of evangelizing the people of that area but as strategic outpost for reaching the Shan tribes of northern Burma and China. For several years after its establishment the mission centered first at Sadiya then at shifted to Jaipur. It was due to the political unrest and instability at Sadiya, the missionaries were moved to Jaipur with the suggestion of C. A. Bruce, a British officer.[64]

Hence, missionary Bronson made the tours from Jaipur to the Namsang village (Naga Hills). With great hope he requested the Home Board of American Baptist (HBAB) to send a missionary to help in Namsang Mission. Mr & Mrs. Cyrus Baker were therefore sent to Namsang Mission on 22 July 1839, Mr. Bronson's sister Miss, Rhoda also accompanied them.[65] The HBAB and Bronson himself took Namsang project in a last attempt to reach the *Shan* Mission. They started school on March 22, 1840, but Baker was interested to work among the Assamese rather than the Nagas. Unfortunately, Namsang Mission was abandoned in 1841 owing to the death of Miss Rhoda and also due to the impracticability of the original objectives of mission and their attention was turned to the Brahmaputra valley. In 1841, Bronson settled down in a new station at Nagaon in Assam.[66]

With a retrospective view of the past history of the Northeast Baptist mission, one can say that God was preparing His plan for something else. His eyes were upon the hills tribal people. The emergence of Baptists ecclesiology in NEI has brought out many far-reaching changes in the lives of people. After the extensive study of the Baptist mission in NEI, it is found that the Baptists are scattered and found in every part of the Northeast region. However, to bring the entire Baptist Ecclesiology and associations with one council, the Council of Baptist Churches in Northeast India was formed. The central functions of the Council are simply means of bringing the great diversity of its people into the

[63] H. K. Barpujari, *The American Missionaries and North East India: 1836-1900 AD* (Guwahati: Spectrum Publication, 1986), xv. (Hereafter referred to as Barpujari, *The American Missionaries* ...).

[64] F. S. Downs, *The Mighty works of God* (Panbazar, Guwahati: CLC, 1971), 31. (Hereafter referred to as Downs, *The Mighty works ...).*

[65] Joseph Puthenpurakal, *Baptist Mission in Nagaland: A Study in Historical and Ecumenical Perspective* (Calcutta: Firma KLM Private Ltd., 1984), 50-51.

[66] Mathew Muttumana, *Christianity in Assam and Inter-Faith Dialogue: A study on the Modern Religious Movements in North East India* (Indor: Satrakasan Sanchar Kendra, 1984), 27. (Hereafter referred to as Muttumana, *Christianity in Assam* ...).

unity of a single denominational structure. Now CBCNEI function as supreme over the affiliated regional convention of Baptist Churches in NEI. The spectrum of knowledge and the outlook of the native people were deeply sharpened by the encounter with the Christian message.

1.2.4. THE WELSH MISSION

The origins of the Welsh Mission in NEI are entirely different from those of the American Baptist. In their case the decision to begin work in the Northeast hills had nothing to do with the government. For more than thirty years mission minded members of their churches in Wales had supported the interdenominational London Missionary Society. Due to feeling that Welsh candidates for missionary service were being discriminated against by the mainly English LMS, it was decided to establish separate Welsh Missionary society in 1840.[67]

Gradually alienation from the LMS led to the creation of a Welsh mission society. The Welsh churches in Liverpool took the initiative with the formation of an autonomous society. Increasingly, it gained the support of all the Welsh Methodists and led to the formation of the Welsh Calvinistic Methodists Foreign Mission Society (WCMFMS) in 1840. Now they had their own society, they began searching for field in which to work.[68] The well-known Scottish Missionary Dr John Wilson recommended Gujarat and another missionary Rev. Jacob Tomlin recommended Khasi Hills in NEI. Finally the matter was decided in favored of Rev, Jacob Tomlin suggestion because the Khasi hills were the closer to Calcutta than Gujarat, which provide inexpensive passage to Calcutta for their missionaries. Thus it was that Rev and Mrs. Thomas Jones arrived in NEI.

The Welsh Mission in NEI began with the mission work with the arrival of missionary Rev. Thomas Jones and his wife. The Presbyterian Church is also one of the largest denominations within Protestant Mission in Northeast India. At present Presbyterian Assembly operates from its central office Shillong, having two fulltime administrative secretaries. The report of 1998 statistic highlights the Presbyterian Church has a total strength of 8,23,456 and 2,568 local Churches. The Assembly of Presbyterian Church is divided into six Synods for administration

---

[67] There were various factors why co-operation with the LMS did not work out. First, there were differences in theology and church structure between the Welsh Church and the predominantly Congregationalist Churches that had come to dominate the LMS. Secondly, an increasing denominational spirit led to further deterioration in the relationship. Another factors may have been that with a predominantly agricultural and working class background, the Welsh candidates were not as well qualified as others in the view of the Directors. Another reason was almost certainly the national one. The LMS Directors and missionaries would have been predominantly English and the Welsh have always considered themselves a nationality distinct from their English conquerors. They have their own language and culture and have always had a suspicions if not antagonistic attitude towards the English.

[68] O.L. Snaitang, *Christianity and Social....,,,* 69.

and pastoral ministry. Following are some of the major regions where Welsh Presbyterian mission took its root.

1.2.5. THE WELSH MISION IN KHASI HILLS

The first Welsh mission began its work in Khasi Hills was with the arrival of Rev. and Mrs. Thomas Jones on 22 June 1841, at Cherrapunji.[69] During that time it was an isolated and a thinly populated village. Lacking good communication with outsiders the people were warlike having no mercy on outsiders. The missionaries had to deal with a people who traditionally had resisted alien influences. With much adversity there was a slow progress in Cherra. As a result Cherrapunji mission field was shifted to Nongsawlia Hill in 1843.[70] Nongsawlia became the first Mission center and is also regarded as the mother church throughout the land. Thomas first effort was literature and education. He re-opened the three schools started by Serampore Mission at Mawmluh, Mawsmai and Cherra, and published various school textbooks. The first two books were '*Ka Kot Pule Banyngkong*' (First Reader) and '*Ka Kot Pule Shaphang Ka Jingkoit Jingkhiah*' (My Mother's Gift).[71]

There were two more missionary families, namely William Lewis and Owen Richards arrived at Khasi field in 1843. The Mission work was mainly concentrated around the Cherrapunji till 1850. Despite of strong opposition from the people, gradually they began to show an interest in the new religion. In response to the new situation a young Khasi women, *Ka Nabon Sawiar* of Mawmluh was baptized in 1848. In 1853 a Church was established at Shella and the following year a school was started at Jowai, Jaintia state. By the end of 19th century missionary progression began among the Lyngngams through the labor of Khasi-Jaintia Christians themselves rather than the work of missionaries.[72]

At the close of 1866 it was reported that there were schools and Churches in almost all Khasi region. This period was significant as Christianity touched the royal families- The '*Nongkrem Syiemship*' a royal family considered to be the most difficult of all Khasi kingdoms to evangelize. The impact was tremendous and the numbers of Christians increased to about 1,659. As an act of faith a bold step was taken to establish five Presbyteries in 1896;[73] The Home Mission was organized in 1900, to work in the area where Christianity had not previously been introduced. The 19th century projected a good signs for the Khasi-Jaintia Presbyterian

---

[69] "Assembly of the Presbyterian Church in NEI", *Golden Jubilee Souvenir 1926-1976* (Shillong: Central Ward, nd), 1."*Ka Pateng Khristan*," *(KPK)* Vol. III, No. 9 (Shillong: September, 1939), 131-132.

[70] Downs, *The Wondrous Works of God* (Shillong: Mrs. M. B. Jyrwa, 1980), 22.

[71] Assembly of the Presbyterian Church in North East India, *Golden Jubilee Souvenir 1926-1976* (Central Ward, Shillong: APC, 1976), 1.

[72] O.L. Snaitang, *Christianity and Social....*, 74.

[73] The five Presbyteries were namely Sohra-Shella, Shillong-Mawlai, Mawphlang-Mairang, Jowai-Shangpung and the Plains.

Church, which has developed indigenous community. Its contribution towards ecumenism was unique and it played an active role in discussions for the Church Union in the region.

1.2.6. THE WELSH MISSION IN NORTH MIZORAM

The Presbyterian mission commenced its mission work in Mizoram with the coming of Mr William Williams a young Presbyterian evangelist, on March 20th 1891.[74] He sowed the first seed of the Gospel among the Mizos who were living in Aizawl, but unfortunately the work was not materialized since the Mizos were engaged in war with British. The mission to Mizos again started with the arrival of Rev. J.H. Lorrain and Rev. F.W. Savidge at Aizawl on January 11th 1894.[75] But, they stayed only three years in Aizawl.

Later, Rev. D.E. Jones, arrived at Aizawl on August 31st 1897 and the following year another missionary Rev. Edwin Rowlands joined him.[76] These two missionaries had the whole of Mizo Hills as their field of service till the coming of other denominations. When Jones first landed in Mizo hills there were not even a single Christian but their untiring toil made much progress, thus when he left in 1927, 17,000 Christians had been received into the church. The beginning of twentieth century was one of the most rapidly growth of Mizoram Christians, which was attributed to a series of 'revival movements.'[77] One of the distinct characteristics of the revival movement among the Mizos was its contribution to the indigenization of Christianity. At present the Mizoram Presbyterian Church Synod has 27 Presbyteries.

1.2.7. AN ANGLICAN MISSION

The Anglican Mission began its work in NEI through two waves. The first were the military chaplains who resided in military towns of Guwahati, Goalpara, Dibrugarh and Tezpur etc. The second wave belongs to missionaries sent to Assam by Society for the Propagation of the Gospel mission to look after the *Adivasi*[78] converts. The earliest contact of Anglican Ministration was a clergyman, Rev. A. Grastin, Chaplain of Sylhet who visited the scattered Europeans, who were beginning to come to Assam valley in 1841. In 1845, Calcutta Anglican Bishop, Wilson appointed Rev. Robert Bland as Chaplain of Assam, where he

---

[74] C.L. Hminga, *The Life and Witness of the Churches in Mizoram* (Mizoram: The Literature Committee, BCM, 1987), 47. (Hereafter referred to as Hminga, *The Life and Witness …).*

[75] J. Meirion Lloyd, *History of Church in Mizoram: Harvest in the Hills* (Aizawl, Mizoram: Synod Publication Board, 1991), 27.

[76] Hminga, *The Life and Witness* …, 52.

[77] Downs, *Christianity in NEI* …, 123.

[78] *Adivasis* were known as Kols, who were probably migrated to the valley of Ganges before the Arians came there. They speak a dialect related to Shan Tribes. The statistic reports in 1901 they were 2, 98,997 numbers lived around Bengal, Assam and other parts of India.

took charge at Guwahati in the same year. Fredrick S. Downs stated that those chaplains were appointed to look after the spiritual interest of European members of their denomination.[79] But, Robert Bland had certain enthusiasm to revive the Anglican Mission for which he made a tour extensively in Assam including Sibsagar, Dibrugarh, Jaipur and Goalpara. It was in his time a new Anglican Church was built at Guwahati, called 'Christ Church,'[80] which still stand.

Apart from the work of Chaplain in the Company, a British officer Capt. J.T. Gordon took over a small Anglican mission in around 1848 at Tezpur. Two German missionaries, C.H. Hessdelmeyer and G. Dauble were assigned to this field to work among the Kacharis, with the promises of financial help from British officials.[81] To assist Hesselmeyer, a young deacon Sydney Endle, a missionary appointed by Society for the Propagation of the Gospel arrived at Tezpur in 1864. In 1865 he was entrusted to work and minister among tea planters and also the Kachari tribesmen. Later in 1869, Endle was appointed Chaplain of Darrang district with the charge of Kachari Mission.[82] From the inception of the Anglican Mission in Assam, it was under the jurisdiction of Calcutta diocese but because of detachment between Assam and Calcutta diocese, Assam was raised to a Suffragan diocese in 1914. Finally, the diocese was created in 1915 with an appointment of Rev. Herbert Pankenham Walsh,[83] who became a first Anglican Bishop in Northeast India.

Till the middle of nineteenth century, Cherrapunji was the residence of the Agent of Governor General and Commissioner of Assam. There were a certain number of troops deployed at Cherrapunji. Accordingly the Bishop of Calcutta asked to Rev. H. Hinde to visit those troops, thus he was made the first Chaplain of Shillong with the additional responsibility of Cherrapunji and Chachar.[84] As such Anglican mission was enterprise at Cherrapunji.

1.2.7.1. AN ANGLICAN MISSION IN GARO HILLS

The Anglican Mission to Garo was made only at the beginning of the last century. It was Fr Edmud Shore, a member of the Anglican Religious community, who in pursuit of his duties as Chaplain of Dacca had to visit Mymensingh (now in Bangladesh), who made contact with a group of Garo converts. He made his

[79] Frederich S. Downs, *Christianity in North East India* (Delhi: ISPCK/CLC, 1983), 111. (Hereafter referred to as Downs, *Christianity in NEI ...*).

[80] Ernest W. Talibuddin, *The Anglican Church in North-East India (1845-1970): A Missiological Reflection* (Delhi: ISPCK, 2002), 16-18.

[81] Downs, *Christianity in NEI ...*, 112.

[82] Muttumana, *Christianity in Assam ...*, 128.

[83] M.E. Gibbs, *The Anglican Church in India 1600-1970* (Delhi: ISPCK, 1972), 352.

[84] S B Taylor, *Annual Report of the Chaplaincy of Guwahati, Shillong and Dhupri for the year 1881* (Shillong: The Assam Secretariat Press, 1882), 23.

first visit to their center at Haluaghat in 1907.[85] This endeavor continued for quite some time under the leadership of Fr Chakravarti, a man who had many potentialities to inspire others. Thus, the mission work continued till 1947. Much later due to communal and political unrest many Garos crossed over to India, many of them were Anglicans.[86] According to the Bishop Adres at the 20th Ordinary Session of the Assam Diocesan Council in 1962, the Diocese had four missionary fields [87] of which Garo was one of them. Surendra Mandda and Behala were the first Garo, who served with great enthusiastically to build congregation in Garo Hills. The Church was built at Kontakpara along which boarding school for boys and girls with the aid of society of the propagation of Gospel.[88] But, unfortunately today there is nothing left.

In the initiatory the Anglican clergy showed little interest in evangelization of native people. But with an amalgamation of Society for the Propagation of the Gospel, it gave new impulses in the matter of evangelization in colonies. Early nineteen century found a little progressed of Anglicanism in Northeast India. At present Anglican parishes expanded to various regions in the plain of Assam and few were found in other parts of Arunachal Pradesh and other hills area. Although, from the beginning the Anglican mission always preserved their identity to show their divergence from the rest of the Protestants in matter of doctrinal and so on. Hence, the Anglican Community failed to grow in Northeast India, partly because of their exclusive activities- tending to the spiritual concerns within the European community.

1.2.8. THE LUTHERAN MISSION

Actually, the Lutheran Missionaries did not succeed much in establishing the Lutheran mission in Northeast India. It was through the tribals emigrants from other parts of India, the Lutheran Church in the region was started. The Gossner Mission began its evangelical activities in Chotanagpur much earlier in 1845. When the outsiders came to Chotanagpur, there was crisis between them and the local people. Thereupon thousands left Chotanagpur to work in other parts of India. Many migrated to Assam to work in tea gardens for their livelihood. Among those who immigrated were Lutheran Christians.[89] Thus, they started a small Lutheran mission in Assam particularly in tea garden. Slowly a Church was built and a native pastor was ordained in 1900. With the request of the local people

---

[85] *A Hundred Years In Bengal: A History of the Oxford Mission 1880-1980* (Delhi: ISPCK, 1979), 39.

[86] Talibuddin, *The Anglican Church in North-East India* ..., 22.

[87] Four Missionary fields were, Mikir Hills (Karbi Anglong), Santhals, Sanitary Workers in Shillong and Garo Hills.

[88] *Asssam Diocesan News Letter, August 1962* (Shillong: Shillong Printing Press, 1962), 32.

[89] C. Becker, *History of the Catholic Missions in North East India: 1890-1915* (Shillong: Kerma KLM Pvt. Ltd., 1980), 49. (Hereafter referred to as Becker, *Catholic Mission* ...).

on July 10, 1919 the Gossner Evangelical Lutheran Church at Chotanagpur and Assam was established. The main station of the Lutheran Church in Assam was in Tezpur, where the church members were mainly from tea-garden workers and emigrants but was an active church during that time.

The second batch of Lutheran mission to work in NEI was the Northern Evangelical Lutheran Church. In reality, they were Santhals, who came to Assam as tribals emigrants from Bihar in search of jobs. They embraced Lutheranism through the work of L.O. Skrefsrud and H.P. Boerresen, who work under the Gossner Mission. As such Lutheranism was flourished in various parts of Assam and also in the neighboring area, particularly in the areas of Boros and Garos. The first three Santhal converts were Siram, Jogot and Rahgu, who took baptism in 1869.[90] Now there were 46,303 Lutheran members with 344 communities and around 60 pastors who are working in various Lutheran mission stations in North East India.

1.2.9. THE UNITARIAN MISSION

A small but interesting group that has its origins in this period in the Khasi and Jaintia Hills is Unitarian Union. It began with Hajom Kissor Singh, who had been converted through the work of the Welsh Presbyterians, who had also provided him with a good education. For unspecified reasons he felt compelled to leave that church. Through a Bengali member who resident in Shillong he was put in touch with C H A Dall, an American Unitarian missionary living in Calcutta. On the basis of correspondence with Dall, Hajim was converted to Unitarianism.[91]

In 1886 the first Khasi Unitarian Church was organized at Jowai with the joined work of Dall and Hajom. Dall died shortly thereafter but Hajom continued to espouse Unitarianism until his own death in 1923. Another English Unitarian Margaret Barr arrived at Shillong in 1936. She had taken her degree from Cambridge in 1923 and was ordained a minister of the Unitarian Church in 1928. Barr wanted to establish a rural center on the Gandhian model, but first became involved in building up two schools that had already been established in Shillong.[92] The Unitarians maintain absolute separation between them and others in various ways, particularly in their faith and beliefs. Despite all these they are growing slowly as a microscopic in the region.

1.2.10. THE ROMAN CATHOLIC MISSION

The word Roman Catholic derives from the Greek term *katholikos*, meaning 'general' or 'the whole world'. This name was adapted to the Church of Rome,

[90] Becker, *Catholic Mission* ..., 138.

[91] Downs, *Christianity in NEI* ..., 114.

[92] The Sunderland Memorial School that was eventually turned over to Khasi management and the other Lady Ried School at Malki which was finally turned over to government and taught by the Khasi teachers.

who opposed to Reformation led by Martin Luther. They strongly believed in the infallibility of Pope especially since the first Vatican Council in 1870. They also stick to the dogma that outside the church there is no salvation. Besides the Holy Bible they also adhere to the Church tradition as authority of their faith.[93] In the light of this, the advent of Roman Catholics to NEI took place from the very early stage of time but was not much successful as the other Protestant missions did.

Main Catholic missionaries activities date from the creation of the Prefecture Apostolic of Assam, Bhutan, and Manipur in 1889. It was made the responsibility of a young German order, the Salvatorian Fathers.[94] Fr. Broy handed over to them and left Assam, later joining the Society of Jesus. In February 1890 four Salvatorians under the leadership of Fr Otto Hopfenmuller[95] arrived in Shillong. It had been decided to shift the headquarters from Guwahati to the provincial capital at Shillong because the hills people showed greater promise than did those of the plains.[96] 'The administer of the diocese of Dacca, as also Bp. Pozzi of Krisnagar, indicated that the hill tribals were more ready to accept Christianity than the Assamese.' Therefore the missionaries did not remain long in Guwahati, but continued their journey on to the Khasi hills. With the arrival of the first missionaries in Shillong on 27th February 1890 the Prefecture Apostolic of Assam was finally established not only de Jure but also de Facto and could begin to develop under the leadership its new apostolic workers.[97]

According to C Becker, the beginning of the new mission at Shillong was indeed very trying and small community. They were mainly Englishmen, Anglo-Indians and a few Catholic servants coming from other parts of India.[98] From this time onwards Fr Otto Hopfenmueller concentrated all his efforts on bringing the local people of Shillong, the Khasis, to the Catholic Faith. There was not a single Catholic among them yet. He writes "If we cannot form a community

---

[93] A. Bendangyapang Ao, *History of Christianity in Nagaland Social Change 1872-1792* (Bangalore: Shalom Ministry Publication, 2004), 257.

[94] The religious society mentioned here is none other than the 'Society of the Divine Savor,' popularly known as Salvatorians. The chief task of the society was the spreading of Catholic Teaching. An earlier society was 'The Catholic Teaching Society' but during the course of its growth, there arose a problem about its name. Hence the name Catholic Teaching Society was apparently quite suitable. But it was often misunderstood. Some thought it was a society of teachers and the learned at the service of Catholic Theology. This had several painful and unpleasant consequences and a search for a new name was made. With the approval of ecclesiastical authorities the society was given the name 'Society of the Divine Savior'. Its members were to proclaim the teaching of Christ after the example of his disciples. This definitive name was given to society in 1904. Its scope remained the same as before.

[95] He was native of Bavaria, chosen to be the first Mission Superior.

[96] Becker, *Catholic Mission ...*, 14.

[97] Snaitang, *Christianity and Social Change...*,78 Also see in Becker , History of the Catholic Missions ..., 13.

[98] Becker, History of the Catholic Missions ..., 14.

of Khasi Christians here, our stay here will be useless,"[99] Thenceforward, he dedicated himself with great zeal and attention to learning the Khasi language. In spite of the difficulties he made great progress. He had to begin the work of the religious formation of the Khasis from the very beginning. After a few weeks, Fr Hopfenmuller began to translate into Khasi the "Our Father" and "Holy Mary". He also paid great attention to the making of a catechism in this language. In 1891 the first Khasi Catholic was baptized and the following year a station was opened at Raliang in the Jaintia Hills to the east of Jowai. Gradually the work spread in the Khasi and Jaintia area and before the end of the century a missionary had taken up residence in Guwahati. Missionary work was also begun among the Chota Nagpur is working in the tea gardens of Upper Assam.[100]

For entirely different reasons the First World War was a turning point for the Roman Catholic Church as well. Though the Salvatorian missionaries had initially thought that the people of the hills would respond more readily to their work than would those on the plains, the Catholic missionaries became increasingly active in the Burahmaputra valley. In addition to maintaining their work in the Khasi and Jainta hills, stations were opened at Dibrugarh in 1908 and efforts were made to secure land for a station at Tezpure. In Guwahati nuns started an Assemese school and orphanage in 1914, but most of the plains work at that time was concentrated in the tea garden areas. Two thirds of the Catholic community in the Northeast was by that time found among the tea garden laborers of Lakhimpur, Darrang, Nowgong, and Sibsagar districts of Brahmaputra valley and the rest were in the Khasi and Jaintia hills.[101]

The main method that the Catholic missionaries used to spread Catholic mission was made in the education and medical work. Shillong became an important center of this work. In 1907 an industrial school had been started there and the following year St. Anthony later to become one of the best colleges in the regions, was opened. In 1909 the Loreto Sisters established their prestigious school for girls there. In 1913 Salvatorian nuns opened for girls school in Shillong as well as a convent for sisters, Catechist-Missionaries of the Immaculate Conception at Gauhati.[102] As a result of their evangelistic work a Catholic community was increased more in number in the Northeast regions.

Unfortunately, the Salvatorians were a German order and their missionaries were therefore nationals of that country. In June 1915 they were given orders by the British Government to quit India. The Archbishop of Calcutta sent a Jesuit. Fr Lefeve, to take over responsibility for the Assam missions, and until 1921 the Jesuits working in Bengal maintained the work as best they could. Though they

---

[99] Otto's letter from Shillong to Fr. J.B. Jordan Superior General, 1 June 1890.

[100] Becker , History of the Catholic Missions ..., 5.

[101] Downs, *Christianity in NEI* ..., 130 also see in Snaitang, *Christianity and Social Change...*, 79

[102] Downs, *Christianity in NEI* ..., 131.

were unable to maintain as many stations as the Salvatorians had, the Jesuits were not simply caretakers. They initiated several new ventures and during the six years of their responsibility the Catholic community continued to grow. According to F.S. Down "by 1921 the Catholic community numbered was increased up to 5, 419."[103]

In the summer of 1921 the Holy See entrusted the Assam Mission to the Salesians of Don Bosco, whose first missionaries reached Shillong at the beginning of the following year. At first they like Salvatorians before them, manned the hill stations but soon they too were active in the plains. Numerous new stations were opened in the old fields and thanks to a Catholic Governor of Assam, they were permitted to enter the Garo Hills in 1933. Educational work continued to expand and so too did the size of the Catholic community. During the Second World War Catholic work was again affected by the expulsion or internment of its German and Italian missionaries, but by this time there were enough belonging to other national groups to enable them to carry on their mission.

In fact the war adversely affected all denominations, with very few Walsh and American Protestant missionaries remaining. In keeping with the rapid growth of the Catholic community in the Northeast, the Prefecture of Assam was made into a diocese, the Diocese of Shillong, in 1934. Despite the substantial growth during the 1920s and 1930s, it was considerably less than that which took place after India gained its independence in 1947. The British had always restricted Catholic mission to Meghalaya and the Assam plains, with the result that they soon moved into the other hills areas.

One of the rapid developments of Christianity in the post-war was the Roman Catholic Church in Northeast India, particularly in the hill regions. At the beginning of the war there were 50,000 Catholics in the region, but in the post-war it was increased to 369,681.[104] This was due to an extraordinary expenditure of resources, both in terms of money and missionary personal. On the other hand it was due to the removal, after independence, of the restrictions of the British had placed upon Catholic missions. Up till independence Roman Catholic had been permitted to work only in Meghalaya and the Assam plain and to a certain extent in Tripura. Now they began to expand throughout the region, the cutting edge of their new thrust being an ever-expanding network of educational institutions.

The expansion of Catholic mission was marked by the creation of new dioceses. Much of that expansion was in the areas in which Catholics had traditionally worked. Diocese of Dibrugarh was established in 1952, the Diocese of Tezpur in 1964, of Silchar in 1969 and Tura in 1973. In 1969 Shillong-Guwahati was made as Archdiocese. Shortly after the independence the first Catholic congregation in Nagaland was formed out of the group of

[103] Downs, *Christianity in NEI* ..., 131.

[104] Downs, *Christianity in NEI* ..., 152.

dissident Baptist from Lotha tribe.[105] From 1949 a priest had been resident in Kohima as chaplain to a small group of Spanish Sisters, but he was not permitted to do missionary work. Nevertheless his successor had established a small Angami Naga Catholic community by 1963.[106] In 1956 at a time when no other missionaries were permitted in the territory, two priests took up residence at Imphal in Manipur. Eventually churches began to be established in the hill regions of that state.

During 1960s special emphasis was given to the development of the work in Nagaland and Manipur. Jesuits, Carmelite Sisters, Clarists, Aduration Nuns, Ursulines Apostolic Carmel and Bethany Sisters opened schools in the two states. The Medical mission Sisters began a medical service center at Kohima. In 1973 the Catholic in these two states were brought under the newly created diocese of Kohima and Imphal.[107] According to the reports of 2002 statistic shows the Catholic diocese claimed its membership increased to 37% with seventh dioceses and two Archdioceses[108] in NEI.[109]

1.2.11. OTHER MISSIONS

The beginning of 20th century marks a tremendous development in both positive as well as negative changes within the Christian missions in Northeast India. Number of other mission groups sprung up all over the region from the established Churches. The main reasons for the emergence of these other groups were the theological differences, dissatisfaction of the teaching in existing Churches, the inconsistency of constitution and the Gospel of Christ and governing of Church by it, awakening of revival movement, differences of opinion, and the leadership crisis within the same flock, a sharp decline in Christian life among the leaders and its members.

Some of those groups are the general Mid-Mission, Salvation Army, Church of God, Jehovah Witness Church, Assemblies of God, Pentecostal Churches, Seventh Day Adventists and the Pentecostal etc.[110] Some of these groups are known for their tendency to seek converts from among existing Christian groups rather than from among non-Christians. Again there are some sectarian groups who were formed as the outcome of the revival movements. In them we could see syncretistic nationalistic and heretical elements. The main emphases in their

---

[105] Ezamo Murry, *The Introduction and Growth of Christianity in the Lotha Area of Nagaland* (unpublished B.D Thesis, UTC, Bangalore, 1976), 35-36.

[106] A Bendangyapang, *History of Christianity in Nagaland: Social Change 1872-1972* (Bangalore: Shalom Ministry Publication, 2004), 257.

[107] Becker, History of the Catholic Missions ..., 131-135.

[108] Diocese of Dibrugarh, the Diocese of Tzipur, Diocese of Silchar, Diocese of Tura and Diocese of Manipur and Nagaland. Shillong and Guwahati was made as Archdiocese.

[109] *Catholic Directory of India*, 2001, p. 270.

[110] Downs, *Christianity in NEI* ..., 151.

worship were re-baptism, healing, prayer, singing, vision and prophecy, speaking in tongue etc., which in one way or the other produce and enhance the feeling of denominationalism.

CONCLUSION

It is obvious that Christian mission activities and colonialism go hand in hand with each other in many parts of the world. Similarly, even in northeastern India Colonialism as an instrument paves the way for Christian mission activities and at the same time helping them to establish their power. Perhaps, it's known fact that Colonialism improved the Christian mission activities and granted resources and moral support in many ways. However, due to such existence of different kinds of church denominations in the region there needs a quest for unity in Northeast India.

Chapter 2

Development of Christian Unity Then and Now

INTRODUCTION

In first part we shall deals with the meaning and concepts of Christian Unity or ecumenical movement in general. Secondly, the most important aspect in this section explores the Christian Unity that was developed among the churches in wider scenario, which gives the paradigm for the development of Northeast India Christian Council, which is the apex body of Christian Unity in the region.

2.1. THE CONCEPTS AND DEVELOPMENT OF CHRISTIAN UNITY

The concept of Christian unity refers to efforts by Christians of different Church traditions to develop closer relationship and better understandings. It also expressed to the efforts towards the visible unity of different Christian denominations in some form. The term is also often used to express as the ecumenical movement is broadly identified as communion towards the unity of the church. Thus, Christian unity signifies the movement or tendency toward worldwide Christian unity or cooperation. However, Christian unity is an attempt on the part of the divided Christian churches of the world to recognize their essential unity and to move toward new concord and reunion. The word *Ecumenism* is derived from the Greek words '*Oikoumene*' "the inhabited world" or "the inhabited earth" and *oikos* 'house' and can be traced from the commands, promise, and prayers of Jesus.[111] But, in current usage it is ordinarily linked to the specific Christian spirit,

[111] Martin E. Marty, "Ecumenical Movement," *The Encyclopedia Americana International Edition*, Vol. 9, (Danbury: Grolier Incorporated, 1996), 623.

movement, and set of organizations that seek religious reconciliation. Therefore the word Christian unity and Ecumenism will use simultaneously in this research.

In the course of history, it distinguished with various meanings and understandings of the word 'Christian Unity' or 'Ecumenism,' starting with the pertaining to or representing the whole inhabited earth, pertaining to or representing the whole of the Roman Empire, pertaining to or representing the whole of the church, that which has universal ecclesiastical validity, pertaining to the world wide missionary outreach of the church, pertaining to the relations between and unity of two or more churches and that quality or attitude which expresses the consciousness of the desire for Christian unity.[112] In present day usage it sometimes means worldwide and sometimes interdenominational. In recent years, ecumenical is sometimes used as a synonym for inter-religious or interfaith, though this usage is still somewhat rare. [113] Perhaps the most common meaning is that which expresses the awareness of and yearning for Christian Unity.

After the International Missionary Conference held at Edinburgh in 1910, Protestants began to use the term ecumenism to describe the gathering of missionary, evangelistic, service and unitive forces. During and after the Second Vatican Council (1962-65) Roman Catholics used ecumenism to refer to the renewal of the whole life of the church, undertaken to make it more responsive to 'separated churches' and to the needs of the world.[114]

Under this term, the Christian churches are primarily considered, but the word embraces in the Greco-Roman world the whole of humanity and the New Testament uses the word in the sense that the Word of God must be preached to the whole world inhabited by the human race (Mt 24:14; Acts 17:31; Romans 10:18). Therefore, one can correctly define "ecumenism as the coming together of all Christians and the churches into one community to overcome the denominational, national, cultural and social limitations, in order that this community may continuously witness and serve the unity of the humanity in Christ."[115]

Primarily, ecumenism concerned with the unity of the churches in Christ is based on the four criterions of the church, One, Holy, Catholic and Apostolic. It is an attempt of the churches not only to repair the damage caused by the divisions in the church from the Council of Ephesus to the present and to witness Christ

---

[112] W. A. Visser 't Hooft, "The Word 'Ecumenical'-Its History and Use," in *A History of the Ecumenical Movement, 1517-1948,* eds. Ruth Rouse and Stephen C. Neill (Philadelphia: Westminster, 1954), 735-40.

[113] Edwin Luther Copeland, "Ecumenical movement: will Southern Baptists ever get with it?" *Religious Studies*, 2/1 (Spring, 1975), 15.

[114] "Ecumenism," *The New Encyclopedia Britannica*, vol-4, edited by Philip W. Goetz (Chicago: Encyclopedia Britannica, Inc., 1815), 362.

[115] *The Ecumenical Church*, Report in Section V of the World Conference for Practical Christentum, Oxford, 1973, 15, cited by Muttumana, *Christianity in Assam and Inter-Faith Dialogue*..., 140.

unitedly but also to offer a credible pattern of unity to the whole of humanity by dedicating the united church for the well being of all mankind on earth. To be ecumenical means to serve and to unite the human race by means of the church founded by Christ.

In order to undertake the great task of uniting humanity on its continuous course towards freedom and peace, the churches must be authentic by being united according to the will of the founder whose Word was received and preached by one church. Hence, the primary task of the churches is to bring their own house in order. Thus ecumenism is normally used in an introversive sense. It is understood as the communion between different denominations in faith and worship, in believing and witnessing the one Lord and in celebrating his salvation acts together by the Eucharistic sharing.

Ecumenism, therefore, may be defined as that movement in which Christians are becoming aware of their world-wide fellowship and their common faith and life in Jesus Christ and are seeking ways to express this basic unity.[116] Ecumenism thus offer a new way for intercultural relationship by accepting churches belonging to different national, cultural and social traditions into a unity independent of every human barrier which no culture or ideology is able to establish.[117] Therefore, the churches in Northeast India must seek Christian unity identity to fulfill their responsibility to preach and to administer the sacraments which are true characteristics of the universal church founded by Christ. Unity is the very life principle and commission of the Lord for the new churches in by which they unite the people above their cultural and social differences, and create not hostile tribal groups in new forms but make them brethren in Christ above the barriers of belief, culture and regionalism.

2.2. BEGINNING OF CHRISTIAN UNITY

There is an increasing concern on the part of churches to find more ways in which to give visible expression to Christian unity. The Christian unity is the phrase used to describe efforts to attain such unity. Until the twentieth century, only sporadic efforts were made to reunite a Christian denomination shattered through the centuries by schisms, the Reformation, and other disputes. Pressure towards unity was inspired and aided in the nineteenth century by the development of the Evangelical Awakening and the Missionary Movement. German Pietism, English Methodism and American Revivalism were all inspired with great missionary zeal.[118] Thus, several missionary societies and organizations were formed and missionaries were sent all over the world to preach the gospel and to convert people to Christian faith. When the missionaries from the different

---

[116] Copeland, *Ecumenical movement: will Southern Baptists ever get with it?...*, 15.

[117] Muttumana, *Christianity in Assam and Inter-Faith Dialogue...*, 141-142.

[118] Kuncheria Pathil, *Ecumenism: Unity and Diversity* (Bangalore: Dharmaram Publications, 2006), 29.

denominations met together in the mission land, they realized increasingly that division among them was a scandal to the non-Christian and an obstacle to the success of missionary work. So, the plea for one united church and the search for the rediscovery of the visible unity of the churches came first from the mission field.[119] It also contributed through the formation of several voluntary movements which were interdenominational, like Bible Societies and the Young Men's Christian Association (YMCA), the Young Women's Christian Association (YWCA), the Students Christian Movement (SCM) and so on.[120]

All these nineteenth century movements, although their primary objective was not the restoration of the visible unity of the churches, in fact, united young men and women and students from all churches in prayer, discussion, Bible studies and common missionary and social action. They were convinced that denominational differences should not prevent them from coming together on the basis of their fundamental unity as Christians. Of which these great Christian unity principle or a new method for the ecumenical conversation was developed.[121] Thus, the contemporary Christian unity was prepared by the voluntary movements of the nineteenth century.

2.3. THE PROMINENCE OF MISSIONARY MOTIVATION

If one looks at the Christian Unity as a whole, undoubtedly its most prominent motivation has been the modern missionary movement. Other streams of motivation were Christian youth and student movements and the efforts to discover and implement the gospel's relation to society. Both of these streams, however, are closely related to missionary motives. It seems natural for missionaries to meet together across denominational lines for Christian fellowship and mutual conference concerning common needs and problems. The famous Baptist missionary, William Carey proposed interdenominational world missionary conferences. On 15th May 1806, Carey wrote to Andrew Fuller, the secretary of the Baptist Missionary Society, proposing the convening of a decennial world missionary conference at the Cape of Good Hope (South Africa).[122]

> ...The Cape of Good Hope is now in the hands of the English; should it continue so, would it not be possible to have a general association of all denominations of Christians, from the four quarters of the world, kept there once in about ten years? I earnestly recommend this plan, let the first meeting be in the year 1810 or 1812 at furthest. I have

[119] William Richey Hogg, Ecumenical Foundations: A History of the International Missionary Council and Its Nineteenth Century Background (New York: Harper and Brothers, 1952), Cited by Pathil, *Ecumenism: Unity and Diversity ...*, 28-29.

[120] Pathil, *Ecumenism: Unity and Diversity ...*, 29; Also see in Snaitang, *A History of Ecumenical Movement ...*, 97.

[121] Pathil, *Ecumenism: Unity and Diversity ...*, 30.

[122] Rose and Neil, *A History of the Ecumenical Movement, 1517-1948 ...*, 355.

> no doubt but it would be attended with very important effects; we could understand one another better and more entirely enter into one another's views by two hours conversation than by two or three years epistolary correspondence.[123]

Andrew Fuller called Carey's proposal a 'pleasing dream.' It was a vision far beyond Carey's times, not to be fulfilled until a century later in the great world missionary conference at Edinburgh 1910, out of which came the International Missionary Council and, less directly, the World Council of Churches.[124] It is a dogma of the missionaries that the western missionary movement was the originator of the modern ecumenical movement. They point out that as the scandal of disunity became a real stumbling block for the discharge of Christian missions in the mission field, the missionaries in the field organized missionary conferences to discuss co-operation and unity.

2.4. WORLD MISSIONARY CONFERENCE, EDINBURGH 1910

The World Missionary Conference met on 14th -23rd June 1910. Here, the delegates representing missionary societies from all over the world met. This World Mission Conference is widely considered the birth place of the contemporary ecumenical movement. The conference was organized by John R. Mott, J. H. Oldham and other pioneers of the ecumenical movement, and was attended 1200 delegates from different level of mission societies.[125] The conference emphasized the need for the cooperation and unity and called the Christians to plant in each Christian nation one undivided church of Christ.[126] The greatest contribution of the conference perhaps the concerns of mission and unity were brought together once for all as in the prayer of Jesus, 'that they all may be one.'

The main slogan of the 1910 Edinburgh conference was "evangelization of the world in this generation."[127] This conference provided an occasion that gave serious attention to the planning for effective mission and evangelism of the whole world consciousness and the concern of unity and mission were seen inseparable as two sides of the same coin. They met together and expressed their oneness in the daily sessions of worship and meetings. The focus of its ecumenical unity was on the world's need of Christ and the urgency of fulfilling the great commission.[128]

---

[123] Kuriakose, *History of Christianity in India: Source Materials* ..., 82.

[124] Edwin Luther Copeland, "Ecumenical Movement: Will Southern Baptist ever gets with it?" *Perspectives in Religious Studies*, 2/1 (September, 1975), 16.

[125] Snaitang, *A History of Ecumenical Movement* ..., 97-98. Also see in Pathil, *Ecumenism: Unity and Diversity* ..., 34.

[126] Pathil, *Ecumenism: Unity and Diversity* ..., 34.

[127] Coorilos Geevarghese, "Towards and Beyond Edinburgh 2010: A Historical Survey of Ecumenical Missiological Developments since 1910," *International Review of Mission*, 99/1 (April 2010), 7.

[128] Snaitang, *A History of Ecumenical Movement* ..., 99.

However, it was a general consensus on these fundamental principles that had enabled the conference to see the possible of cooperation and working together in spite of divergent theological heritages.

It was in 1910 that a very significant missionary conference was held at Edinburgh, Scotland. They sought to discover by consultation how the churches could help, instead of hampering or competing with, one another, to pool whatever knowledge and experience each had gained. Out of this conference emerged three new movements, International Missionary Council, the Faith and Order Movement and the Life and Work Movement, which paved the way for the formation of the World Council of Churches in 1948 at Amsterdam.

2.5. THE INTERNATIONAL MISSIONARY COUNCIL

The first was the International Missionary Council (IMC), formed in 1921 in order to achieve a greater measure of practical co-operation among missionaries. In these councils, soon to be knit together in the International Missionary Councils, the younger churches and the missionary bodies of the older churches joined for consultation and cooperation in their common tasks. In two aspects, therefore the ecumenical movement owes a basic debt to christian missions, first because it is the missionary outreach which has brought about a day in which the church is world-wide, secondly because the International Missionary Council was the first organizational embodiment of the ecumenical spirit in the churches themselves.[129] Besides providing a small, permanent organization to carry on its work continuously, it has held four great world conferences; at Jerusalem in 1928, at Tambaram (Madras), India in 1938, at Whitby, Canada in 1947 and at Willingen, Germany in 1952.

The function of the IMC were to stimulate thinking and investigate on missionary questions, to help co-ordinate the activities of the national missionary organizations in different countries through common consultation, to help to unite Christian public opinion in support of freedom of conscience and religion and of missionary liberty; to help bring the Christian forces of the world in seeking justice in international and inter social relations, especially where politically weaker people are involved; to be responsible for the publication of the International Review of Missions and to call another missionary conference as and when this should be desirable.[130]

With the approval of the IMC's authorized administrative committee that met in 1959 and 1960 on the required documents for merger and the constitution of the commission of the World Mission and Evangelism, the IMC became one of the departments of the World Council of Churches (WCC) at the third WCC

[129] Bengt Sundkler, "Daring, in Order to Know: The IMC from Edinburgh to New Delhi," *International Review of Mission*, 51/201 (January, 1962), 4-11.

[130] Snaitang, *A History of Ecumenical Movement ...*, 107-108.

assembly in New Delhi on 19th November 1961. Thus, IMC became known as the division of World Mission and Evangelism of the World Council of Churches.

2.6. THE FAITH AND ORDER MOVEMENT

A second movement developing from the 1910 meeting was the Faith and Order Movement. One of the purposes of this was to explore together the reasons why denominations differed from each other, when they worshipped the same Lord and used the same Bible. Immediately following the Edinburgh Conference, when on the initiative of the Protestant Episcopal Church in the United States of America, a plan for holding a World Conference on Faith and Order was lunched.[131] After an interim of seventeen years, the Conference was met in Lausanne, Switzerland in 1927.[132] For the first time official representatives of the separated bodies of Christendom studied together the areas of agreement and of difference, in the hope that someday, under the leading of the spirit, the ground of full unity might be found. The second Faith and Order Conference was held at Edinburgh, Scotland in 1937.[133] The Faith and Order Movement was formed with the specific purpose, to call for the common proclamation of the gospel required the visible unity of the church which again called the churches to face squarely their doctrinal and theological differences, settle their disputes and thus heel the divisions and re-establish mutual communion.

2.7. THE LIFE AND WORK MOVEMENT

The third great movement stemming from 1910 was the Life and Work Movement, came to its most vivid organizational expression at the Stockholm Conference in 1925.[134] Its purpose was to make possible co-operative undertakings other than missions. Here for the first time the new sense of responsibility in the churches for making Jesus Christ the Lord not only of the individual' heart, but of every realm on social, economic and political life, came to a clear focus on an international scale.[135] There had already been important united efforts along this line in some countries[136] but Stockholm signalized the rise of a world-wide concern for a more united and therefore stronger impact of the churches on human life in its every-day affairs. The Oxford Conference of 1937 on 'Church, Community and

131 W. A. Visser'T Hooft, ed., *The First Assembly of the World Council of Churches*, vol. V (New York: Harber & Brothers, 1949), 13.

132 W. A. Visser't Hooft, *The Genesis of the World Council of Churches* (Geneva: WCC, 1982), 21.

133 Hooft, ed., *The First Assembly of the World Council of Churches* ..., 13. Also see in H. N. Bate, ed., *Faith and Order: Proceedings of the World Conference Lausanne* (London: Student Christian Movement, 1927), ix.

134 Hooft, ed., *The First Assembly of the World Council of Churches* ..., 12.

135 Hooft, ed., *The First Assembly of the World Council of Churches* ..., 12.

136 These united efforts are the federal Council of the Churches of Christ in America and in the C.O.P.E.C. conference in Britain.

State,' which focused attention on christian strategy in relation to economics, international order and education, marked the next significant stage in this development.[137]

There were others who believed that the ecumenical need of the hour was to promote fellowship and peace in a world torn apart by the world war and the work for just and free society on the basis of the christain principle of truth, justice and love. To serve this purpose the Life and Work Movement was formed.

It was quite natural that these three movements, with different emphasis, but having many of the same people interested in each, should think of joining forces. Out of the meetings at Oxford and Edinburgh in the summer of 1937, there came a proposal to form a World Council of Churches through the merging of the Faith and Order and Life and Work Movements. Although, the International Missionary Council continued its separate existence for more than two decades, it was fully co-operative with the World Council of Churches and became a division of the larger body in 1961.

2.8. WORLD COUNCIL OF CHURCHES

Although, necessary plans for organization of the World Council of Churches had been completed by 1939, the coming of World War II prevented their implementation. It was in 1948, at Amsterdam that this organization finally came into being.[138] The historical influences which have brought it into being have been many, some of them was reaching back for more than a century. But, the ecumenical movement as we know it today is the fruition of the prayers and efforts of a single generation.[139] More particularly, the World Council of Churches is the confluence of three streams which have poured their contributions into a central channel. These are the missionary movement which has made the church a world-wide community. The Life and Work movement, which has brought the churches together in their attempts to make Christianity more effective in its relation to society and the Faith and Order movement, which has to explore the difference in basic Christian conviction that must be reconciled if the unity of the church as one visible body of Christ is to be attained.[140]

The constitution began with a statement which describes the nature and basis of this council. It states, "The World Council of Churches is a fellowship of churches which accept out Lord Jesus Christ as God and Savior."[141] It offers a minimal statement of the basis for fellowship and co-operative work, therefore

---

[137] Hooft, ed., *The First Assembly of the World Council of Churches* ..., 13.

[138] Hooft, *The Genesis of the World Council of Churches* ..., 64.

[139] Hooft, ed., *The First Assembly of the World Council of Churches* ..., 12.

[140] Hooft, ed., *The First Assembly of the World Council of Churches* ..., 12. Also see in F. Hrangkhuma, *An Introduction to Church History* ..., 370.

[141] Visser' T Hooft, *The First Assembly of the World Council of Churches* ..., 197.

at the third general assembly in 1961 a revised statement was adopted. It states, "The World Council of Churches is a fellowship of churches which confess the Lord Jesus Christ as God and Saviour, according to the Scripture and therefore seek to fulfill their common calling to the glory of one God, Father, Son and Holy Spirit."[142] There was keenly aware of the churches responsibility in a secularized and non-Christian world as such to facilitate the more effective action of the Christian church in the modern world the World Council of Churches was created.

The WCC was the product of a number of streams and strains. One derives from the world missionary conference at Edinburg in 1910, the event from which modern ecumenism measures its anniversaries. In 1961 the International Missionary Conference an extension of the original meeting joined forces with the WCC. A second strain came from the world churches efforts to work and serve together. This part of the movement was called Life and Work and met in two great conferences at Stockholm in 1926 and at Oxford in 1937.[143] Many Christian were uneasy, however about unitive efforts based on anything short of doctrinal consensus or at least of profound discussion of valid differences. Out of their concern the Faith and Order movement was born. Faith and Order held four world conferences beginning in 1927 at Lausanne. The formal entrance of the Eastern Orthodox churches of Russia, Bulgaria, Poland and Rumania in 1961 enhanced and complicated the WCC's life, since tens of millions from communist nations were now represented.[144]

Several useful purposes are served by the World Council of Churches. Carrying on the work of the earlier movements, it promotes biblical and theological study by interdenominational committees and facilitates common undertakings. Through various means it seeks to encourage the development of an ecumenical spirit. As men and women from various backgrounds are brought together in study groups or for meetings on various matters, they became more aware of their kinship in Christ. Valuable books and pamphlets have been published through commission of the council, and there are several special commissions and committees which have permanent staff members, enabling the work to be prosecuted without loss of continuity. Special committees also sponsor theological studies, keep abreast of international affairs and encourage an informed christian conscience at points of tension. It provides aid to refugees and furnishes a channel through which churches may give relief to distressed areas, help interested young

[142] Hrangkhuma, *An Introduction to Church History ...*, 372.

[143] Madeleine Barot, "1946: Its Significance for the WCC," *Ecumenical Review*, 39/2, (April, 1987), 216-221.

[144] Marty, *Ecumenical Movement ...*, 623.

people find opportunities for ecumenical education abroad and stimulate interest in evangelism and numerous other practical matters.[145]

The World Council seeks to cultivate a deeper sense of Christian unity, to make it possible to co-operate in many areas where a single denomination could not effectively operate and to encourage Christians to fulfill their mission under God more faithfully. Feeling deeply the need for unity to become more visible, the council tries to be an agency through which that unity can be expressed. It is not easy to forget the differences and there are many forces including misunderstanding and ignorance which work against this co-operative work. However, there is a determination to overcome obstacles for Christ's sake.

2.9. THE NATIONAL COUNCIL OF CHURCHES

In addition to the World Council of Churches for co-operation on a worldwide scope, there are agencies particularly devoted for co-operative Christian work on national and regional levels. Organized in 1950, it was the heir of a number of earlier movements, particularly the Federal Council of Churches. In the face of complex problems, a growing Protestantism had previously sought new ways of co-operating in evangelism, missions and Christian education in the latter part of the nineteenth century. Among these earlier interdenominational organizations were the Y.M.C.A, the Y.W.C.A., the International Society of Christian Endeavour (ISCE), the Evangelical Alliance (EA), the Uniform Lesson plan, the World Students Christian Federation (WSCF) and various others. In 1908 the Federal Council of Churches (FCC) was constituted and became the main channel for co-operative work.[146]

In 1950, the Federal Council and most of the special purpose organizations were merged into the National Council of the Churches of Christ in America. The preamble states the basis of the new organization as follows, "in the providence of God, the time has come when it seems fitting more fully to manifest oneness in Jesus Christ as Divine Lord and Savior, by the creation of an inclusive co-operative agency of the Christian churches of the United States of America to continue and extend the following general functions."[147] In continuing the work of the Foreign Missions Council and the Home Mission Council, it provides a useful means of exchanging information and coordinating activities of many denominations. Through a commission it calls together representatives of the churches to plan uniform lessons for Sunday school. Many practical interests are served through the channels afforded by the agencies of this interdenominational organization. At many points, it can provide channels of co-operation and communications,

[145] Hendrik Kraemer, "The Formation of the World Council and Its Significance for the Relations of the Churches to one Another," *Ecumenical Review*, 1/3 (Spring, 1949), 260-266.

[146] "National Council of Churches events marks 100 years of Ecumenism," *Christian Century*, 127/25 (December, 2010), 17.

[147] Maring and Hudson, *A Baptist Manual ….*, 200.

and make it possible for certain tasks to be done together which would not be done at all without such co-operation. The very nature of the church as one under Christ demands that the branches of the church can work together and maintains close working relationship with many local types of council of churches.

2.10. THE BAPTIST WORLD ALLIANCE

In addition to World Council of Churches for interdenominational co-operation, there are also channels through which various Baptist groups work together. There are numerous Baptist groups around the world. In order to help maintain some sense of their common identity, to assist one another and to co-operate in some mutual tasks, there are various agencies through which they work. It is under the banner of the Baptist World Alliance (BWA), organized in 1905 in London that Baptists people in all parts of the Christian world are united.[148] Its purpose is stated in the preamble to the constitution of the alliance, "the Baptist World Alliance, extending over every part of the world, exists in order more fully to show the essential oneness of Baptists people in the Lord Jesus Christ, to impart inspiration to the brotherhood and to promote the spirit of fellowship, service and co-operation among its members, but this alliance may in no way interfere with the independence of the churches or assume the administrative functions of existing organizations."[149]

It is in this purpose of imparting inspiration through the infrequent meetings and in affording links by which the sense of fellowship between Baptists can be strengthened, the Alliance has been most useful. At some point it has helped to safeguard and promote full religious liberty in places around the world where such liberty has been denied or threatened. With a minimum staff of permanent workers, it cannot accomplish much beyond these things. However it is of value for these contributions.[150] There are other Baptist agencies through which certain activities can be co-ordinated apart from Baptist World Alliance. The co-operation in this venture was limited largely to simultaneous emphases upon evangelism, for each group carried out its own program and methods differed greatly. Indeed, enthusiasm for co-operation and fellowship among the Baptists are encouraging.

2.11. PARADIGM FOR THE DEVELOPMENT OF NORTH EAST INDIA CHRISTIAN COUNCIL

Historically, the Modern Missionary Movement came in the form of a number of missions from Europe and America. Each propagated its own type of teachings and its own system of organization and discipline. This resulted in the inevitable

---

148 Richard V. Pierard, "The Baptist World Alliance: An Overview of Its History," *Review & Expositor*, 103/4 (Fall, 2006), 707-732.

149 E. Glenn Hinson, "The Baptist World Alliance: Its Identity and Ecumenical Involvement," *Ecumenical Review*, 46/4 (October, 1994), 406-412.

150 Townley Lord, *Baptist World Fellowship* (Nasville: Broadman Press, 1955), 24.

birth of a number of separate Christian communities, like Anglican, Methodist, Presbyterian and so on. Though they maintained their denominational positions, they formed the habit of consulting together on common problems. A measure of co-operation in evangelistic methods, in running institutions and in matters of discipline, became necessary and developed an unwritten convention of comity.[151] There was more unity feeling and co-operation between the denominations in India. As a result several experiments in church union in India were made by Indian Christians at various levels like Christo Samaj in Calcutta, National Christian Alliance in Western India and the National Church in Madras.[152] With this there came an urge to come together into one Indian Christian community, unhampered be denominational differences and disregarding mission allegiances. Conferences were held by Indian Christians belonging to different missions, pointing out to the authorities of the churches and missions and the need for working towards a larger unity. The Indian Christians began to cultivate the desire for unity in action, in spite of their differences in doctrines and worships. This led to the formation of various Christian union movement in India like, National Missionary Councils, local union of Presbyterian in South India in 1910, the South India Union Church in 1908, the Church of South India in 1948, the Church of North India in 1981 and the Communion of Churches in India (CSI, CNI, and MTS) are some of the union movement that led to the development of Church Union Movement in NEI.

2.12. OVERVIEW ON THE CHURCH UNION MOVEMENT IN INDIA

2.12.1. CHURCH OF SOUTH INDIA

In the history of Indian Church the formation of Church of South India is unique event because it was the first time that Episcopal and non-Episcopal churches united to form one church. The first proposal for a union of the churches in South India has come from the Anglican Bishop V. S. Azaria. This witnessed the formation of Church of South India (CSI), which was inaugurated at St. George Cathedral in Madras on 27, September 1947.[153] It came into being as the result of three different churches in south India, uniting namely, The Wesleyan Methodist church, The Anglican Church, and the South India United Church (SIUC).[154]

---

[151] Comity is a principle, in which each mission was recognized as occupying certain territories and it was agreed that other mission should abstain from entering and wirking I those territories. Ref. C. B Firth, *An Introduction to Indian Church History* ..., 234.

[152] Isaac Devadoss, "A Historical Survey of Ecumenism in India," *Ecumenism in India Today* ..., 16.

[153] V. V. Thomas, *Conciliar Ecumenism: The Beginning of the Former CSI-CNI-MTC Joint Council* (Bangalore: BTESS/SATHRI, 2008), 7.

[154] K. M. George, *Church of South India Life in Union* (1947-1997 (Delhi: ISPCK, 1999), 1.

The SIUC was itself the result of a federated union which had taken place in 1908 between the Presbyterian and Congregational Churches in South India.[155]

The formation of the CSI can be traced directly to the Modern Ecumenical Movement and the International Missionary Conference (IMC) in 1910 at Edinburgh. The recommendation for cooperation in mission among the churches led to joint evangelistic outreach by several Churches in South India from 1918. The awareness of the scandal of disunity and the discovery that all the churches had the same gospel to proclaim and the same testimonies to give induced the leaders of the churches to call a conference on church union at Tranquebar in May 1919. Bishop Azariah of Dornakal was one of the pioneers of this move.[156] At this conference, a joint committee was formed to plan for the union of the churches. It took 28 years of negotiations before the churches decided to unite.[157]

At first the Anglican Churches insisted on the historic episcopate as the basis for union. The South India United Church insisted on the spiritual oneness among the churches as the basis. They all finally agreed to adopt as a basis what was known as the Lambeth Quadrilateral (LQ), namely acceptance of the Bible, the two ecumenical creeds, i.e., the apostle and the Nicene, the two universal sacraments of baptism and the Eucharist and the historic episcopate. The CSI adopted the threefold ordained ministry of bishops, presbyters, and deacons.[158]

The primary aim of CSI is to achieve the unity of all the christian churches in South India by which the evangelization of India would be easier. The ordained ministers of all the united churches were accepted as ministers of new church. This was based on the affirmation that God had blessed with 'undistinguished regard' the ministries of the uniting churches and on the theological insight that ministry belongs to the church and not the church to the ministry. The ministries were considered as having been united when the churches were united. All ordinations in the CSI are by Episcopal laying on of hands.[159] The structure of CSI consists of local congregations, diocese, and synod. Each diocese has a bishop and one of the diocesan bishops is elected as moderator for a term basis. The very fact of the formation of Church of South India was a great challenge to the other churches in India, particularly the churches in NEI.

---

[155] K. M. George, *Church of South India Negotiation Towards Union 1919-1947* (Kerala: K.M. George, 1997), 18.

[156] Thomas, *Conciliar Ecumenism* ..., 6-7.

[157] J. Russell Chandran, "Church of South India," *A Dictionary of Asian Christianity*, edited by Scott W. Sunquist (Grand Rapids, Michigan: William B Eerdmans Publishing company, 2001), 175.

[158] Chandran, *Church of South India* ..., 175.

[159] Chandran, *Church of South India* ..., 175.

2.12.2. CHURCH OF NORTH INDIA

In the spirit of Church Union in South India, the Congregational Churches and the Presbyterian Church in India joined together in Dec. 1924 to form the United Church of Northern India (UCNI). The first General Assembly of the UCNI (1924) sent out invitations to other churches and mission agencies to explore the possibility of a wider union. The Wesleyan Methodist Church responded and proposed that invitations be sent to all the churches which were willing to come together for a consultation to discuss the possibility of a union of churches.[160] As a result the First Round Table Conference on the issue of union was held on 10-11 April 1929, with the representatives of six churches, namely the UCNI, the British-related Baptist, the Anglican, the British and Australian related Methodist and the American related Methodist, a meeting was convened at the Methodist Church's Lall Bagh Girls School, Lucknow.[161] This meeting paved the way for negotiation for the organic union of churches.

The Second Round Table Conference was held in November 1930 at Delhi, with the Anglicans now present as official participants. There were also visitors from Presbyterian churches who had not previously been involved as well as from the South India Joint Committee.[162] As follows the Third, Fourth, and Fifth Round Table Conferences were held in 1939, 1941, and 1947 respectively, through which the Basis of Negotiation and an agreement on the mode of unification of the episcopates of the Methodist Church in Southern Asia (MCSA) and the Church of India, Pakistan, Burma and Ceylon (CIPBC) was developed, a Negotiating Committee (NC) was also formed. The first meeting of this Negotiating Committee was held at Calcutta 27-30 March 1951 and produced the first plan of church union. This plan was further revised by the Negotiating Committee at meetings held in 1952 and 1953 and the second edition was published in 1954. At the request of the churches in Pakistan and the same plan also provided for an identical union of churches in Pakistan. In 1957, the third edition of the plan was adopted by the Negotiating Committee and was referred to the seven negotiation churches for decision.[163]

In March 1965 the Negotiating Committee produced the fourth and final edition of the plan of church union in north India and Pakistan, which became the basis of the union from which the Church of North India has evolve. The final plan was drawn up by and referred to the Baptist churches in Northern India

---

160 Pritam B. Santram, "Church of North India," *A Dictionary of Asian Christianity*, edited by Scott W. Sunquist (Grand Rapids, Michigan: William B Eerdmans Publishing Company, 2001), 173.

161 James Killock, *Breakthrough for Church Union in North India and Pakistan* (Madras: CLS, 1965), 3, cited by V.V. Thomas, *Conciliar Ecumenism: The Beginning of the Former CSI-CNI-MTC Joint Council* (Bangalore: BTESS/SATHRI, 2008), 10.

162 *Plan of Church Union in North India and Pakistan* (Madras: CLS, 1965), iii.

163 Santram, *Church of North India* ..., 174.

(CBCNI), Churches of the Brethren in India (CBI), Disciple of Christ (DC), Methodist Church (MC), Methodist Church in Southern Asia (MCSA) and the Church of India, Pakistan, Burma and Ceylon (CIPBC), and United Church of Northern India (UCNI).[164] Although, these seven churches participated in the negotiations, one of them, the MCSA (now known as Methodist church of India (MCSA) having earlier accepted the plan in 1965 with the required two third majority, later in Aug 1970 rejected the plan and opted out of the proposed church union. The remaining six churches (CBCNI, CBI, DC, CIPBC, MC, British and Australian conferences and UCNI) acting through their respective constitutional procedures and appropriate legislative and executive bodies, accepted the fourth edition of the plan 1965, and entered into the union which was inaugurated on Sunday, 29 November 1970 at Nagpur, establishing the Church of North India (CNI).[165]

The union was not meant to absorb one church by another. The united church values and is enriched by the diverse spiritual and liturgical heritage of the uniting churches. The unity is in baptism, ministry, sacramental communion and mission. It is unity in diversity. Members of CNI are assured full freedom of belief and practice insofar as these do not conflict with the faith and order of the whole church. This was a significant signpost for the development of the spirit of Church Union Movement negotiation among the churches in NEI.

2.12.2.1. Some Theological Insights of the Debate in the Formation of the CNI

During the time of negotiation process, CNI Negotiating Committees were faced many obstacles which almost brought the process to a standstill. But, the Committee would finally succeed to bring the revised edition of the plan of Church Union (1965). The difficulties were chiefly centered around mainly on three issues; the place of the episcopate; acceptance of the ministry of different churches and the tradition of infant and believer's baptism.

2.12.2.1.1. Episcopate

In CNI negotiating churches have two Episcopal form of government. The Methodist Church in Southern Asia lays stress on the constitutional form of episcopacy, while the Anglican Church also treasures the historic continuity of its Bishops with the early church. Despite this difference which was a source of considerable basis for bringing together the two episcopates was finally evolved. The episcopate of the church of North India will be both constitutional and historic. It will be constitutional because its bishops will be appointed and will perform their functions in accordance with the constitution of the church. It will be historic, because it will have historic continuity with the early church. However,

---

[164] Snaitang, *A History of Ecumenical Movement* ..., 154.

[165] Santram, *Church of North India*..., 174-175.

the CNI will not be committed to any particular theological interpretation of episcopacy.[166]

2.12.2.1.2. Baptism

After a long period of negotiation between the negotiating churches for the acceptance of uniform Christian baptism because the negotiating churches accept both infant baptism and believer's baptism, some recognize only baptism of believers. However, it finally found which could satisfy the convictions of all. Since British Baptist Churches are included in the Church of North India negotiation, they accept both believer's baptism and the infant baptism as two alternative practices.[167] In the case of parents who desire their children to be baptized, there is a provision for the blessing of children in their infancy. Admission to communicant membership for the baptized is through confirmation by a bishop or its equivalent rite.[168]

Baptist representative have stated that their churches will be able to enter the union, since in the Plan 'provision is made for the dedication of infants and the administration of baptism by immersion as the seal of conscious faith and profession of faith is required of those baptized in infancy before admission to membership in full standing in the church.[169]

2.12.2.1.3. Ministry

The negotiators in North India sought to have a unified ministry from the outset. The different churches followed different practices in ordaining their ministers for example Episcopal ordination, ordination by the presbytery and congregational ordination. These ordination rites also reflect differing views regarding the ministry which are held in the churches. The problem was how to bring about unified ministry which would have validity for all the differing traditions coming into the union. Finally, the negotiators had to evolve an acceptable basis for the unification of the ministry. This is embodied in the intention of the representative act of the unification of the ministry.[170]

On the ministry of women the Plan (1965) says two things; firstly "the office of deaconess as practiced in the early church" and secondly, "the admission

---

[166] James Massey, "A Church According to the Best and Earliest Traditions," in *Church of North India; According to the Best and Earliest Traditions of the Church: Papers and Reports presented at the Theological Workshop of CNI Evaluation Commission held on 11th and 12th August, 2007*, edited by James Massey, (New Delhi: CNI Evaluation Commission, 2008), 18.

[167] James Massey, "A Church According to the Best and Earliest Traditions,"..., 19.

[168] Santram, *Church of North India*..., 175.

[169] Quoted in Forward to Union, *The Church of North India, A Hand Book* (Delhi and Lucknow: CNI, 1968), Cited by James Massey, "A Church According to the Best and Earliest Traditions,"..., 19.

[170] James Massey, "A Church According to the Best and Earliest Traditions,"..., 19.

of women to ordained ministry."[171] Later this section of Plan was included in the constitution as part of the Faith and Order of the church in section VII (b).[172] In regards to women ordination the Church of North India has taken positive stand on 4th October 1980. The resolutions are as following;

1. The church of North India admits women into the ordination ministry.
2. If in any diocese of the church of North India the need arise for a woman to be ordained into ministry of the word and sacrament the bishop concerned may do so with the approval of the Diocesan council.[173] As a result in many Dioceses of the Church of North India women are part of the ordained ministry.

2.12.3. COMMUNION OF CHURCHES IN INDIA/THE JOINT COUNCIL OF THE CSI-CNI-MTC

The Communion of Churches in India (CCI) is a representative body of three main Churches in India; The Church of South India, The Church of North India, and the Malankara Mar Thoma Syrian Church.[174] The three churches are in full communion with each other. Prior to 2004, the CCI was known as the "Joint Council of Churches in India" which was constituted of the same member churches. The formation of the Joint Council was one of the important ecumenical achievements in the Indian Church in twentieth century. It was formed through decision taken by the highest decision-making bodies of each of the three. The first meeting was held on July 4 5, 1978 at Nagpur.[175] Its objective has clearly been stated in the preamble thus, 'The Joint Council of the CSI-CNI-MTC, has been constituted as the visible organ for common action by the three churches which recognize themselves as belonging to the one Christ Jesus in India, even while remaining as autonomous churches, each having its own identity of traditions and organizational structure.'[176]

In 1973, Theological Commissions from each of the three churches met to consider exploring possible areas of cooperation and unity. The first meeting of the Joint Theological Commission (JTC) was held in January 1975 at Madras.[177] The object of the Commission define as;

---

[171] *Plan of Church Union in North India and Pakistan*, fourth edition, Madras, 1965, Page, B.

[172] *The Constitution of the Church of North India*, (Revised), January 2006, 2.

[173] *Minutes of the Fourth Ordinary Meeting of the Synod of the Church of North India*, 3rd to 6th Oct., 1980. Cited by James Massey, "A Church According to the Best and Earliest Traditions,"..., 20.

[174] V.V. Thomas, *Conciliar Ecumenism* ..., xiv.

[175] V.V. Thomas, *Conciliar Ecumenism* ..., 35.

[176] Snaitang, *A History of Ecumenical Movement* ..., 174.

[177] Devadoss, A Historical Survey of Ecumenism in India," Ecumenism in India Today ..., 24.

> ...to explore the possibilities of close cooperation between the CNI, CSI and MTC and to discuss the question of faith and order and other relevant issues. The aim of JTC was to search for the possible ways that there might be union between these churches and also to explore possibilities of working together especially in the field of evangelization in India and other areas of cooperation in the fulfilment of the mission of the Church.[178]

During their third meeting in September 1976, the JTC passed the proposal for a new model of union for these three churches, which was accepted and inaugurated in 1978.[179] As the Mar Thoma Church has oriental traditions which it wishes to preserve, the Church did not agree to lose its identity by merging with the other churches. The CSI and CNI, formed by the merging of different denominations from the Western tradition, did not have difficulty with the idea of again merging to form a new church.[180]

The Joint Council is not a traditional church negotiation aimed at organic union but it is an attempt to manifest organic oneness through a common structure, while retaining the autonomy of the three churches. According to the preamble of the Constitution the object of the Joint Council is;

1. To serve as the common organ of the three churches and of the whole church of Jesus Christ in India.
2. To help the churches and to fulfil the mission of evangelization of the people of India and to witness to the righteousness of God revealed in the Gospel of Jesus Christ by striving for a just society.[181]

However, one major task was to find a common name for the fulfilling all the aspirations of the three uniting churches for the future united church in India. The new name was adopted and announced at the meeting held on 11-14 November, 2000 at Calcutta.[182] The Communion of churches in India has been constituted as the visible organ of common expression of the life and witness by the founding churches which recognize themselves as belonging to the one church of Jesus Christ in India, even while remaining as autonomous churches, each having its own identity of traditions and organizational structures.

---

[178] George, *Church of South India Life in Union* ..., 150; Cited by Devadoss, A Historical Survey of Ecumenism in India," Ecumenism in India Today ..., 24.

[179] Dhirendra Kumar Sahu, *United and Uniting; A Story of the Church of North India* (Delhi: ISPCK, 2001), 89.

[180] "*The Communion of Churches in* India," in *en.wikipedia.org/wiki/Communion_of_Churches_in_India.*

[181] *The Constitution of the Joint Council of the CNI, CSI and MTC* (Delhi: ISPCK, 1981); cited by Sahu, *United and Uniting*..., 89.

[182] Sahu, *United and Uniting*..., 89.

The formation of the Communion of Churches in India (CCI) marked the beginning of a new development of church relationship and common action among the CNI, the CSI, and the Mar Thoma Church. The representatives of the three churches came together to affirm their preparedness to explore new ways of growing in mutual understanding and a deepening of their experience of oneness in Christ. In a declaration read out at a public function to celebrate the event they said "We see this as a divine moment to affirm unity in an increasingly divided world. We affirm that this vision for unity and action will capture a holistic vision as we respond to God's call to discipleship."[183]

The CCI had a number of important insights and affirmations, particularly in relation to the basic principle on which Ecumenism will be practised in coming years. The model of 'organic union' with its implied requirement of a fusion of particular traditions has given way to a vision of unity that required the upholding of plurality. It was realised beyond doubt that in the Indian context the churches cannot experience their oneness in Christ without accepting the worth of diversity among them. Diversity is not something to be tolerated but to be accepted as essential to unity. The message to the churches stated, "Diversity is to be celebrated while unity is to be affirmed. The Indian panorama is diverse, socially, culturally, religiously, economically and in several other ways. Diversity should enrich the community rather than fragment it. A similar scenario is seen in the life of the church. Therefore, respecting and accepting each other's uniqueness amidst plurality as a reality is essential to foster the unity of the churches and humankind."[184] The CCI always encourage and look forward to a reality that transcends every human borderline that stands in the way of realisation of God's ultimate plan to sum up all things in Christ. Church fellowship should not be regarded as an end in itself, it aims at the unity of humankind and of creation in its totality.

2.13. CONCLUSION

Above cited missionary conference became most influential instrument in shaping the idea of One, Holy, Catholic and Apostolic church. The impression of forming such Christian unity is a divine summons to the Christians to rediscover their visible unity, which they had lost in the course of history and thus to realize the prayer of their Lord and Master Jesus Christ, that 'they all may be one'. Subsequently, various Christian organizations and churches developed different models of Christian Unity. These missionary conferences and movements became the contributory factors in the process of Christian Unity discussion in many parts of the world, even in Northeast India.

---

[183] Abraham P. Athyal, "*Towards a New Ecumenical Vision*," in www.csichurch.com/article/.. *./communion _of_churches_in_india.htm,1.*

[184] Athyal, *Towards a New Ecumenical Vision* ..., 1.

Chapter 3

Formation of Christian Unity in Northeast India

INTRODUCTION

The spirit of Christian Unity began to spread across the globe, from the subsistence of Modern Missionary era, which has even reached the region of Northeast India. In this section we worked on historical sources and theological basis for the development of Christian Unity in NEI. The formation of Christian unity in North East India so called 'North East India Christian Council' (NEICC) was decisive moment among the churches in the region. However the Christian Unity negotiations could not achieve what they intended when the council was formed will be discuss in this chapter.

3.1. BEGINNING OF CHRISTIAN UNITY IN NEI

The history of Christian Unity in Northeast India is no doubt that North East India Christian Council (NEICC), which has been the main church based organization that strives for Christian Unity in NEI. It had its origin in the Bengal Christian Council (BCC) in 1926. For which J. Fortis Jyrwa stated that;

> For a number of years the Welsh Presbyterians and the American Baptist were part of the Bengal Christian Council. But, in course of time, it was considered unprofitable to continue this organized union between the two provinces because problems in Assam were different from those in Bengal. Ultimately, the American Baptist dropped out though the Welsh Presbyterian continued for some more time."[185]

[185] J. Fortis Jyrwa, "Church Union Movement in North East India; A Historical Perspective," in *Church Ministry and Mission: Eassy in Honour of K.I. Aier* ..., 58.

The Assam Baptist Christians and Welsh Presbyterian were part of it till the Assam Christian Council (ACC) was constituted in 1937. There were certain inconveniences to be together with Bengal Christian Council (BCC), as such the Welsh Presbyterian mission initiated a meeting at Shillong on September 22, 1936.[186] The main purpose of this meeting was "to discuss together preliminary ways and problems in which they had a common interest" with a view to enhance mutual help, co-operation in matter of literary works, exchange of representative of church assemblies, establishing a joint theological college for higher studies and promote a closer relation among the Christians.[187] There attended six mission representatives in the meeting namely the American Baptist Mission, Santal Mission of the Northern Churches, Gossner Evangelical Lutheran Mission, Co-operative Baptist Mission of North America, English Baptist Mission, Welsh Presbyterian Mission and two Churches: the Church of God and the Church of India.[188]

The Assam Christian Council report said that, 'while no definite action towards organizing a council could be taken, it was expressed that such a council would be desirable and a committee was appointed to draw 'a scale of representation of churches and mission…'.[189] However, office bearers were appointed to carry out the meetings and to carry out the necessary efforts for the church union. Following this, an appeal was sent out to all the churches and missions to send representatives to discuss together the issue for the possibilities of forming a council.[190] As a response to appeal on April 15, 1937 a joint meeting of authorized representatives met from various churches and missions and was unanimously voted for the formation of a separate Christian council in Assam. An Executive Committee consisting of six members[191] was also formed and a draft constitution was drawn up and accepted by it.[192] Following this, on November 23, 1937 the meeting of joint conference at Shillong, and the meeting declared

[186] J. Fortis Jyrwa, "Church Union Movement in North East India Historical Perspective," in *Good News For North East India*, edited by Renthy Keitzar (Guwahati: CLC, 1995), 23.

[187] *Assam Christian Council, Minutes and Proceedings of the Annual Session*, March 29-31, 1940.

[188] *Assam Christian Council, Minutes and Proceedings 1940…*

[189] *Assam Christian Council, Minutes and Proceedings 1940…*, 9.

[190] Jyrwa, "Church Union Movement in North East India Historical Perspective," in *Good News For North East India …*, 23.

[191] Following names are the Executive Committee; Chairman Bishop of Assam, Vice-Chairman Rev. J.W. Robert, Secretary & Treasurer Rev. Adamo, Mr. C. Goldsmith Member, Rev. F.J. Paper Member and Rev. L. Gatpoh Member.

[192] *Assam Christian Council, Minutes and Proceedings 1940…*, 9.

the council constituted as the 'Assam Christian Council.'[193] Also this meeting declared its aims to bring closer unity and co-operation.[194]

A significant spadework had been done during 1937 and 1938. A programme was arranged for the ACC to meet at Guwahati on December 3-5, 1938, which was considered to be the first church union meeting under the banner of the ACC. [195] The following affiliated units sent their delegates;

1. The Assam Baptist Mission and Assam Baptist Convention
2. The Welsh Presbyterian Mission and Church
3. The Anglican Communion
4. The B.M.S and Church, Lushal Hill
5. The Gossner Evangelical Lutheran Mission and Church and
6. The Bible Society of North East Region[196]

The aim and purpose of the Assam Christian Council was;

1. To encourage Christian fellowship, co-operation and comity by common counsel among the various Christian bodies (Church and Mission) in Assam.
2. To co-operate in matter of common interest such as education, publication of Christian literature and in the preaching of Gospel of our Lord and Savior Jesus Christ.
3. To create and maintain public opinion in the province;
4. To consult other Christian Councils as and when necessity rises;[197]

When it was revised in 1947 two more proposals were added:

5. To co-operate with the NCC of India, Burma and Ceylon;
6. To take all possible steps to give effect to the principle that in the Christian enterprise the church is central and permanent.[198]

With these objectives, the Assam Christian Council had been steadily growing and made several attempts to bring closer unity and co-operation among the churches in North East India.

---

[193] *Assam Christian Council, Minutes and Proceedings 1940…*, 10.

[194] *Assam Christian Council, Minutes and Proceedings 1940…*, 13.

[195] *Assam Christian Council, Minutes and Proceedings 1940…*

[196] Jyrwa, *Church Union Movement in North East India A Historical Perspective* in *Church Ministry and Mission: Eassy in Honour of K.I. Aier* ..., 61.

[197] *Assam Christian Council, Minutes and Proceedings 1940…*, 3.

[198] *Assam Christian Council, Minutes and Proceedings of the 10th Annual Conference*, 1947, 13.

3.2. FURTHER DEVELOPMENT OF CHRISTIAN UNITY

Initial efforts to develop the unity and co-operate with a wider objective of Christian unity in NEI was made by the Assam Christian Council. The council met annually and had a permanent full-time secretary for proper maintenance of the office. It was after the Western Missionaries handed over the ecclesiastical administration to the indigenous church leaders, that a definite movement towards church union gains momentum in NEI. It was, however, only a decade and a half after the indigenous leaders took over the entire responsibility, which the churches in the region began to seriously consider church unity. Then the ACC proposed church union discussion with the object to determine whether its constituent churches were interested in forming a church union of their own. In spite of many indigenous differences, the leaders of churches and missions came more forward to form church unity in NEI. In 1942 report there is a section on 'Fuller Co-operation among Christian Bodies in Assam,' which reads as follows:

1. That the churches affiliated to the council accept members from other churches in the council on receipt of certificate of membership particularly in places where there is a congregation of the church to which the applicant belongs.
2. That in cases where full membership cannot be given, an associate membership be established giving full Christian fellowship and privileges of worship but not qualifying for holding office.
3. That all attempts to establish a new church in village where one church already exists be discouraged.[199]

At the ACC annual meeting at Shillong in 1940, there was a special section entitled "Co-operation" as the secretary's report presented:

> There is a very definite trend towards closer co-operation on the part of most of our churches and it is hoped that we shall soon see the day when we will take counsel with one another regarding such matters as such membership, Christian workers whether evangelist or village teachers opening of new work or closing of old.[200]

Again in 1942 it was reported that although such a project to form a united theological college might not be immediately practicable, it must aim to have one united Protestant Church in Assam.[201] During 1940s the theme of unity and co-operation dominated the thinking and proceedings of the leaders of the Council.

---

[199] Jyrwa, "Church Union Movement in North East India Historical Perspective," in *Good News For North East India* ..., 25.

[200] *Assam Christian Council, Minutes and Proceedings 1940*..., 13.

[201] Assam Christian Council, Minutes and Proceedings of the 5th Annual Conference, 1942, 5.

They talked about subject like "Unity among Christian people and means to securing the same," and "the means to the healing of divisions."[202]

The seventh Assam Christian Council annual meeting was held in 1944 at Shillong, where they gave more importance to 'Unity of the Church' in NEI.[203] Based on the theme they made three resolutions as follows;

1. That the council requested the President to draft a message to be sent to all affiliated bodies emphasizing the spiritual aspect of church union in Assam and urge its members to search their hearts and mind and pray about this great question of church union.
2. That the council request all affiliated bodies to give attention to the resolutions in the minutes regarding church union and the message of the President and to give their authority to the appointment of a committee to consider the possibilities towards a united church in Assam.
3. That the council urges all affiliated bodies to depend their fellowship by means of some or all of the following suggestions; (a) join wherever possible in acts of united worship with those of other churches, (b) from time to time invite ministers and pastors of other churches to occupy their pulpits, (c) agree to take part in a special annual week of witness for Assam and on one day during the week join with other churches in a united co-operate act of witness.[204]

As per the resolution of the meeting, the President of the Council dispatched a letter to all the Christians who were represented at the Council elucidating of disunity of the church in NEI and which inscribe that:

> At the recent meeting of the Council held at Shillong, the grave scandal of disunity among us was considered very carefully …It was decided that an appeal should be sent out to all the constituent churches to beg them to face up the evil of separation and endeavour to find the way …to approach each other in the spirit of humanity and self-giving then only will there be hope of a real and abiding Union between us.[205]

The constituent member of the churches took seriously the matter of President's letter and they responded positively. At this time the Assam Christian Council has grown steadily in term of membership from the original-founding members, which were only seven in number at the initial stage, but by 1945 it

[202] Jyrwa, Church *Union Movement in North East India: A Historical Perspective* in *Church Ministry and Mission: Eassy in Honour of K.I. Aier* …, 63.

[203] *Assam Christian Council, Minutes and Proceedings of the 7th Annual Session*, January 1944.

[204] *Assam Christian Council, Minutes and Proceedings of the 7th Annual Session*, January 1944, 25. (Hereafter, *Assam Christian Council, Minutes and Proceedings*, 1944 …).

[205] *Assam Christian Council, Minutes and Proceedings*, 1944 …, 11.

increased up to six Ecclesiastical bodies[206] and six Missions members[207] in addition to the Bible society.[208] The Assam Christian Council discontinued its affiliation with the Bengal Christian Council (BCC) in 1945. The reasons for the partition from BCC was that the concerns in Assam Churches were so different from those in Bengal that the Christians in Assam found no significance in remaining within the BCC. But, a request was made to the BCC that the minutes of two Councils be exchanged.[209]

The meeting of the Assam Christian Council, which was held at Shillong on August 22-26, 1945 resolved to form a Committee for church union and stated that, 'the Council at its last session requested all affiliated bodies to give authority to the appointment of a committee to consider the possibility of a united church in Assam.'[210] It was further reported that, 'the eight affiliated bodies of the Council had voted in favor of forming such a Committee.'[211] And the task was authorized the Executive Committee to appoint the Committee and the Committee should study the South India scheme and other reports, which are available from the National Christian Council of India (NCCI).[212]

The movement towards union gathered more momentum to the extent that in 1947, reports of church union consisted of statements like "we aim not a United Church of Assam but a United Church of India, and ourselves part of this…"[213] and 1949 reports also state that, "…to stress the point that our ultimate goal is not a United Church in Assam but a United Church of India."[214] The emphasis was to create a wider sense for the United Church in NEI. Therefore the Committee expressed this in various manners in order to carry out their objective of united church. It was clearly projected that the affiliated church bodies held seriously the question of church union not only in terms of co-operative efforts but also in terms of organized union of churches.

The ninth session of the ACC was held at Guwahati from January 15-19, 1947. The Committee made attempts to study both, the South India Scheme of

[206] The following names were the Six Ecclesiastical Bodies; Assam Baptist Convention, Presbyterian Church of Assam, Assam Diocese of the Anglican Church, Baptist Church of South Lushai, Gossner Evangelical Lutheran Church, and Church of God.

[207] The followings are the Six Mission members; American Baptist, Welsh Presbyterian, British Baptist, Santal Mission of the Northern Church, New Zealand Baptist, British and Foreign Bible Society.

[208] Downs, *Christianity in North East India…*,156.

[209] Jyrwa, *Church Union Movement in North East India: A Historical Perspective* in *Church Ministry and Mission: Eassy in Honour of K.I. Aier …*, 64.

[210] *Assam Christian Council, Minutes and Proceedings of the 8th Annual Conference*, 22-26 Aug., 1945, 9. (Hereafter, *Assam Christian Council, Minutes and Proceedings*, 1945 …).

[211] *Assam Christian Council, Minutes and Proceedings*, 1945 …

[212] *Assam Christian Council, Minutes and Proceedings of the 6th Annual Conference*, 1943, 3.

[213] *Assam Christian Council, Minutes and Proceedings*, 1945 …, 11.

[214] *Assam Christian Council, Minutes and Proceedings of the 12th Annual Conference*, 1949, 9.

Church Union Movement and the Round Table Conference of North India.[215] After a careful study of the above stated, the Committee felt that, the following points would be desirable and adopted the Round Table Conference basis of negotiation and suggested some alternations and additions as Basis of Union which are as follows;

1. Doctrine: While recognizing the value of the Apostles and Nicene Creeds and their adoption as statement of faith, this should not produce other statements, further and more up to date, being put forth.
2. In Relation to Baptism: - A note should be added that Baptism might be by immersion or pouring of water on the candidates, upon professions of faith or in infancy. When only adult Baptism is practiced a service for the blessing of children may be encouraged.
3. Holy Communion: Holy Communion is the means of Union with Christ and with each other and that the term 'the means of grace' should be avoided. The term 'sacrament' should be excluded from the basis of Union.
4. Ministry: To secure this unified ministry the authority of the whole church must be represented at ordination, 'Bishop and Presbyters' alone have the authority to set aside the candidate for the ministry by the laying on of hands, but the lay have their part of it in selection and approving the candidate and in the prayers at the actual service.[216]

At this time, the proposal of Assam Christian College (ACC) in Barapani was being materialized and it was changed into Union Christian College (UCC), as emphasis would then be placed on the united efforts of the various Christian bodies of Assam. The actual foundation of UCC in 1952 was certainly a great success of various churches in Assam as they moved together towards closer co-operation and unity.[217] But unfortunately, it is the only successful college, which united efforts of North East India Christian Council so far.

The eleventh proceeding session of the Assam Christian Council was met at Shillong from August 26-29, 1948 where the Church Union Committee brought a report and after discussion of the report, the general Council suggested to remove the word "Baptism" from the report.[218] Again the Council was assigned further study of the Round Table Conference plan and the South India Union scheme for more guidance on this important matter. The Church Union Committee introduced a form of admission into the fellowship of the church amongst the affiliated bodies of the ACC in 1950. This form of commendation was approved

[215] *Assam Christian Council, Minutes and Proceedings*, 1947 ..., 12.

[216] *Assam Christian Council, Minutes and proceedings*, 1947 ..., 13.

[217] Jyrwa, *Church Union Movement in North East India: A Historical Perspective* in *Church Ministry and Mission: Eassy in Honour of K.I. Aier* ..., 64.

[218] *Assam Christian Council, Minutes and Proceedings of the 11th Annual Conference*, 1948, 9.

and forwarded for the approval in the general session of the ACC in 1951. At the Annual Session of the ACC at Shillong in 1951, both the formula of ordination and infant baptism was revised and was re-formulated that the infant baptism was not the custom, but a service of dedication of infants.[219] During the 22nd annual session of the ACC meeting at Shillong from April 29-May 3, 1959, the Church Union Committee recommended to the ACC for the formation of North-East Faith and Order Conference in the region.[220]

During these few decades the Church Union Committee rendered a tremendous work for the development of church unity in NEI. Hence, the permanent headquarter for a church union was set at Shillong and the committee appointed the first fulltime secretary Rev. L. S. Diengdoh and an Office clerk in 1959.[221] Till 1960s the church union movement was not really a movement but the idea was taken for granted that the spiritual union of churches as manifested by the ACC, would lead to some kind of organic unity. In a real sense it was merely a consultation and observation of the union movement in other parts of India, specially the Church of South India and Church of North India.

3.3. FORMATION OF NORTH EAST INDIA CHRISTIAN COUNCIL (NEICC)

The year 1963 and 1964 was significant in the history of the Churches in NEI as it provided the basis for the Church Union Movement in the region. Since 1930's, consultations and general discussions for the church union pondered about whether the affiliated churches in NEI should form part of the CNI or to work towards a union within North-East itself. In view of certain objections and the practical difficulties involved in relation to the churches, the Council decided to have a separate church union in NEI. Even the two churches namely, the Eastern Himalayan Church Council and the Anglican diocese of Assam, who were members of CNI had expressed their preference to join the church union of North East India Christian Council, if it comes into being.[222]

In such circumstances the Church Union Committee proposed for the formation of a united church in the region. In the view of that decision and appreciation from the other churches, the Council appointed a Special Committee to study and find out a suitable basis of union for further discussion and action. In the strictest sense, the real movement for union began only after the Annual session of the NEICC at Kalimpong in 1963, when the Church Union Committee

---

[219] *Assam Christian Council, Minutes and Proceedings of the 14th Annual Conference*, 21-26 August, 1951, 28ff.

[220] *Assam Christian Council, Minutes and Proceedings of the 22nd Annual Conference*, 29 April – 2 May, 1959, 44.

[221] Jyrwa, *Church Union Movement in North East India: A Historical Perspective* in *Church Ministry and Mission: Eassy in Honour of K.I. Aier* ..., 65.

[222] Downs, *Christianity in North East India* ..., 157.

was given the mandate to organize what was known as the first Faith and Order conference in the region.[223]

3.4. NORTHEAST INDIA FAITH AND ORDER CONFERENCES

3.4.1. FIRST FAITH AND ORDER CONFERENCE

The first Northeast Faith and Order Conference organized at Union Christian College (UCC), Barapani from January 7-10, 1964, was a significant event in the history of ecumenism in NEI. It marked the beginning of a new development of church relationship and common action among the protestant churches in Northeast region. There were twenty-four delegates and speakers representing the twelve constituent bodies.[224] And it was expressed that the forming of a church union in NEI would be possible and should be encouraged. The Assam Christian Council (ACC) was renamed as Northeast India Christian Council (NEICC) for wider vision and task, but the constitutions and functions were all the same. However the following recommendations were made to the NEICC:

1. That the council requested its affiliated bodies to decide whether they would be willing to consider the possibility of forming a United Church for NEI.
2. That the council calls another Faith and Order conference at the UCC in January 1965.[225]

In spite of many difficulties and problems regarding the church union negotiation, the Special Committee could successfully convene to form a first Northeast Faith and Order Conference in the region. Though the numbers were gradually dwindling, enthusiasm still ran high among those present in the first Conference.

3.4.2. SECOND FAITH AND ORDER CONFERENCE

With mandate from the meeting of the NEICC in 1964, the Church Union Committee convened a second Northeast Faith and Order Conference at UCC, Barapani from December 29, 1964 to January 1, 1965 with the purpose of drawing a tentative basis for the union. The representatives from ten constituent member Churches, fifteen delegates, a speaker, and the Council officers from ten affiliated bodies attended.[226] The conference produced "the Plan of Church

---

[223] Toshi Aier, "Church Union Movement in North East India: A Reflection," in *Perspectives: Current Issues in Theological Thinking*, edited by Akheto Sume (Aolijen, Mokokchung: Jongshinokdang Trust, CTC, 2002), 143.

[224] NEICC, The First Draft of A Basis of Union for the Churches in NEI (1965), 4.

[225] NEICC, *Faith and Order Conference, Minutes of the Meeting of the Committee*, 7-10 January 1964, 1.

[226] Ten affiliated bodies were CBCNEI; Eastern Himalayan Church Council; KJPS; Tripura Baptist Union; CIPC; MPS; North Bank Baptist Association; Baptist Church of Mizoram; Baptist

Union and Draft Constitution of a Basis of Union for the churches in Northeast India."[227] The committee noted the willingness to enter into discussions of church union on the basis of the Draft and it was hoped that this would be the beginning of official negotiations. [228] The First Draft's introduction is as follows:

> This is by no means a full plan of Union but represents the thinking of the participants on the points which are likely to be crucial ones in any negotiations. The conference had before it various schemes of Union for churches in other parts of the world and is very heavily indebted to the 'Proposed Basis of Union' prepared by the Ghana Church Union Committee.[229]

In May 1965 at the annual session of NEICC, the Church Union Committee presented the First Draft of a basis of union and it was approved.[230] Thus, it was felt that the churches should first unite in mutual trust, leaving the settlement of their differences to be worked out in the context of the larger fellowship. The participants considered the special needs and traditions of the churches in NEI as well as the possible future relationship between the proposed united church and other churches in India. They attempted to draw up a scheme that would be relevant to conditions in their own area, while at the same time maintaining a larger ecumenical perspective.

3.5. NORTHEAST INDIA CHRISTIAN COUNCIL CONFERENCES

3.5.1. CONFERENCE 1965

In the pursuance of the Church Union Committee the Council convened a Church Union Conference at Shillong from November 27-30, 1965.[231] This was attended by officially appointed delegates of six churches and one mission as well as observers from two additional churches and one mission. [232] Two church bodies that had agreed to participate officially were not able to send delegates. Those that agree to participate officially represented 86% of the Protestant Christians

---

General Conference Mission Society and Australian Baptist Missionary Society.

[227] Appendix- I

[228] Jyrwa, "Church Union Movement in North East India Historical Perspective," in *Good News For North East India* ..., 27.

[229] Jyrwa, "Church Union Movement in North East India Historical Perspective," in *Good News For North East India* ..., 27.

[230] NEICC, The Second Draft of A Basis of Union for the Churches in NEI ..., 3.

[231] *Assam Christian Council, Minutes and Proceedings of the 29th Annual Conference*, 1966, 68. (Hereafter, *Assam Christian Council, Minutes and Proceedings*, 1966 ...).

[232] The Participants from the CBCNEI, Eastern Himalayan Church Council, KJPS, Tripura Baptist Union, CIPBC, MPS, BCMT, NBBA, Baptist General Conference Mission Society, and Australian Baptist Missionary Society.

in Northeast India. The observer represented a further 7%.[233] The delegates represented various churches and missions with optimism and keenness to enter into the church union negotiations. But in this conference, it was discovered that most of the churches had not studied carefully the first draft. This was one of the reasons, that it was resolved and agreed to revise the draft with the addition of a preamble and the same was to be submitted to churches for consideration.[234] So, the Draft was dispatched to all the affiliated churches for study and comments from the Office. But, unfortunately many of the affiliated churches did not receive the draft and those who did receive, did not take it seriously nor studied it carefully.

However, during the Conference profitable discussions were held on problems of church union in general, Church Membership, Sacraments: Baptism and the Holy Communion, Church Ministry, Organization etc. and it was agreed to revise the first draft with the addition of preamble and the same was to be presented before the affiliated churches of the Council. There are some important points mentioned in the preamble to the second draft because they reflect the motive and basis for the proposed church of NEI as follows:

1. It is the will of God as revealed in the scriptures that His people should live together in fellowship and division should come to an end in NEI in order to follow the will of God and to give a stronger witness.
2. The proposed church of NEI will not solve all problems but it will certainly provide greater strength to face those problems. It will bring about greater sharing of leadership and resources; it will bring together the christians to make a common witness to the vast non-Christian community. With great responsibility we have to proclaim the gospel to all men, we cannot afford to be weakened by our divisions.
3. We should ask, "Will this united church bear witness to the love of Christ?" Instead of a question such as this how will this united church benefit our community? United witness is the will of God and essential to the proclamation of the gospel of Jesus Christ in NEI.[235]

At the Conference the second Draft was formulated as a 'Basis of Union'[236] for the churches in the region.[237] Therefore the second Draft and F. S. Downs paper entitled 'Church Union: Theological and Non-theological Factors' were

---

[233] Jyrwa, "Church Union Movement in North East India Historical Perspective," in *Good News For North East India* ..., 28.

[234] Downs, *Christianity in North East India* ..., 159. Also see in Jyrwa, "Church Union Movement in North East India Historical Perspective," in *Good News For North East India* ..., 28.

[235] Jyrwa, Church Union Movement in North East India: A Historical Perspective in *Church Ministry and Mission: Eassy in Honour of K.I. Aier* ..., 67.

[236] Appendix - II.

[237] NEICC, The Second Draft of A Basis of Union for the Churches in NEI ..., 4.

printed and circulated to all the affiliated Churches for consideration and discussion.[238] Many Churches took it seriously and even translated the above two papers into their local languages, on the other hand many local Churches did not consider the matter seriously. Even then the issues were under discussion in various constituents of the NEICC, and many accepted the Second Draft as the basis of Union. In 1968 the Church Union Committee reported at the NEICC Annual session at Haflong that the seven bodies[239] had sent positive replies of their willingness to consider the possibility of forming a united church of NEI.[240] However, some of the churches like Salvation Army, The Baptist Churches of Mizo District and the General Conferences, North Bank Mission were still in the process of consideration of the second Draft. That shows the draft were an unfavorable to them.

3.5.2. CONFERENCE 1969

In order to impart a sense of urgency and to avoid stagnation of Church Union Movement in NEI, a Committee summoned second Church Union Conference at Shillong from19th –20th September 1969.[241] It was attended by a larger number of higher-level church officials than any of the earlier meetings and it produced a draft constitution. The Conference formed a Drafting Committee to prepare the plan of union and the draft constitution of the church of NEI.

As it was assigned to the Drafting Committee, the plan of union and draft constitution was prepared and presented to the Council during the annual session in 1970. The Council also gave a mandate to the convener and the Drafting Committee to make some correction and revisions in the light of discussions at higher level and finally resolved to send the revised Draft to be prepared by the Drafting Committee to the affiliated bodies for their views and comments. The Council accepted the Draft in principle at the NEICC session on May 6-10, 1970 and was published after making some corrections and revisions by the Drafting Committee. The revised plan of church union and draft constitution of the Church of NEI was printed and circulated to all affiliated bodies in July 1970 for study and action.[242] Also it encouraged the churches to favourably consider the proposed plan for a united church in NEI and participate in a common witness.

Unfortunately it was reported from the affiliated churches that the plan of the Church Union Movement, which was officially reached at the annual

---

238 *Assam Christian Council, Minutes and Proceedings*, 1966, 26.

239 Seven Christian bodies were CBCNEI, Eastern Himalayan Church Council, Khasi Jaintia Presbyterian Synod, Tripura Baptist Church Union, Church of India, Pakistan, Burma and Ceylon, Mizoram Presbyterian Synod, and GBBCU.

240 *Assam Christian Council, Minutes and Proceedings of the 31st Annual Conference*, 1968, 53.

241 *Assam Christian Council, Minutes and Proceedings of the 32nd Annual Conference*, 1969, 37.

242 *North East India Christian Council, 32nd Annual Conference*, Resolutions of the Church Union Committee, September, 1969, 1.

session of the NEICC in May 1971 was not acceptable to all. The churches like Khasi-Jaintia Presbyterian Synod (KJPS), Cachar Hill Tribes Synod CHTS), Darjeeling Diocese, Mizo Presbyterian Synod (MPS) and Mara Independent Evangelical Church (MIEC) were in favour of the plan of Church Union and Draft Constitutions. Whereas, the CBCNEI, Tripura Baptist Church, Goalpara Baptist Church and the Church of God were reported to be still in the process of studying about it.[243] It was also noted that these views did not mean official commitment by the churches concerned. Such a response compelled the Church Union Committee to make further plan for the united churches in NEI.

3.6. CONTROVERSIAL PERIOD 1971

The most spectacular expression of unity among Christians in NEI has been a Council called North East India Christian Council which had its origin in the Bengal Christian Council 1926. Later in 1937 a joint Conference of Churches and Missions in Assam decided to form a separate church union in NEI. This NEICC was effectively cherished for just a few years till a storm of controversy arose when the draft constitution for church union was discussed at different levels of the constituent churches during 1970s. Most of the constituent churches approved the draft as a basis for church union negotiations, mainly the Presbyterian Churches.[244]

However, the Council of Baptist Church in North East India (CBCNEI) consultation which met at Guwahati from August 15th-16th 1971 found the Draft Constitution of the Church of NEI unacceptable.[245] On the basis of the CBCNEI consultation the Church Union Committee was met on June 10, 1972 at 5 P.M in the library of the Cherra Theological College and it was resolved that;

> The council notes with regret that the second consultation of the CBCBEI which met at Guwahati on 15th and 16th August 1971 found the draft of the proposed church of North East India unacceptable in its present form and that the main objection was related to baptism, centralized church government, and the office of the Bishop and its term etc., in this connection, the council also noted that idea of united church of North East India had been in the air since the nineteen fifties and that it was since 1963 that steps were taken to give concrete shape to this objective by the holding of two Faith and Order Conferences and two Church Union Conferences. In all these conferences as well as in annual season of the Council ever since, the leaders of the CBCBEI

[243] Jyrwa, "Church Union Movement in North East India Historical Perspective," in *Good News For North East India* ..., 30.

[244] Downs, *Christianity in North East India* ..., 163.

[245] North *East India Christian Council, 35th Annual Conference*, Church Union Committee Resolution No. XV: D, 1972, 42.

> like Dr Downs, C. C. Jones, Rev. J. Thumra, Rev. K. I. Aier etc had contributed substantially and had virtually accepted the plan of church union and draft constitution of the church of the NEI in its present form subject to adjustments to be made at the negotiating stage and subject to ratification by the units. The principles relating to Baptism, Church Government, Office of Bishop etc., have been adapted to suit the conditions of Baptists of all shades. In the circumstances the present approach of the CBCNEI to the plan of union appears to be rather negative in respect of some vital matters. But, as they say that they are prepared to discuss a new plan of church union, it is hereby resolved that the CBCBEI be request to give their alternative proposal in respect of the specific objection raised by them so as to enable the council to improve the plan of union.[246]

The main objection was related to baptism, centralized church government, the office and form of Bishop etc. The Executive Committee of the CBCNEI decided to abstain from any further discussion on church union after the matter had been discussed at representatives of its constituent Associations. The CBCNEI contributed a lot for the enlargement of the Church Union Movement in NEI in spite of some disagreement on draft constitution. The CBCNEI was not only participating in the Church Union Conference but they also contributed for the formation and development of the united church in NEI.

As a consequence, the NEICC had no option but to request the CBCNEI to give their alternative proposals in respect of the specific objections raised by them. Therefore the NEICC requested the CBCNEI three times to offer their alternative proposals in respect of their objections: the first at the 35th annual session of NEICC in1972, second at 36th annual session in 1973 and the third at 39th annual session of NEICC in 1976. But, there was no positive response till 1977 from CBCNEI. There were even some affiliated members of NEICC who did not express their views and ideas of the draft plan but kept silent. Those affiliated members were: Northern Evangelical Lutheran Church (NELC); Church of North India, Assam; Gossner Evangelical Lutheran Church (GELC); Church of God; Manipur Presbyterian Synod and Christ National Church.[247] The Council reminded those affiliated members to give their opinion before the next Council session in April 1977, particularly to CBCNEI.

But at the 40th NEICC Annual Session at Barapani in 1977, it was reported that new developments arose in the CBCNEI and Cachar Hill Tribes Synod respectively. These two member churches have clearly signified that they are not

---

[246] E.H. Pakyntein (Convenor), "Reports of the Church Union Committee," *The NEICC Proceedings of 35 Annual Session*, Cherrapunji, Meghalaya, May 10th -14th, 1972.

[247] *North East India Christian Council, Minutes and Proceedings of the 39th Annual Meeting*, 1976, 54.

prepared to enter into negotiations.[248] Further official negotiations could not take place on church union discussion, without the CBCNEI presence, since CBCNEI is the single largest body within the NEICC. Therefore, the whole Church Union Movement lost its original momentum and for the time being church union discussions came to a halt.

3.7. RE-OPENING OF CHURCH UNION CONSULTATION

Despite earlier failures, the church leaders did not give up the ideas and momentum to have united church in the region. Thus, they attempted to overcome the impasse from 1980s onwards. Since then there had been several consultations and meetings were organized to resume the Church Union Movement in NEI. Following are some of the important consultations.

3.7.1. CONSULTATION 1982

With hope and prayer the Church Union Committee tried to revive the lethargic spirit by calling a consultation in 1981, though unfortunately it did not succeed. This was followed by a successful consultation held at Kohima, Nagaland from May 6th to 9th, 1982.[249] Delegates from various churches associations, and societies participated in the consultations. The objective and the function of the consultation was the Christian fellowship of co-operation and comity by common counsel among the various bodies of the North-East region. At the consultation there was a special session of the ecumenical development where the participants had discussion on the vital aspect of the role of the NEICC.[250] It is to bring churches closer to each other in obedience to the prayer of our Lord that 'May they be one, Father, may that be one in us, as you are in me and I am in you'. (John 17: 21-22).

3.7.2. CONSULTATION 1984

Another Consultation was successfully held at Guwahati in 1984. During the Consultation the members expressed their views and ideas from two aspects, the difficulties and the possibilities in respect of church union in the region. In the view of difficulties the members openly expressed that the hierarchical structure of church union administration and the practice of baptism in the church union plans was one of the main hindrances for the church union negotiations from the beginning. On the other hand, in view of possibilities the member expressed the urgency of unity and co-operation among the Christians in the region as a

[248] Jyrwa, "Church Union Movement in North East India Historical Perspective," in *Good News For North East India …*, 30.

[249] *North East India Christian Council, Minutes and Proceedings of the Annual Consultation*, Kohima, Nagaland, 6-9 May 1982, 27.

[250] *North East India Christian Council, Minutes and Proceedings of the Annual Consultation*, Kohima, Nagaland, 6-9 May 1982, 27.

necessity. It is possible to have inter-communion, however, in a federal setup. Again the acceptance of membership from one denomination to another denominational church without requiring re-baptism is a possibility.[251]

The Council of Baptist Church in North East India rejection of the Draft of Union on matter of baptism and hierarchical structure of church union administration was based on the fact that the North East India Christian Council had come a long way from Episcopalian system in proposing a modified form of Presbyterian type of government.[252] This system was unacceptable to the Baptist members. Therefore it needed more clarification in line with the ways suitable to tribals administrative set up. The consultants' main finding was the necessity of united church in the region, so they urged to hold more consultations to find ways and means to come to a more reliable church union in the region.

3.7.3. CONSULTATION 1985

The church leaders made attempts to revive the spirit of unity by holding a Consultation to discuss thoroughly the issue of united church during August 9-11, 1985 at Laban, Shillong.[253] There attended 35 representatives from 14 affiliated Christian bodies. In this consultation, they tried to find a new approach to the plan of church union, which had lost its thrust in 1970s. The principal objective of the Laban Consultation was to find a suitable pattern of church union in NEI.[254] Thus, the participants unanimously resolved to search for a new pattern and recommended to the Council a few points, which are as follows:

1. The first point recommended a new pattern of church government to be invented for the proposed united church and that pattern be a 'modified form'[255] of Presbyterian system of government giving sufficient autonomy to the regional churches or associations.
2. The second point recommended the 'Rules of Comity,' which was adopted from NCCI, be made to revise to suit the North-East context. It is, of course, necessary to have 'Rules of Comity' relevant to our situations. The one in use now is obsolete for it was made during the

---

[251] *North East India Christian Council, Minutes and Proceedings of the Annual Consultation*, Guwhati: April 26, 1984, 4.

[252] *North East India Christian Council, Minutes and Proceedings of the Annual Consultation*, Guwhati: April 26, 1984.

[253] Lalhmangaiha, "A Critical Review of Laban Consultation," *Presbyterian Review*, IX/33 (January-March, 2003), 33.

[254] *North East India Christian Council, Minutes and Proceedings of the Annual Consultation*, Laban, Shillong: 1985, 3. (Hereafter, *North East India Christian Council. Minutes and Proceedings*, 1985 ...).

[255] Modified form will be a mixture of good things drawn from both the Presbyterian and Baptist Church administration. Perhaps it may be the so-called 'Centralization' pattern of administration.

missionary period. It is a long felt need to make our own 'Rules of Comity' for we are facing many problems at various mission fields.

3. The third point recommended the Council's resolution on re-structuring NEICC which runs thus, "It was decided that the matter be referred back to the Executive Committee for study and working out a draft plan including financial implications for a thorough discussion and decision to be arrived at the next Annual Session".
4. Point four and five together accepted the Council resolution No. VIII. 1(b) P.15 in 1986. The understanding of church plays an important role in the life and work of the church. Hence, more discussion is needed at grassroots level.
5. Point six advocates creation of better relationship and co-operation between the Roman Catholic and the NEICC through dialogue.
6. The seventh point was highly recommendable, if at all church union is projected. Accordingly "the Church Union Movement began and ended with the church leaders only and the people were not in a position to make any reaction because they were ignorant about the development of the union movement in the absence of information". Materials should be made available in order that discussion at grassroots level may take place and the common people may involve in the whole enterprise.
7. The last point makes a serious study on Lima Documents (1982) on Baptist, Eucharist and Ministry, in the churches of the NEICC with the view to educating the people on these issues and for a better understanding of the ecumenical views of church unity.[256]

The Laban Consultation was quite a successful one because the participants took more seriously regarding the possibilities and in that it tried to find a new approach to the plan of church union, which came to a halt in 1972. Indeed the Laban Consultation made a breakthrough of Church Union Movement in NEI and has laid the foundation for the future course of decisions and actions.

3.7.4. CONSULTATION 1986

In the light of the Council instructions, again the Drafting Committee met at Guwahati in August 1986. The Committee forwarded to revise the plan of Union and Draft Constitution of the united church of NEI to the Executive Committee of NEICC. Drafting Committee consisting of seven members was appointed for church union in NEI, to study in depth the previous Draft for church union

[256] *North East India Christian Council, Minutes and Proceedings*, 1985..., 20.

in NEI and to make available a new Draft as early as possible to the Executive Committee for study and suggestions.[257]

There were some changes made in the revised Plan and Draft constitution. These were the omission of 'bishop' from the special ministry, which was the greatest change ever. Other significant omissions were the references to 'priest' or 'priesthood' and liturgical worship. A significant change of terminology was also made from 'Sacraments' to 'Ordinance' and from 'priest' to 'Presbyter.'[258] Even there was a new important inclusion in the revised Plan of Union and Draft constitution that read as follows;

1. A new provision was added for the minister who is unable to administer either one of the baptism.
2. Not only ordained ministers, but also those who have been licensed by the church were allowed to administer the Holy Communion.
3. The provision that the UCNEI will involve the definite form of procedure of ordination to be followed by all Uniting Churches is also made.[259]

After having a serious consultation by the Drafting Committee a revised Plan of Union was drafted and circulated to all the affiliated bodies for their opinions, considerations and actions. The council hopes that a new phase will be soon taking place in the history of church union plan in NEI. But, it was unfortunate that the issue had been silent for some years and lost its original enthusiasm for the plan of church union in the region.

In mid 1990's, the Church Union Committee realized that the Council in 1986 appointed a sub-committee to renew 'Rules of Comity' but there was no report about the implementation of the assigned task. It also took the poor attendance of the Church Union Committee meeting in the previous two years as an indication of the Council's declining interest in the idea of united church. In an attempt presumably to revive the concern for church union the Committee met in 1995 and resolved to make two recommendations which are as follows;

1. That the Sub-Committee for revision of 'Rules of Comity' be needed to revive and their report and recommendations be accepted by the Executive Committee of the Council.

---

[257] *North East India Christian Council, Minutes and Proceedings of the 49th Annual Meeting,* 1986, 20.

[258] NEICC, Plan of Union and Draft Constitutions (Revised 1986), 4.

[259] NEICC, Plan of Union and Draft Constitutions,

2. That church leaders conference is convened to discuss the plan of church union in NEI drafted by the Laban Consultation at the earliest possible.[260]

The Church Union Committee expressed the needs of church unity in NEI, but the Council did not take up seriously as proposal for few years. However the proposed church union did not lose its keenness, even though there were a few units who dropped their relation with the NEICC.

3.7.5. CONSULTATION 2001

In spite of many barriers, the Executive Committee of the church union called another consultation at Williamnagar, Meghalaya from May 20-23, 2001.[261] It was reported that the NEICC has 29 affiliated members from various church traditions of which 18 units participated at the consultation. One of the greatest achievements at the Williamnagar consultation was that the member participants took the matter seriously and made their own recommendation to hold a consultation on church union. Also there were two more units; Evangelical Baptist Church from Manipur and Mizoram Evangelical Fellowship were received as members of the NEICC at this consultation[262] which shows the need to maintain its ecumenical concept in its structural organization and evangelical conviction in its mission.

3.7.6. CONSULTATION 2002

There was another Annual Session and Consultation of the NEICC held at Phudumawrie Presbyterian Church, Shillong from May 9-12, 2002.[263] The theme of the Session was "Christ the Answer for the Problems of the World." The whole meeting was centered on the gospel of "Peace", which was much needed in North-East region. The attendance of the units was comparatively better than that of the previous year. It recorded 110 official delegates against 75 in the previous session.[264] The meetings testified the true ecumenical sense amongst the units that all the delegates freely and frankly expressed their views and ideas without any confusion. It was recommended at Willamnagar consultation 2001 to hold a consultation on church union, but it could not be materialized. As

---

[260] *North East India Christian Council, Minutes and Proceedings of the Annual Conference,* 1995, Resolution No. 6.

[261] *North East India Christian Council, Minutes and Proceedings of the 64th Annual Consultation,* 2001.

[262] *North East India Christian Council, Minutes and Proceedings of the 64th Annual Consultation,* 2001, 3.

[263] *North East India Christian Council, Minutes and Proceedings of the 65th Annual Consultation,* Phudmawire Presbyterian Church, Mawlai, May 9-12, 2002.

[264] Vanlalchhuanawma, "North East India Church Council Marches Towards Peace," *Presbyterian Review,* VIII/30 (April-June, 2002), 2.

such, the committee in 2002 consultation, once again resolved to hold the same consultation as proposed in the previous session at Williamnagar consultation. Some of the important resolutions of the Session are noted below;

1. The Executive Committee recommendation to inaugurate peace center during the Session was forwarded to the Council.
2. It was resolved that the KJP Synod is unable to send Chaplain to UCC, Barapani till 30.6.03, the Baptist Church of Mizoram will be requested to provide one with salary.
3. The proposal to initiate Bible Society for NEI, which has been dragged on for some years now, was reviewed. It was also resolved that the units be reminded to send their comments and considered opinion on the revised modalities to the NEICC office before March 31, 2003.
4. On the recommendation of Nomination Committee, elected NEICC Officers of for 2002-4. President Rev. Zabhu Terhuja, V-President Rev. Zaihmingthanga, Secretary Rev. Lalhmangaiha and Treasurer Rev. K. Nonhpluh.[265]

The president of NEICC inaugurated the "Peace Center" during afternoon session on 11 May 2002. This consultation therefore is especially significant in the history of the NEICC and of the church union committee.

3.7.7. CONSULTATION 2003

In pursuance of the Church Union Committee decision, a Consultation on church union was held at CBCNEI, Guwahati from January 23-25, 2003.[266] Although the attendance in terms of number was not so large, the representation was rather extensive since nine units of NEICC were represented. The main focus on the Consultation was 'Reflection of church union Efforts in NEI'. The following comments and recommendations came out of the ensuing discussion;

1. In view of the prevailing socio-religious situation in NEI it is a high time that the NEICC reconsider the urgency of unity and co-operation among the Christians in the North-East region.
2. It was recognized that the proposal made by the Church Union Committee to send the Plan of Union and Draft Constitution of the church in NEI to the units for translation, scrutiny and for their considered opinions on it had not been implemented.

---

[265] *North East India Christian Council, Minutes and Proceedings of the 65th Annual Consultation,* Phudmawire Presbyterian Church, Mawlai, May 9-12, 2002. Resolution No. 3.

[266] *North East India Christian Council, Report and Minutes of the 66th Annual Consultation,* 2003.

3. As the proposal to adapt models of the CNI and CSI apparently contributed to the failure of Church Union Movement in NEI, a model of union more suitable to the NEI context may be explored.
4. It was proposed that all the Church Union Committee members and participants be requested to study thoroughly the Draft Plan of church union in NEI, which was prepared in 1970 and their considered opinion be sent to the NEICC Office and the Office be entrusted to compile the suggestions and send the same to the members of the Church Union Committee and the participants of the consultation.
5. A common concern was the neo-imperialistic Hindutva movement in North-East region that the Council has to make a suitable response to the situations.[267]

On the basis of the consultation the urgency of Christian solidarity and the possibility of church union of some kind was recognized. As regards to the model of union, the consultation assumes that it needs no imitation of some model from elsewhere, but one has to be devised to best suit the Northeast people and the context.

3.7.8. NEICC ANNUAL SESSION 2003

The 66th Annual Session of the NEICC was held during May 8-11, 2003 at the Chawnpui Presbyterian Church, Aizawl, Mizoram.[268] There were 105 delegates representing different associations and churches around NEI attended it. One of the main features of the Session was a 'Press Release', which was read on Sunday 11th May 2003. Through this press release, an appeal was made by the Council to the concerned communities to stop fighting's and killings and to try to bring about peace at all levels.[269] This Annual Session of the NEICC 2003 made some resolutions as follows;

1. The NEICC resolved to form a committee for Peace Center (inaugurated in 2002), consisting of 11 members each from the NEICC and the PCI to be responsible for the implementation of the Peace Center programme.
2. It resolved to accept the following churches as members of the NEICC: Ri-Bho Synod, KJP Synod Sepngi, KJP Synod Mihngi and Meetei Christian Organization.

---

[267] *North East India Christian Council, Report and Minutes of the 66th Annual Consultation*, 2003, 4. (Hereafter, *North East India Christian Council, Report and Minutes*, 2003…).

[268] *North East India Christian Council, Report and Minutes of the 66th Annual Consultation*, Aizawl, Mizoram, 2003.

[269] Lalhmangaiha, "NEICC Annual Session 2003," *Presbyterian Review*, IX/34 (April – June, 2003), 22.

3. It resolved to request the Mizoram Presbyterian Church Synod to kindly send and sponsor a pastor for Union Christian College, Barapani.
4. It resolved to extend the service of the Secretary Lalhmangaiha for another term (3 years).
5. A request was made to the Manipur Baptist Convention to host the next NEICC Annual Session in Imphal 2004.[270]

3.7.9. NEICC ANNUAL SESSION 2006

The sixty-nine annual session of North East India Christian Council, which was held at Thadlaboh Presbyterian Church, KJP Synod Mihngi, from 11th -14th May, 2006, under the theme "Spirit Filled Community" (Acts 2:44-47).[271] Although, there were many problems like communication difficulties, sudden bands, road blocks etc. that could hinder the council meeting, it was encouraging to see that majority of the members could attend and participate in the Annual Session. During this annual session, after some clarification by the secretary, it was resolved to accept the Presbyterian Independent Church of North East India as one of the affiliated members of the council.[272] In an attempt apparently to revive the concern for church union the Committee met in 2006 and resolved to make two observations and comments which are as follows;

1. The Committee is concerned about the implementation of its previous recommendation that the NEICC Secretary be entrusted to personally contact the Council'c constituent bodies on church union issues.
2. The committee also expressed its concern about transmission of the important council's concerns and resolutions to the member bodies. For instance, the concerns and recommendations of the Executive Committee and Standing Committees.[273]

From the foregoing observations and comments the committee proposed to make the following recommendations;

1. That hereafter the NEICC Office be expected to convey the important council's concerns and resolutions to the member bodies for discussion and necessary action.
2. That with a view to the socio-cultural evils invading and disintegrating the churches in North East India, the NEICC Executive Committee

---

[270] *North East India Christian Council, Report and Minutes*, 2003…,

[271] *North East India Christian Council, Reports and Minutes of the 69th Annual Conference*, KJP Synod Mihngi, May 11-14, 2006.

[272] *North East India Christian Council, Reports and Minutes of the 69th Annual Conference*, KJP Synod Mihngi, May 11-14, 2006, 5. (Hereafter, *North East India Christian Council, Report and Minutes*, 2006…).

[273] *North East India Christian Council, Report and Minutes*, 2006…, 57.

requests its member bodies and churches to organize Unity Crusade/ Campaigns wherein a team of the Council would minister the word.

3. That the proposal in the previous annual meeting to make a fresh Church Union Draft is becoming more important and urgent.
4. That for the purpose of making a fresh draft the church union committee be enlarged to ensure representation from more of the constituent bodies.
5. That a time span for making the said draft be specified.
6. That the draft, when ready be submitted to the Executive Committee for approval and necessary action.[274]

Based on the theme "Spirit filled Community" the council put more emphasis and importance on "Mission and Evangelism" in the whole of the North East India in order to fulfill God's commission and to be observed by the people of other parts of India that is regarded as a Christian majority area. At the same time the finding committee reports that the member of the churches be encouraged again and again to attend the council on time and in full force for better and solidarity relationship among the churches and the leaders in North East India.

3.7.10. NEICC ANNUAL SESSION 2008

The 71st Annual Session of NEICC which was held at Town Baptist Church Mokokchung, Nagaland, from 14th -18th May 2008, with the theme "Empowering Local Congregation for Mission."[275] This was one of the most significant gatherings because it was hosted by the federation of Clark Theological College, Aolijen and Town Baptist Church Mokokchung, which is an active member of the Nagaland Baptist Church Council, and indeed one of the most dynamic units of the NEICC.[276] The participants in this Conference felt that the council was of great value to them, and expressed the desire and need for such a consultation to be repeated regularly.

3.8. CONCLUSION

To show more active existence of NEICC in NEI the committee always tried their best to hold the annual session every year. The existence and the importance of the Council have been widely felt. The number of members in the council is also increasing year by year. At present there are 36 affiliated units and 9 associate members in NEICC.[277] Special mention should be made that the attendance in the Annual Session is improving in the sense that almost all churches are represented

---

[274] *North East India Christian Council, Report and Minutes*, 2006..., 58.

[275] *North East India Christian Council, Proceedings of the 71st Annual Sessions*, Secretary Report of the NEICC, Mokokchng, Nagaland, May 14-18, 2008.

[276] *North East India Christian Council, Proceedings of the 71st Annual Sessions*, Secretary Report of the NEICC, Mokokchng, Nagaland, May 14-18, 2008, 31.

[277] Appendix - III.

at all sessions. The NEICC also is developing its infrastructure that will have definitely facilitated it to do more work for the common interest of the people in Northeast region. It may be identified here that perhaps, the general weakness of the movement is whatever attempt has been made so far started with the top leaders of the Council's units and ended with them. Hence, there is an urgency to reach the grassroots levels and the general mass of the Christian public with the message of unity and cohesion.

Chapter 4

The Participation of Council of Baptist Churches in North East India (CBCNEI) Towards Christian Unity

INTRODUCTION

The Baptist missionaries came with a strong commitment and great enthusiasm to do missionary work among the tribal world in NEI. The stupendous involvement and establishment of various mission activities like educational, medical, social, etc., caused to the spread of Baptist Churches into every corner of NEI. In NEI within the greater Protestant family of Christians in the past century, the Baptists have played a significant role, with the establishment of the Council of Baptist Churches in North East India (CBCNEI), which is the apex body of the Baptist Churches in North East India. In this chapter we shall deal with the Council of Baptist Churches in North East India and its attitude towards the Christian Unity discussion in the region.

4.1. THE COUNCIL OF BAPTIST CHURCHES IN NORTH EAST INDIA

The Council of Baptist Churches in North East India is one of the largest Baptist groups in South East Asia. The seed of the Gospel was planted by the first American Baptist Missionaries at Sadiya, Upper Assam in 1836.[278] Since then the CBCNEI has had a long history of partnership with the American Baptist Churches in its life and mission in carrying out the commission of the Lord. The

[278] Downs, *Early Christian Contacts with North East India ...*, 73.

transfer of responsibility from the "foreign mission" to "national leadership" took place in 1950. CBCNEI's primary function is "to bring the great diversity of its people into unity of single denominational structure."[279] It is an instrument of unity for mutual assistance, fellowship, inspiration and above all else, mission. The Council is actively involved in mission and evangelism, Theological education, Campus and Hostel Ministries, Healing Ministry, Christian Education, Peace Building, Relief and Development, Leadership Development Training Programs and Seminars.[280]

The Baptist missionaries were the first to establish their mission as well as the indigenous churches in the region. The time of the establishment varies from church to church, as each mission started its activities at different times. But, all the missions agreed to the principles of self-government, self support and self-propagation as the best means to intensify evangelization in the region. Therefore they took necessary measures in training native clergy and other evangelical works. The American missionaries who first landed in the region of North East India were Nathan Brown and O. T. Cutter. The group sailed up the Brahmaputra River and arrived in Sadiya in March, 1836 and there they were confronted with dense jungles, hostile tribals and rugged hills. [281] Yet, hoping they had been led to a fruitful place they began to learn Assamese language, set up their printing press and gave themselves to the task of translating, publishing and teaching. Thus began the work of the Baptist in the North Eastern corner of India.

From its inception the field work in North East India was largely the responsibility of the American Baptist Mission until the missionaries left the region. From the early days of the missions in NEI there were joint meetings of missionaries and nationals to plan the work. They were properly speaking, only mission stations because the appointments and financial, support came directly from the American Baptist Foreign Mission Board. But, these stations were the pre-models for the future churches.[282] Later on those churches together formed a convention called, 'the Assam Baptist Christian Convention.' The convention exercised only very little influence and power on the administration of the church and whatever power they had was restricted only to the churches in the Brahmaputra Valley.[283]

From 1900 onwards it became the 'Assam Baptist Missionary Union.' After 1910 the Union began to meet annually. The two organizations, the Assam Baptist Convention and the Missionary Union continued to function separately

---

[279] *Sesquicentennial Celebration* (Guwahati: CBCNEI, 1986), 2.

[280] *Sesquicentennial Celebration* ..., 2-3.

[281] CBCNEI, *Introducing the Council of Baptist Churches in North East India* (Guwahati: The CLC, 1972), 2.

[282] Downs, *The Mighty works of God*..., 186; Cited by Muttumana, *Christianity in Assam and Inter-Faith Dialogue*..., 108.

[283] Downs, *The Mighty works of God*..., 186.

till 1950. These organizations grew in its stature and finally in January 1950, it was decided in a joint meeting to form a single organization called, 'the Council of Baptist Churches in Assam.'[284] This council has been gradually extended to the whole Baptists of the North East India and thus 'the Council of Baptist Churches in North East India' (CBCNEI) came in to existence.[285] Accordingly, almost all the Baptist churches, associations and missions in Assam, Arunachal, Manipur, and Nagaland were brought within the council.

It was not easy for the churches and associations and regional conventions with their own programmes to fully understand the difference between the old Mission structure and the gradually emerging indigenous denominational structure. Many still regarded the Council as something apart from themselves, something from which they should receive, not something to which they should contribute. The failure of the churches to raise even that small portion of the central budget allocated to them each year was evidence enough of this. Consequently, while at the local associational and convention levels the structure was almost completely self-supporting, at the central level there continued to be reliance upon grants made by the American Baptist Churches.[286]

The CBCNEI has now over 5446 churches in 84 organized associations with 7,53,606 membership. The CBCNEI Head Quarter is in Guwahati, Assam. They are again administered under six regional conventions, namely, Assam Baptist Convention, Arunachal Baptist Church Council, Garo Baptist Convention, Karbi Anglong Baptist Convention, Manipur Baptist Convention and Nagaland Baptist Church Council.[287]

4.1.1. The Principles of CBCNEI

4.1.1.1. Organization and Vision of CBCNEI

CBCNEI stands to serve and empower its member Baptist churches in Northeast India, so that they will be effective in the transformational ministries within their own communities.

4.1.1.2. Service of the CBCNEI

1. Enhance fellowship and cooperation of member churches that represent 250 tribes
2. Provide youth, women, lay leaders, pastors, Sunday School teachers, missionary, and worship training
3. Promote ministry with street children, students and people of other faith.[288]

---

[284] Muttumana, *Christianity in Assam and Inter-Faith Dialogue...*,

[285] *Sesquicentennial Celebration* ..., 2.

[286] F. S. Downs, *History of the Council of Baptist Churches in North East India* **(Since 1836)** in http://www.cbcnei.com/index.php?option=com_content&view=article&id= 49&Itemid=69.

[287] CBCNEI, *Introducing the Council of Baptist Churches in North East India* ..., 3.

[288] Ajoy K. Lama, *CBCNEI,* http://cbcnei.com/news-events.htm.

4.1.1.3. CBCNEI Mission Define

1. to serve and empower the Baptist churches in Northeast India so that they will be effective in transforming the societies within their own communities;
2. to encourage and equip our Baptist Churches in witnessing Jesus Christ so that all people groups may come to know Jesus Christ and experience life in its fullness;
3. to foster Baptist unity in Christ in the face of divisive forces working against it;
4. to be an agent of peace and reconciliation against ethnic, relgious, political voilence; and
5. to advocate justice and render humanitarian service to the poor and the marginalized.[289]

4.1.1.4. Ministries of CBCNEI

Since its inception the ministry of the CBCNEI has been holistic. We believe that it is essential for an individual to be wholly-healthy physically, spiritually, and emotionally. Therefore, the Council seeks to serve and empower our churches so that they will be more effective in transforming our individuals and communities.

4.2. CBCNEI'S PARTICIPATION IN CHURCH UNION DISCUSSION

As it has been mentioned in earlier chapter, the Council of Baptist Churches in North East India (CBCNEI) is a forum of Baptist Council which consists of six Baptist Conventions[290] in Northeast India. It is not a super-union with powers above the local and association of Baptist churches, but a federation for co-operation between the Baptist churches in NEI. The federation fully respects the independence of the association and local churches. Not a transnational church structure in its own right, it is a forum for spiritual fellowship and cooperation between the autonomous Baptist Churches that participate in it.

The Baptist Council CBCNEI was there at the ACC consultations, along with other member churches including the Presbyterian Church and the other Protestant Churches, as a sign of an active involvement in, and commitment to, the ecumenical journey. Consequently, the CBCNEI has been actively involved in the church union movement discussion of the North East India Christian Council (NEICC) from its formation. It had even appointed a special sub-committee on church union to keep the council informed as to the developments and trends in connection with the church union movement in India, and to consider any

[289] *CBCNEI*, http://cbcnei.com/news-events.htm.

[290] The six Baptist Conventions are; Arunachal Pradesh Baptist Convention, Assam Baptist Convention, Manipur Baptist Convention, Garo Baptist Convention (Meghalaya), Karbi-Anglong Baptist Convention, and Nagaland Baptist Church Council.

inter-church movement which may be referred to it by the council or its affiliated bodies.[291]

In the 1965 CBCNEI annual session, the above responsibility was handed over to the theological education committee which was entrusted to assume responsibility to represent the CBCNEI in future discussions in church union.[292] The CBCNEI executive committee meeting in 1965 recommended that along with the theological Education Committee, two delegates from each affiliated convention can attend the first church union conference of the NEICC to be held in shilling from November 27-30, 1965. As such the delegates from the CBCNEI participated in it though enthusiasm was more or less lukewarm. As Edward Singha, the then General Secretary, CBCNEI reported the very fact that the CBCNEI, which formed sixty percent of the Christian population in the North East, attended it in large numbers was encouraging.[293]

The CBCNEI was not only participating, but also contributing in no small measure to the movement. During the first Church Union Conference, the already mentioned booklet by F. S. Downs, "Church Union: theological and Non-theological factors," which was an important paper related to Church Union was published and distributed to all the affiliated bodies along with the "Second Basis of Church Union." He also wrote a booklet in reply to "A picture of an Organic Church Union," by T. Likok, the then Literature Secretary of Ao Baptist Association.

The CBCNEI also contributed to the formation of the basis of union and the plan of union and draft constitution. The CBCNEI had prominent leaders in the union movement in the person's of F. S. Downs, J. H. Thumra, K. I. Aier, and E. Singha. These leaders have contributed substantially and virtually accepted the plan of union and draft constitution of the united church of Northeast India in that form subject to adjustment at the negotiating stage and subject to ratification by the units.[294]

The CBCNEI was also represented by seventy one delegates in the church union consultation held at Guwahati from August 15-16, 1970. All these clearly show that the CBCNEI was enthusiastic about the proposed church union. But unfortunately, this enthusiasm remained at the higher levels of the conventions. There was much fear at the association and local level which actually represents the common Christians. Realizing this fear among the local congregations, E. Singha said;

---

[291] *Council of Baptist Churches in Assam and Manipur. Minutes of the 7th Annual Session,* Nowgong, 1957, 42.

[292] *Council of Baptist Churches in North East India. Minutes of the CBCNEI Executive Committee Meeting,*1965 ..., 7.

[293] *Council of Baptist Churches in North East India. Minutes and Proceedings of the CBCNEI Annual Conference,* 1966 ..., 18.

[294] The NEICC Annual Session Proceedings, 1972, 42.

> We Baptist should never be afraid of the word union. No one is going to force us into any union, until we have fully and prayerfully studied and we are convinced of it. But, on the other hand, we shall never hesitate to unite with our sister churches when we clearly understand the call of the Holy Spirit to do so. Baptists have much to contribute to and much to learn from other churches.[295]

The fact is that CBCNEI had participated and also contributed positively towards the development of the church union movement discussion in NEI from the very beginning. But unfortunately, when it reached a certain stage there arose differences of opinion within the CBCNEI affiliated churches in regard to the draft of the basis for the church union movement in North East India.

4.3. CBCNEI ATTITUDE TOWARDS CHRISTIAN UNITY IN NEI

As has been mentioned above, church union was a dream for some in leadership at the council level, and they put every effort to make that dream come true. Yet, for the general Christian public, church union was a subject that was unheard of, about which they were not well informed. Ultimately, it was from this group that church union movement faced the greatest opposition.

4.3.1. The First Period 1937-1962

As was mentioned earlier, from the very beginning of the formation of the Assam Christian Council (ACC), the aim was to enter into actual church union. But during this period, the church union movement was not really a movement. It was simply a period of observation of the trends of union movements in other parts of India, especially the south India and north India union movements. This period was dominated by discussions on subjects of comity unity and the search for the possibility of forming of united church in NEI. Nothing more can be said of the reaction of the CBCNEI towards church union movement during this period than to simply say that it had actively participated in all the discussions held on union under the ACC.

4.3.2. The Second Period 1963-1977

Though the CBCNEI had been a part of the church union discussions from the earliest stage, due to conflicting opinions within its own membership, no serious consideration was given by the CBCNEI for entering into any kind of union till 1970. This is made clear by the statement made in the 20th Annual session of the CBCNEI in 1970 by K. I. Aier. He said;

> The CBCNEI is the single largest church body in North East India. Most of the church bodies in the NEICC look to the CBCNEI for

[295] *Council of Baptist Churches in North East India. Minutes and Proceedings of the CBCNEI Annual Conference,* 1964, 13.

> leadership. Khasi and Mizo Presbyterian churches have decided to join this union scheme. The CBCNEI as a council has not taken up this matter seriously yet. This is indicative that we have not been fair to this church union.[296]

The conflict in opinion was that some within the CBCNEI felt it should join the union while others strongly opposed it fearing that they would lose their Baptist heritage and distinctiveness. The reason for the CBCNEI's rejection of the second draft of the NEI church union was on the grounds of Baptism, centralized church government and the office and term of bishop which are alien to the Baptist polity and doctrine.

During the NEICC Faith and Order Conference held at Union Christian College, Barapani in 1964, all affiliated bodies were asked to decide, before the next council session of the NEICC in May 1965, whether they would be willing to consider the possibility of forming a united church for NEI and to notify the secretary of the council of their decision.[297] This matter was discussed during the CBCNEI executive committee meeting held at Resu in 1965 and the executive committee felt that the CBCNEI was not ready yet to commit itself to church union but they were interested in studying the matter.[298] But, till 1969 no definite response was given. It was only in 1969 at the Field Directors' Conference held at Guwahati that this issue was extensively discussed. This conference resolved to recommend the CBCNEI to request the associations to state their preference in respect of church union. The feeling was expressed that the people were not well informed to make a constructive decision and that a conference of associations leaders prior to the NEICC meeting would be a more helpful approach.[299]

Accordingly, the CBCNEI Executive Committee requested the theological Education Committee to commence a CBCNEI consultation on church union inviting two key leaders from each association. Thus, the first CBCNEI church union consultation was held at Guwahati from August 17-20, 1970. But, nothing concrete could be decided. They again forwarded the draft constitution and church union plan to the associations and conventions requesting them to bring their specific observations and recommendations in writing to the next consultation on church union.

The second CBCNEI church union consultation was held at Guwahati from August 15-16, 1971 under the auspices of the CBCNEI Theological Education Committee in which about eighty representatives from about thirty

---

[296] *Council of Baptist Churches in North East India. Minutes and Proceedings of the CBCNEI 20th Annual Conference*, Kohima, February, 18-22, 1970, 21.

[297] *North East India Christian Council. Minutes of the Faith and Order Conference*, 1964..., 1.

[298] *Council of Baptist Churches in North East India. Minutes of the CBCNEI Executive Committee Meeting*, Resu, 1965, 14.

[299] *Council of Baptist Churches in North East India. Minutes of the CBCNEI Executive Committee Meeting*, Guwahati, 1969, 15.

five associations out of forty four attended.[300] Besides the CBCNEI central staff, a few visitors, one from Tripura Baptist Christian union and three from Goalpara Baptist Church Union attended.[301] This shows how other Baptist bodies in the region depended on the CBCNEI's decision on this important matter.

At the meeting the following topics were presented and discussed

1. The practical implications of the Draft Constitution by J. H. Thumra
2. Negative approach to Church Union by O. M. Rao
3. Do we need one united church in NEI? by E. Stafford

From the reports and discussions it was realized that the churches and associations had not studied and discussed among themselves the draft plan and the constitution. The casual attitude of the associations in the CBCNEI to the subject of church union makes one wonder whether the CBCNEI affiliated bodies were really interested in it. Nevertheless, at the end of the conference Rev. E. Stafford, the chairmen of the Theological Education Committee reported;

> It was discovered that the consensus opinion of the majority of the members present was that the CBCNEI may consider joining the church union of NEI, provided that the present draft plan and constitution is revised and presented again to the satisfaction of the churches concerned.[302]

A resolution was adopted and forwarded to NEICC (North East India Christian Council);

> That the second draft of the NEI church union plan is unacceptable in its present form. The general feeling is that at the present time the CBCNEI churches cannot give any definite word on church union. The churches would be prepared to discuss if a new plan of union in NEI is presented taking into consideration the main objections raised at the consultation, namely baptism, centralized church government, the office and term of bishop etc.[303]

This matter was brought to the annual session of the NEICC at Cherrapunji in 1972. The council regretted the CBCNEI's decision but nevertheless resolved that the CBCNEI be requested to give its alternative proposal with respect to the specific objections it had raised, so that the matter could be discussed further;

---

[300] Stafford, E. Papers. *A Brief Report of the Church Union Consultation* ..., 1.

[301] Stafford, E. Papers. *A Brief Report of the Church Union Consultation* ..., 1.

[302] Stafford, E. Papers. *A Brief Report of the Church Union Consultation* ..., 1.

[303] Stafford, E. Papers. *A Brief Report of the Church Union Consultation* ..., 1.

> The NEICC wants the church union to be kept alive and requested the CBCNEI to prepare a draft and place in the church union committee for consideration and discussion in the month of October 1974. The NEICC also would appreciate special representatives from the CBCNEI to the committee to support the view of the CBCNEI.[304]

But, till 1974 the CBCEI remained silent. It was only in the latter part of 1974 that the CBCNEI Executive Committee voted to inform the NEICC that because of differences of opinions among its churches, the Executive Committee of the CBCNEI was of the opinion that church union negotiations would not be very constructive at the present time.[305] The Executive Committee also opined that seeing and feeling the attitude of the people towards the union proposal any further discussion of the same should be deferred.

A cursory reading of the official reasons given[306] by the CBCNEI throughout the different consultations and conferences so far its hesitation and refusal to enter union negotiations gives one the impression that the reasons were genuinely theological. But, a deeper probing will reveal that beneath the official reasons given, which are theological, lie non-theological reasons. In the case of Baptists rejection of infant baptism was a rejection of what they believed to be a doctrine of divine grace as a kind of magic which operates on an unconscious subject (infant) through a mechanical ritual and which therefore stands in the way of true operation of grace through faith. For the Baptists, membership in the church depends on profession of faith which is possible only when the subject is old enough to understand and make a mature decision. This is a very central Baptist doctrine. But on the other hand knowing this difficulty, the NEICC had taken great care in the plans of union to indicate that infant baptism would not be forced on churches that practices believer's baptism. The chief mark of the visible church is baptism (by immersion) and where there is no baptism there are no visible churches. This arrangement was acceptable to the Presbyterians who, though they practice infant baptism, were willing to accept Christians who took believer's baptism.

As for the centralized church government, the CBCNEI's rejection of this is understandable in the light of the Baptists' love for local autonomy. Church union was looked upon by many Baptists as a prelude to an authoritarian ecclesiastical government. But, on the other hand, when the NEICC in 1972 requested the CBCNEI to make its proposal on subjects where it had raised questions, the CBCNEI, if it was really interested, could have made proposals that would have

---

[304] *North East India Christian Council. Minutes and Proceedings*, 1972 ...,13.

[305] CBCNEI Executive Committee Meeting, August 29-30, 1974, 26.

[306] CBCNEI reason for rejection was on the ground of Baptism, centralized church government, the term and office of bishop etc.

been acceptable to its convictions and churches. It's all in the CBCNEI sides, but the CBCNEI chose to keep silent.

Some Baptist feared entering into union would rob them of something vital in their Christian witness. They feared that a United Church would become liberal. But, this fear was unfounded. The churches that were part of the union discussion in the North Easy India were all Evangelical. In fact they can be termed as, 'Evangelical Charismatic-Orthodox,' with strong belief in mission, evangelism and church growth. Therefore, it was illogical to conclude that such churches coming together would make the United Church liberal. Two conservative churches coming together would not make one liberal church but rather they should make one stronger conservative church. Even today, many Baptist leaders still harbor fear that church union would result in overall decrease rather than increase in effectiveness in witness.

After the three years of complete silence, it was only in 1974 that the General Secretary of the CBCNEI wrote to the NEICC stating;

> During consultation meeting among ourselves in the past, we had sharp differences of opinion on the subject. The members of the Executive Committee therefore felt that opinion up of the negotiating process once again at this stage might cause serious problems among ourselves.[307]

That difference arose among the CBCNEI members in the light of the draft of the basis for union is understandable. But, when the CBCNEI was requested to make its own proposals, that differences occurred is beyond comprehension. The CBCNEI was given the opportunity to dictate its own terms on matters relating to baptism and church government. Had they made proposals, whether they would have been accepted or not by other NEICC members is not concern here. The General Secretary further wrote;

It is noted that the CBCNEI will not in any way stand on the progress of church union consultation among the NEICC to feel free to go ahead with your union plan.[308]

Such kind of negative response at this stage was not so discouraging for all the member churches of the church union discussion. The CBCNEI knew that church union discussion could not progress without it since it represented majority (sixty percent) of the total Protestant population in North East India. With the CBCNEI negative response, the church union talks came to a standstill in 1977. The report of the NEICC Annual meeting held at Barapani in 1977 stated that;

---

[307] K. Imotemjen Aier, to the General Secretary NEICC, 1974.

[308] K. Imotemjen Aier, to the General Secretary NEICC, 1974.

> New development of opinions arose in the CBCNEI and Cachar Hill Tribe Synod...These member churches have clearly indicated now that they are not prepared to enter into negotiation.[309]

The fact was that not only those two above stated member churches (CBCNEI and Cachar Hill Tribe Synod) have clearly indicated that they are not prepared but also there were units which also did not state their view clearly. In other words the church union movement lost its original momentum completely. All talk about the third draft plan of union was dropped from 1980 onwards.

4.3.3. The Third Period 1981 Till Date

When the issue of union was revived in 1981 the NEICC had gone as far a creating the Drafting Committee which brought out the plan of union and draft constitution of the united Chruch of North East India in May 1986.[310] Later it was revised and circulated to all the affiliated bodies for study and consideration. The Executive Committee meeting of the CBCNEI in May 1988 discussed the plan of union and draft constitution but decided that it was not in favor of Church Union at that stage in view of the upcoming restructuring of the CBCNEI itself;

> ...resolved that in view of present phase of restructuring of the CBCNEI, we defer to a future time, any negotiation for Church Union under the auspices of the NEICC, and at the same time call upon the NEICC to strengthen its existing fellowship.[311]

Regarding the proposed restructuring of the CBCNEI, it was more or less a kind of federal set up where the conventions, like the parallel Presbyterian Synods, could affiliate with bodies like the NEICC, NCCI, BWA, CCA, BCM, WCC etc. In this way conventions would have the privilege of representation and participation in many of the national and international bodies. But the CBCNEI has till date not shown any positive sign to enter negotiations leads one to ask whether the restructuring was yet another excuse. Till date the CBCNEI affiliated Baptist Churches stance has been quite clear, that they have refused to participate further on the church union discussion due to some factors. Having probed into the reasons the CBCNEI gave for its decision not to enter Church union negotiations, we have discovered that the real reasons were not theological alone but more on non-theological issues.

The report of the church union committee which was accepted by the Council, however pointed out that the situation in North East India called for closer cooperation and unity more than ever before. J. Fortis Jyrwa rightly pointed

---

[309] *North East India Christian Council, Minutes and Proceedings,* 1977..., 15.

[310] *North East India Christian Council, Minutes and Proceedings,* 1977..., 16.

[311] *Council of Baptist Churches in North East India. Report of the CBCNEI Executive Committee Meeting,* Guwahati, 1988, 5.

that "What is needed now is to re-examine the problems because Church Union is not a dead issue in North East India as some tend to think." Now the question is what kind of union are we talking about which suits our context and which can be of help in our common witness and service? New avenues for closer cooperation and other alternative forms of union best suited to the Christian Churches and situation in North East India should be explored and considered.

A close examination of the above stated historical fact shows that, the NEICC had become the most important ecumenical agency of Protestant Churches in Northeast region. It represents majority of the Protestant Churches with the aim and objective of having ultimate church union platform in the region. It had its origins in the Bengal Assam Christian Council that was formed in 1926. Later at a joint Conference it was decided to form a separate body for the NEI and the Assam Christian Council came into being in 1937. However, it is only since 1964 that concrete steps were taken to give shape to this laudable objective by holding two Faith and Order Conferences and two Church Union Conferences. Later, a Drafting Committee prepared a Draft Plan of church union and the same was again revised in the light of discussions at higher level and a copy was sent to each Unit for prayerful examination and comments. The response was unfavorable from many of the affiliated churches, particularly CBCNEI, due to which the Church Union Movement lost its momentum and came to be inactive for quite a long time. Nevertheless, after a long gap of almost 35 years, in the 1980s the spirit of forming a church union in NEI was revived by the church leaders by holding various meetings and consultations at different level within the constituent units.

4.4. CBCNEI AND WORLD COUNCIL OF CHURCHES (WCC)

In the course of history, CBCNEI have reached this point in a spirit of co-operation and Christian unity pilgrimage from milestone to milestone. It is a joyous fact as well as the fruit of the light of Christ and the energies of the Holy Spirit, which CBCNEI became the full members of World Council of Churches. The hope of becoming the CBCNEI to be a full membership with was rekindled. The CBCNEI Executive took the decision to apply for membership at the WCC and the AGM formally approved it. Dr Lama, the former General Secretary, accordingly sent the application two years before. The WCC sent a delegation as the follow up of our application for membership to WCC from June 12-15, 2014. During the visit they wanted to see some of the institutions, hospitals and churches. Due to time constraint, we were able to lead them only to ETC, JCMS, Golaghat Mission School, CLC, Guwahati Baptist Church and the Satribari Christian Hospital. We were also requested to organize Inter-denominational Leaders' Meeting at CBCNEI Conference Hall on June 13 where many church leaders from different denominations attended.[312]

[312] *Baptist News CBCNEI, October - December 2014*, Report o the General Secretary May 27 to October 17, 2014, Edited by Solomon Rongpi, Guwahati, Assam: CBCNEI, 2014.

As its zeal for the CBCNEI to be the member of WCC, that the WCC Central Committee, at its meeting held at Geneva from July 2-9, decided to accept CBCNEI as a member of the WCC subject to the approval of the next Central Committee Meeting held on 2016 Norway. During these years CBCNEI office bearers were invited to participate in the programs of WCC to show our interest and contributions. There are many benefits of having membership in WCC. We can participate in the Global communities on any issue that the world is facing today. We can avail scholarships for higher studies especially for Ph. D. scholarship. We can also bring inter-national programs to our area so that we can be exposed and the world community will also be exposed to North East India. There are many countries that are not aware of the existence of NEI and the issues we are facing today. We will also have the right to explore job opportunities in and through the WCC.

CBCNEI under the leadership of Rev. Dr Solomon Rongpi is jubilant over the achievement of yet another milestone in extending broader ministry as it acquired full membership in the highest ecumenical body in the global church during the WCC Central Committee Meeting held at Tronsheim, Norway, from 22-28 June 2016. Since then CBCNEI became the WCC member from 2016. The WCC describes itself as "a worldwide fellowship of 349 global, regional and sub-regional, national and local churches seeking unity, a common witness and Christian service." Rev. Dr Solomon Rongpi delivering the acceptance speech on behalf of the Baptist Churches in North East India was a proud moment of achievement for the members of CBCNEI.

> It is indeed a moment of joy and jubilation to be a member of the WCC, sharing common vision that WCC has. I believe that God will continue to lead us and guide us as we continue to celebrate life of togetherness and envision oneness in Christ.[313]

As Baptist in NEI travel together it is important to mark milestones on their way. The churches can continue to work together and seek together to extend the peace of Christ by participating in the Christian unity.

4.5. CONCLUSION

The coming of Baptist mission to Northeast India marked a new beginning in the history of Christian mission, because the Baptist missionaries were the pioneers in Northeast territory to establish permanent Christian mission activities in both the plain and hills. Though, it does not undermine the hard work of other Protestant Christian denominations and the Roman Catholic mission in NEI. In spite of the painstaking labours invested upon it, church union efforts in NEI are yet to see its real success. Though, at present, it is very difficult to ascertain whether the

---

313 *Baptist News CBCNEI,, April - June, 2017,* Report o the General Secretary May 27 to October 17, 2014, Edited by Solomon Rongpi, Guwahati, Assam: CBCNEI, 2017.

Christian Unity in NEI will ever succeed or not. Hence, it is generally accepted that there is a prospect for its success if the multifaceted hurdles are overcome through a right approach in the union movement. One of the major challenges for the Christian unity is to identify the basic hindrances towards unity and find the solution for it. The following chapter will sketch the challenges of Church Union Movement before the Baptist Churches in NEI.

Chapter 5

Challenges of Christian Unity Before the Baptist Church

INTRODUCTION

This section is to explore what are the issues and challenges faced by Baptist Church towards the Church Union Movement in Northeast India. Retrospect, the Baptist Churches in Northeast India began, as all infants, since 1836, under the American Baptist Missionary Union (ABMU), which was struggling to survive in the midst of traditional beliefs and practise. Today, however, the Baptists with the largest population in the region have become the leading Protestant denominational family. The Baptists have come a very long way in their growth and development in mission work as well as in numbers. But, the intention of this study is not to appreciate the positive and negative side of the work of the mission, rather to explore the challenges of Christian unity before the Baptist Church in NEI, both from theological and non-theological factors.

5.1. BAPTIST ECCLESIOLOGY

Historical evidence says that Baptists came into existence in England in the early seventeenth century. They apparently emerged out of the Puritan-Separatist movement in the Church of England. Some of these earnest people read the Bible in their own language, believed it, and sought to live by it. They formed separate congregations which accepted only believers into their membership, and they baptized converts upon their profession of faith. Their opponents nicknamed them "Baptists," and the name stuck.

5.2. ISSUES AND CHALLENGES

Subsequently the issues and challenges towards the further formation of church unity in NEI will be discussed. The fact is that the failure of Church Union discussion in Northeast India was not only Theological challenges but also Non-Theological forces as well. Let us see what are the theological and non theological that hindered to the progress of Christian unity in Northeast region.

5.2.1. THEOLOGICAL CHALLENGES

From the very beginning of the formation of North East India Christian Council, there were certain practical objections arising from theological challenges. Therefore, the church disunity exists where a communion is separated from other communions on account of theological differences, regarding essential doctrines of the faith and order and other church discipline will be discussed in this section.

5.2.1.1. BAPTISM

Baptism proves to be one of the major difficulties in the relationship between Baptist and other churches. While the majority of Christendom practices infant baptism, Baptist have a commitment to believer's baptism by immersion, and this presents clear difficulties in trying to reach agreement about the meaning and practice of this central sacrament within the life of the church. There continue those who hope and seek to build deeper ecumenism on the basis of a common baptism, but this is always likely to be problematic for Baptist's.[314] The generally accepted Baptist's practice of baptism is when a person in the context of the Christian community hears the story of Jesus as the story of God's love for him or her and responds to it, which often speaks of a faith-event. Believers thus experience the forgiveness of sins and acceptance by God. Faith opens the believer not only towards God but also towards his or her fellow human beings as God's creatures.

Thus, the believer seeks fellowship in a Christian community and, at the same time, he or she wants publicly to confess their faith in word and deed.[315] The public celebration of baptism, whereby the believer is baptized by immersion in the name of the Trinitarian God, marks the entry into the church and, at the same time, provides the believer with the possibility of publicly placing his or her life under the Sovereignty of Christ; to this the congregation responds with the pledge of prayer and fellowship. Baptism is often followed immediately in the same worship service by the first participation in the Lord's Supper.[316] As such, the whole service concretely expresses the beginning of a living faith in God, the

---

[314] *Baptists and Ecumenism*, Unpublished paper written for an Ecumenical Officers' Consultation in November 2007.

[315] Jeffrey Gros, "Baptism Today: Understanding, Practice, Ecumenical Implications," *Worship*, 83/3 (May, 2009), 264-266.

[316] T. Bergsten, "Baptism and the Church," *The Baptist Quarterly*, 18/3 (1959), 125-131.

personal commitment to Christian discipleship, and entry into full communicant membership of the local Baptist church.

Baptists practice believers' baptism by immersion for the following reasons:

(a) It is the practice indicated by the New Testament,
(b) Immersion is the best symbolic re-enactment of the believer's dying and rising with Christ and of Christ's total claim upon, and renewal of, the whole bodily existence of the believer,
(c) The emphasis on believers' baptism takes seriously the voluntary nature of faith on one hand, and the responsibility and dignity of the individual in his or her relationship to God on the other
(d) Baptists want to emphasize the nature of the church as the gathered community of believers. Thus, only those who have committed themselves to the Sovereignty of Christ are given full communicant membership.[317]

These affirmations imply a rejection of infant or any other form of baptism.[318] It is to note that baptism was one of the main obstacles towards the further development of church union discussion in Northeast India. In 1947 church union committee annual session at Guwahati resolved to adopt the Round Table Conference and it was added that the Baptist children are members of the church and share in the privileges and obligations of membership so far as they are capable of doing so.[319] Since then some members of the Council of Baptist Churches felt that the definition on baptism may be ignored. So, the Council requested the drafting Committee to make a further study for more guidance in this issue. Thus, the Committee added in the Plan of Union and Draft Constitution that:

> The Church of North-East India allows both Infant Baptism and Believers Baptism but not both on the same person and shall receive as communicant members all those who have been baptized or confirmed. It assures freedom of expression for the particular convictions of different traditions.[320]

---

[317] Thorwald Lorenzen, "Baptism and Church Membership: Some Baptist positions and their Ecumenical Implications," in *Journal of Ecumenical Studies*, 18/4, (Fall 1981); 561-574. This is a paper presented at the Consultation on Believers' Baptism organized by the W.C.C. Commission on Faith and Order, and held at the Southern Baptist Theological Seminary, Louisville, Kentucky, March 28-April 1, 1979.

[318] T. Lorenzen, *Baptists and Ecumenicity*, 1980, 268, cited by Mathew, *Christianity in Assam and Inter-Faith Dialogue* ..., 184.

[319] *Assam Christian Council, Minutes and Proceedings*, 1947 ..., 12.

[320] *NEICC,* The Plan of Church Union and Draft Constitution of the Church of NEI (Shillong: NEICC, 1970), 7.

The Baptist Churches under the Council of Baptist Churches in NEI could not accept the two forms of baptism (infant and adult) proposed in the union plan. The concern is that there shall be no restriction placed upon the person who wishes to receive believers' baptism regardless of whether he/she has been baptized as an infant. Generally, the Baptists believe and practice 'believer's baptism,' which implies adult baptism. Immersion baptism has been the usual mode of believer's baptism. It is believed that baptism is a symbolic act, an outward expression of faith before the church, after the candidate has been baptized he or she is admitted into the fellowship of the body of believers through partaking of the Lord's Supper.[321] This above argument became a more controversial issue in church union negotiations. It became the bone of contention in the subsequent union discussions. Disagreement on the nature, meaning, and practice of baptism is one of the major obstacles in the continuing realization of a consensus among the Christian churches. Nevertheless this issue continues to be a source of some tension due to varying practices and understandings.

5.2.1.2. THE LORD'S SUPPER

In Baptist's concept, Lord's Supper is one of the church ordinances and so it must be consistent with the faith and practice of the Baptist Churches. Although, a major segment of the Christian regards the celebration of the Lord's Supper as the central act of Christian worship. The meaning and purpose must not be forgotten and it has to be done or administered rightly by the church. It is confined to a local congregation or an official polity. It is always an integral part of the worship service in a church or in a formal gathering of the church like convention and must be accompanied by the preached word.[322] As a rule it is normally administered only by a licentiate pastor or by ordained minister in the church. Baptists usually do not use special vestments during celebration of the Lord's Supper (in NEI Baptist churches), however a decent dress is permissible. Believers' baptism by immersion should be required of those who receive the Supper or participate in the Lord's Supper or take the communion and one should also be an active member of a Baptists church.[323]

---

[321] William L. Hendricks, "Baptism: A Baptist Perspective," *Southwestern Journal of Theology*, 31/2 (Spr., 1989): 22ff; also see in Rao, *Baptist Distinctives ...*, 122.

[322] *Uniform Practices of Baptist Churches in North East India (CBCNEI)*, Published by The Theological Education Committee, Council of Baptist Churches in North East India, Guwahati, 8-9; Arthur B. Crabtree, "Eucharist in Baptist Life and Thought," *Journal of Ecumenical Studies*, 13/2 (Spring, 1976): 296ff; J. B. Middlebrook, "Baptism as Entrance into the Church and Its Relation to the Lord's Supper," in *Concerning Believers' Baptism*, ed., by F. C. Bryan (London: Kingsgate Press, 1943), 57; F.S. Downs. *Manual of Worship* (Guwahati: CLC, 1975).

[323] *Uniform Practices of Baptist Churches in North East India (CBCNEI)*, Published by The Theological Education Committee, Council of Baptist Churches in North East India, Guwahati, 9-10.

Consequently, a diversity of practices of the celebration of Lord's Supper can be seen in the Baptist Churches in CBCNEI area. This perhaps shows a background of several Baptists traditions that enterprise their missions in Northeast India.[324] This is also one of the reasons that different traditional set up find it difficult to have cooperation among them, and it does not give serious thought to develop wider church union movement in the region of Northeast India.

However, only persons who have been baptized as believers by immersion in the context of a recognized Baptists church can be admitted to the communion table.[325] Of course, such a practice presupposes that believer's baptism by immersion has been administered on the authority of a Baptists church. Thus Baptism is seen as an essential mark of the church; consequently, it is a necessary prerequisite for church membership.[326] This baptism can only be administered to believers, and the only permissible form is immersion.[327] Obviously, among Baptists disciplinary qualifications for participating in the Lord's Supper are restricted to immersed believers only.[328] The believer is baptized into communicant membership of the local church. In this case, only baptized believers in some churches only Baptists, and in a few churches, only members of that particular local Baptist church are invited to participate in the Lord's Supper. Baptism is a perquisite for participating in the Lord's Supper or to take communion and one should also be an active member of a Baptist church.[329] Such issues can be also a source of difficulty, and it would be easy to see them as nothing more than obstacles to be overcome.

---

[324] The background of several traditions of Baptist origin in North East India are the American Baptists mission covered upper Assam areas of Brahmaputra Valley, Nagaland, Manipur, Meghalaya (Garo/Achik) and Arunachal Pradesh. Southern/General Baptists covered South Mizoram and Tripura and North Bank of Assam. Australian/New Zealand Baptists covered Lower Part of Assam. The Northern Evangelical Lutheran Church is present in Bodo/Santhal areas of lower Assam. The Baptist Missionary Society (BMS) donated its Guwahati property to the American Baptist Foreign Missionary Society (ABFMS) currently the Council of Baptist Churches in NEI (CBCNEI), Panbazar.

[325] W. Morgan Patterson, "Lord's Supper in Baptist History," *Review & Expositor*, 66/1 (Winter, 1969), 25-34.

[326] William H. Whitsitt, *History of Communion Among the Baptists* (New York: J. K. Lees, 1880), 1 ff.

[327] James B. Taylor, *Restricted Communion: or, Baptism an Essential Prerequisite to the Lord's Supper* (Charleston, South Carolina: Southern Baptist Publication Society, 1856), 124.

[328] Arthur B. Crabtree, *Eucharist in Baptist Life and Thought* ..., 303.

[329] Edward T. Hiscox, *Principle and Practice for Baptist Churches* (Grand Rapids, Michigan: Kregel Publication, 1970), 56.

5.2.1.3. AUTHORITY OF SCRIPTURE

Baptists have emphasized the primacy and sufficiency of the Scripture as their authority for the faith and practice.[330] More than most church groups, Baptists have manifested startlingly opposite characteristics in their history. Because of their emphasis on the Scripture, on a strict puritan and on the absolute necessity of personal faith and personal holiness,[331] most Baptists have remained conservative, in matters of both faith and morals. The Baptist Faith and Message Adopted in 2000 stated that "the sole authority for faith and practice among Baptists is the Scriptures of the Old Testaments and New Testaments. Confessions are only guides in interpretation, having no authority over the conscience."[332]

While Baptists ascribe ultimate authority to the Triune God, they identify Scripture as the supreme earthly source of authority that derives its authority from the Triune God who is the authorizing subject, the principal factor, and the living presence of the biblical story.[333] As a result, Baptist Churches do not regard the practice of human authority over any local churches. Scripture as their authority for Christian faith and practice hints at a rejection of other possible sources of authority.[334] One of the reasons for the objection of the draft plan of North East India Christian Council by the Baptist Churches of the CBCNEI was the inclusion of human authority over the local churches, which was considered to be a direct contradiction with the principle of Baptist conviction.

5.2.1.4. THE PRIESTHOOD OF ALL BELIEVERS

Throughout history, the Baptists have held the doctrine of priesthood of believers as one of the cardinal beliefs and most cherished practise in the church.[335] Thus, the idea of the priesthood of believers is virtually inseparable from the Baptists

---

[330] Steven R. Harmon, "Scripture in the Life of the Baptist churches: Openings for a Differentiated Catholic-Baptist Consensus on Sacred Scripture," *Pro Ecclesia*, 18/2 (Spring, 2009), 187 ff.

[331] Lumpkin, *Baptist Confessions of Faith* ..., 361-362

[332] *Statement of Faith* adopted in June 14, 2000 by Southern Baptist Church, http://www.bible-researcher. com/ baptistfaith.html#family.

[333] James Leo Garrett Jr., "Sources of Authority in Baptist Thought," *Baptist History and Heritage*, 13/3 (July, 1978), 41ff.

[334] William Latane Lumpkin, "Appraisal of Intent in Baptist Affirmation of Biblical Authority," *Perspectives in Religious Studies*, 1/2 (Fall 1974), 156ff.

[335] The priesthood of all Christians has been understood distinctive. Because of their convictions about the priesthood of believers, Baptists preach (1) justification by faith, (2) believer's baptism, (3) regenerate church membership, (4) the church as a fellowship of believers in a spiritual democracy, (5) private interpretation of Scriptures, (6) freedom of thought, (7) religious liberty, (8) separation of church and state, (9) divine calling for every Christian's occupation, and (10) responsibility for the extension of the kingdom of God on the part of every Christian. Further Ref. William L. Pitts, "The Priesthood of all Christians in the Baptist Heritage," *Southwestern Journal of Theology*, 30/2 (Spring, 1988), 34-45.

doctrine.[336] Virtually every Baptist would have argued that there is no more basic belief to Baptists than the idea of the priesthood of the believers. Properly understood, it is one of the bedrock foundation stones upon which all of Baptists other doctrines are based.[337] The Bible assumes throughout the competency of the human soul, the capability of each person to hear and respond to God.[338]

Baptists' story is studded with numerous examples of a courageous defence of the principle of the priesthood of believers. Virtually all Baptist confessions of faith[339] have spoken pointedly in support of religious liberty, the right of a free conscience before God for every person. The Baptists application of the priesthood of all believers has frequently emphasized the privileges given to each believer without stressing also the responsibilities which fall upon each believer. The priesthood of the believers is a cherished Baptists doctrine which sets forth both the privileges and the responsibilities of Christians.[340]

Baptists have often emphasized that the priesthood of all believers supports belief in the following practices;

(a) All Christians have the right to interpret Scripture for themselves.
(b) Every member of a Baptist church possesses voting rights in the conduct of church business.
(c) All Christians have the authority and obligation to develop personally their own religious beliefs.[341]

As such, the priesthood of all believers means that each person must take the full burden of moral responsibility in approaching God.[342] J. N. Tennent had rightly pointed that;

> No other church has insisted, as the Baptists have done, on the centrality of the New Testament connection between baptism and personal faith, the importance of this great symbolic act of surrender to God within that society all are equal, and all are called to the worshipping life; the 'priesthood of every believer' and the impossibility of substituting any

---

[336] William L Pitts, "The priesthood of all Christians in the Baptist heritage ..., 34-45.

[337] W. Barry Garrett, "Priesthood of Believers," *Encyclopedia of Southern Baptists,* ed., Norman Wade Cox (Nashville: Broadman Press, 1958), 1113.

[338] J. Terry Young, "Baptists and the Priesthood of Believers," *Perspectives in Religious Studies,* 20/2 (Summer, 1993), 131-146.

[339] The London Confession of faith, 1644; The Standard Confession, 1660; The Philadelphia Confession, 1742; The New Hampshire Confession, 1833 etc.

[340] Thomas D. Lea, "The Priesthood of All Christians According to the New Testament," *Southwestern Journal of Theology,* 30/2 (Spring, 1988), 15-21.

[341] James Leo Garrett, "The Priesthood of All Believers," *Baptist and Reflector* (January 9, 1964), 9.

[342] William H. Stephens, "The Priesthood of Believers: Baptist Doctrine Study for 1988," *Southwestern Journal of Theology,* 30/2 (Spring, 1988), 5.

> liturgical act for personal communion with God and the self-offering to God, are cardinal points of Baptist belief.[343]

Underhill thereby connects adult baptism to the priesthood of all believers and sees both resting on a passion for spiritual liberty. For Garrett the central idea of the priesthood of all believers is the traditional notion that every Christian has direct access to God.[344] This interpretation clearly centers on the notion of individualism and elimination of a mediator. The notion of the priesthood of all believers as service to one's fellow human beings is alluded to in the biblical exposition, but is not developed in the essay.[345] Robert Handy also wrote the article on 'Baptists'; where he interpreted the priesthood of all Christians as lay participation of the church.[346] Again on the writings of Herschel Hobbs on "Baptist Beliefs," he rests his argument on the ideas of soul competency and priesthood; Basic in the principles of Baptists is the concept of the competency of each individual soul before God. This involves the 'priesthood of believers' whereby every believer may read and interpret the Scriptures as he is led by the Holy Spirit.[347] Hobbs emphasized that the priesthood of all Christians means the believer's direct access to God through faith. He argues that the most unique Baptist distinctive is the competency of the soul and the right of every man to interpret the Scriptures for himself.[348] Cyril Eastwood probably has authored the most extensive, and most intensive, study of the idea of the priesthood of believers (2 volumes, The Priesthood of All Believers, and The Royal Priesthood of the Faithful).[349] His conclusion is that "the doctrine of the priesthood of the believers is not incidental but central in Baptists theology."[350]

---

[343] J. N. Tennent, "The Priesthood of Believers," in *Sixth Baptist World Congress: Official Report,* ed. J. H. Rushbrooke (Atlanta: The Baptist World Alliance, 1939), 170.

[344] Garrett examined the biblical basis and meanings for the doctrine (a pure life, worship, intercessory prayer, evangelism). Then he presented four additional theological arguments for the idea. (1) Creation: man was created with the capacity for fellowship with God without a need for a mediator. (2) God's commandments: the commandments are addressed to individuals. (3) Nature of salvation: salvation is a personal experience which no one can produce for another. (4) Individual responsibility: each person is his own priest. Ref. Garrett, "The Priesthood of All Believers" …, 9ff.

[345] W. O. Carver, "Baptist Churches," in *The Nature of the Church,* ed., by R. Newton Flew (New York: Harper & Brothers, 1952), 288ff.

[346] Robert T. Handy, "Baptist," in *A Handbook of Christian Theology* (Cleveland, Ohio: World Publishing Co., 1958), 28-31.

[347] Herschel H. Hobbs, *What Baptists Believe* (Nashville, Tfenn.: Broadman Press, 1964), 7.

[348] Herschel H. Hobbs, *The People Called Baptists and The Baptist Faith and Message* (Shawnee, Okla.: Oklahoma Baptist University, 1981), 18.

[349] Cyril Eastwood, *The Priesthood of All Believers: An Examination of the Doctrine from the Reformation to the Present Day* (London: The Epworth Press, 1960), 56; and *The Royal Priesthood of the Faithful: An Investigation of the Doctrine from Biblical Times to the Reformation* (Minneapolis: Augsburg Publishing House, 1963), 77.

[350] Cyril, *The Priesthood of All Believers…*, 47.

From the above view it is clear that the doctrine of the priesthood of all believers is a fundamental belief among Baptists. One of the basic principles of Baptist Church government is that all its members are equal because all of them are priest before God. They believe in the priesthood of all believers where each one is endowed with the right to approach God by grace through faith in Christ without the mediatorial role.[351] The Baptist acknowledgement of the priesthood of all believers in Christ convinces the spirit of democracy in their government of the church. From the standpoint of the doctrine of the church, believers are united as brothers and sisters in the corporate body of the church, each fully sharing in the rights and responsibilities in the life and work of the church. Therefore the advocate of an organic church union in North East India is seen as standing contradiction against the convictions of the Baptist principles.

5.2.1.5. RELIGIOUS LIBERTY

The Baptists concept of the ideas of religious liberty and priesthood of believers are not identical but they are very closely related in the thinking of many Baptists.[352] From a biblical point of view human beings are very special. Each person is made in the image of God, according to Gen 1:26-27. What does it mean to be made in the image of God? The dominant idea held by twentieth-century interpreters is that being made in the image of God means that humans are made in relationship with God. Or as some put it, humans are made addressable by God; humans can sense the leadership of God in their lives and can express themselves to God.[353]

Baptists' emphasis on the worth and dignity of the human person, along with all of the questions of religious liberty, is acutely related to this rich concept of humans made in God's own image. Humans have inalienable, God-given rights. We are made in such a relationship to God that we need no intermediary to stand between us and God. And, furthermore, each individual person has the inalienable right to approach God without the interference of another.[354] This basic religious liberty is God-given that all persons are capable of approaching God directly, without interference or the assistance of an intermediary. All persons have full freedom to worship or not to worship according to their own interests and need, with no coercion from the state, the church, or individuals.

Religious liberty, according to Mullins, is a very deep, fundamental part of the Baptist understanding of Christian faith. 'With Baptists, religious liberty is born of the direct vision of God. . . . Always it has been a passion deep as life

---

[351] Edge, *The Doctrine of the Laity* ..., 9.

[352] The preamble to "The Baptist Faith and Message," The Most Recent Baptist confession of faith, states, "Baptists emphasize the soul's competency before God, freedom in religion, and the priesthood of the believer," linking these three ideas. Baptists take this closely related cluster of ideas very seriously because they feel that they are scripturally based.

[353] Young, *Baptists and the Priesthood of Believers* ..., 131-146.

[354] Young, Baptists and the Priesthood of Believers...,

welling up from the depths of being in eternal faith and hope.'[355] Religious liberty, or soul freedom, was no minor emphasis with Mullins. It was as deep as his belief in God and God's creative work. 'Religious liberty rests upon man's original creation in God's image. Mullins then concluded, 'this is the being and these endowments which demand that great boon we call religious liberty.'[356] It would allow no religious creed or confession of faith to stand between the individual conscience and God. Mullins insisted on the inalienable right of each person to have direct access to God for himself/herself, and to have an equal voice in the church.

The Baptist Church's government is based on the belief that all its baptized members are equal because all of them have full freedom or liberty before God and Church. The Baptists acknowledgment of the religious liberty in Christ convinces the spirit of democracy in their government of the Church. It is for this reason that Baptists, have stood apart in seeming indifference to the call of ecumenical concern.

5.2.1.6. FORM OF BAPTISTS WORSHIP

The problem of disunity did not happen just because of the divergent peoples' culture in the region but also because of the form of worship that varied from one denomination to another. Each denominational group was deeply rooted in their own worship set up, which did not easily facilitate the ecumenical spirit of unity. Snaitang says that;

> The proposal for a united church came at a time when the denominational form of worship had a deep rooted foundation among the people. Some churches followed a well-prepared liturgy others adopted a free worship with unwritten spontaneous prayers. There were churches that insisted on a congregational participation in worship and had shaped their members on collective orchestral prayers. Churches which had their own form of worship from beginning and through their life and existence were not prepared to part with it for the sake of union.[357]

Worship cannot, in the Baptists tradition, be a solitary experience; it is the joining of minds and spirits and voices in the praise and adoration of God.[358]

---

[355] E. Y. Mullins, "The Baptist Conception of Religious Liberty," in *The Life of Baptists in the World*, edited by Walter B. Shurden (Nashville: Broadman Press, 1985), 57.

[356] Mullins, *The Baptist Conception of Religious Liberty...*, 58.

[357] O. L. Snaitang, *A History of Ecumenical Movement: An Introduction* (Bangalore: BTESSC/SATHRI, 2010), 169.

[358] Those who come from the rich and colorful history of ritual and liturgy in worship would find the services of worship in the Baptist Church in many places surprisingly barren of such meaningful forms. The worship service will seem informal, lacking in beauty and all too dependent

This perspective helps to explain the vigour of hymn-singing in Baptist churches. In harmony with the earlier mentioned democratic emphasis, in decisions of the church, so also in the event of worship, all are expected to participate. Such participation is an expression of mutuality. Therefore, it is fair to say that such an attitude toward the worship in Baptists church gives them more freedom and also a space for the lay people responsible.[359] And there is no doubt that Baptists have grown in numbers because of this kind of freedom.

The Church Union Movement that was negotiated in NEI is in view of the essence of Christian unity in a visible organic structure reflecting one church under a single hierarchy. What was unknown during the infancy of the church is therefore projected as a sign of Christian unity. What has just been said has a bearing on aspects of Christian disunity wider than those domestic in our church. It is possible for members of one communion to be disturbed by forms and practices in another to which they are unaccustomed. Therefore it was foreign for Baptist to amalgamate their pattern of worship with the other traditional practices and concepts of worship in the name of ecumenism.

5.2.1.7. BAPTIST CHURCH MEMBERSHIP

Membership in the Baptist Church is based upon certain qualifications and must always be approved by the congregation. The requisites for the church membership practice in Baptist churches are through voluntary, covenant and believers' baptism.[360] No one becomes a member simply because he or she was

---

upon the inspiration of the moment or lack of it. There is an informality which almost becomes a formality, a lack of structure which becomes a structure, a spontaneity which sometimes covers and conceals a lack of seriousness in dealing with the great spiritual realities which must undergird the experience of true worship. But, on the other hand, there will be some hearty participation by the congregation, some hearty singing of great old hymns, and some earnest prayers which come from the heart rather than from some ancient printed page. It is a reflection of where the Baptists are somehow, down to earth where the people live, and out of the context of that real world their worship reflects their serious commitment to a Gospel which offers comfort for the burdens of the 'now' and hope for the promise of the 'tomorrow. For ref. Robinson, *The Life and Faith of the Baptists* ..., 50.

[359] Thomas R. McKibbens, "Our Baptist Heritage in Worship," *Review and Expositor*, 13/1 (January, 1978), 26-34.

[360] The requisites for the church membership practice in Baptist churches can be conveniently summarized in three basic forms. They are through voluntary, covenant and believers' baptism. Through Voluntary=Baptists emphasis in the view of the church among Baptists is the insistence that membership in the church is voluntary, the result of a personal and responsible choice. One is not born into the church, or made a member by virtue of being born into a family of Christians. Although the emphasis is sometimes interpreted in such a way that it seems to omit or to overlook the divine initiative in redemption, and thus to reduce church membership to the same level as that of membership in any voluntary organization, this is not the intention. What is intended rather is that church membership is to issue from the individual's personal commitment to Jesus Christ as Lord, and thus to be in harmony with the Baptist understanding of salvation and Christian discipleship. Insistence that one receive baptism and become a member of the church only

a member of another Baptists church, somewhere else, before moving to local Baptist church. One must join the church, and the wish to join must meet with the approval of the congregation. Baptists acknowledge that the church is a creation of the spirit of God and only exists because God has first acted in Christ or us men and for our salvation. Yet they believe that they have sound scriptural and theological grounds or insisting that none is eligible for baptism and church membership except after personal profession of faith, approved by the church.[361]

Accordingly Baptists hold that the church is composed of those who have been born again by the Holy Spirit and who have been brought to personal and

---

upon one's own personal decision means that for Baptists, the stage in Christian life signified by confirmation in the Catholic church is combined with that of baptism, and thus there is no place in the Baptist understanding for the rite of confirmation as a separate event. Ref; G. McLeod Bryan, ed., *Documents concerning Baptism and Church Membership: A Controversy among North Carolina Baptists. Perspectives in Religious Studies* Special Study Series 1 (1977), 16. Through Covenant= A primary emphasis, closely related to this concept of voluntary membership, is that of the covenant. There are two types of covenant usually practiced by the Baptist Churches. Firstly, among Baptists in general, the understanding of covenant is that acceptance by solemn commitment of one's place within the community of faith along with fellow believers under God that is attested when one is baptized. Baptism therefore is not a private event but is performed publicly, in the presence and with the approval of the congregation into which the new convert is brought. The covenant, then, is the sum total of commitments, largely unwritten, accepted in one's entrance into the company of believers. But the second reference of the term "covenant" is a written statement. Thus the written statement of the covenant which are commonly used are; "As we trust we have been brought by divine grace to embrace the Lord Jesus Christ, and by the influence of His Spirit to give ourselves up to Him, so we do now solemnly covenant with each other that God enabling us we will walk together in brotherly love; that we will exercise a Christian care and watchfulness over each other and faithfully warn, rebuke, and admonish one another as the case may require; that we will not forsake the assembling of ourselves together, nor omit the great duty of prayer, both for ourselves, and for others; that we will participate in each other's joys, and endeavor with tenderness and sympathy to bear each other's burdens and sorrows; that we will earnestly endeavor to bring up such as are or may be under our care in the nurture and admonition of the Lord; that we will seek divine aid to enable us to walk circumspectly and watchfully in the world, denying ungodliness and every worldly lust; that we will strive together, in so far as God prospers us, for the support of a faithful evangelical ministry among ourselves and for the spread of the gospel unto the ends of the earth; that we will endeavor by example and effort to win souls to Christ, and that through life, amidst evil report and good report, we will seek to live to the glory of Him who hath called us out of darkness into His marvelous light."Ref; R. D. Patton, "Baptists and Regenerate Church Membership: Historical Perspectives and Present Practice," *Baptist History and Heritage,* 13 (1978), 28-32. Through Believers' Baptism= Believers' baptism is one of the most necessities among the Baptist Churches for the church membership. That means that only persons who have been baptized as believers by immersion in the context of a recognized Baptist church can be admitted to membership. Baptism is seen by these churches to be an essential mark of the church; consequently, it is a necessary prerequisite for church membership. This baptism can only be administered to believers, and the only permissible form is immersion. The believer is baptized into communicant membership of the local church. Ref; A. Gilmore, *Baptism and Christian Unity* (London: Lutterworth Press, 1966), 81.

[361] Russel F. Aldwinckle, *Of Water and the Spirit: A Baptist View of Church Membership* (Canada: The Baptist Federation of Canada, 1964), 7.

saving faith in the Lord Jesus Christ. A living and direct acquaintance with Christ is, therefore, held to be basic to church membership. Membership in the church of Christ is not based on the accident or privilege of birth, either in a Christian country or in a Christian family. Moreover, this view of church membership indicates that the church is entered voluntarily and that only believers may participate in its ordinance. All baptized members are equal in status although they vary in gifts.[362] Baptists acknowledge the principle that church membership is entered upon by one's own personal acceptance of Jesus Christ as Savior and Lord and submission to baptism in obedience to his command. Therefore, it is hard for the Baptists to accommodate 'others,' who do not belong to its own fold. The acceptance of 'others' is seen standing in direct challenges against the convictions of the Baptist churches.

5.2.1.8. BAPTIST POLITY

Church polity is an operational and governance structure of a church or Christian denominations. It also denotes the ministerial structure of the church and the authority relationships between churches. Polity is closely related to Ecclesiology, the study of doctrine and theology relating to church organization. In Baptist polities local churches are autonomous and national organizations can offer assistance or coordinate activities but have no legitimate authority to make decisions for local congregations.[363] However, the basic Baptists polity planks as local church autonomy, the lordship of Christ, the authority of the Bible, personal salvation, believer's baptism, separation of church and state, and the priesthood of the believer[364] have all worked together to tend to keep the Baptists polity more autonomy and distinctive.

Basic to Baptists polity is the belief that the standing of a local church with any of the general Baptist bodies should not affect its standing with other general bodies. As the local church is independent and autonomous, so are the Baptist bodies independent and autonomous. Each church has its own theological standings and practices for more than a century. They (Baptists) have been for long been accustomed to their particular church polity and distinctive form of discipline and practice in church life. So, to bring about the change the polity at this juncture is not an easy thing rather it hampering most ecumenical discussions in NEI.

---

[362] Patton, "Baptists and Regenerate Church Membership: Historical Perspectives ..., 29.

[363] Foy Valentine, "Baptist Polity and Social Pronouncements, "*Baptist History and Heritage,* 14/3 (July, 1979), 52-61.

[364] Nathan L. Baker, "Baptist Polity and Para-church Organizations," Baptist *History and Heritage,* 14/3 (July, 1979), 62ff.

5.2.1.9. DENOMINATIONALISM

In Northeast India, when the church union talks began in the early 1930s, there were different denominational churches which already existed and which had different roots. Henceforth, different Christian missionaries introduced Christianity in the region that led to the creation of separate denominational churches in the whole Northeast area. Some of the regions were converted by the Wesleyan Mission, others by American Board of Mission, others by the Free Church of Scotland, and so on. Mission work continued among the bodies, pursued by different missionary societies, and as a result the different denominational churches emerged in these small regions of North East India. The Christians in Northeast India started competing with each other, emphasizing only to their own denominations.

Therefore, when it comes to the denominational setting, the internal unity of these denominations themselves is often strained and complicated for ecumenical task. It is a common sight in NEI church buildings with names such as, Ao Baptist Church, Mizo Presbyterian Church, Mizo Baptist Church and so on. Most Churches like Baptists, Presbyterians and other Churches had registered phenomenal growth not only in numbers but in terms of geographical area across the region, forming their own administrative set up, maintaining an extensive network of school education, establishing medical institutions, possessing property and strengthening their ecclesiastical ties with their respective mother churches either in America and Europe and became ardent members of their respective confessional bodies.[365]

While considering the development of different denomination in Northeast region F. S. Downs testified that it was due to a historical fact:

> We belong to our present denominations due to the accidents of history and birth. The overwhelming majority belongs to the denominations they do because their parents did. The various Protestant groups in the area are organized into separate Church bodies simply because the mission that established them came from different countries. Thus we are what we are by a series of historical accidents, by virtue of decisions made not by the christians themselves but by missionaries and mission societies sitting around tables with maps and red pencil demarcating comity areas. Under such circumstances it hardly became us to be overly zealous about the virtues of our supposed theological distinctive.[366]

In such a way the Christian community in NEI was divided into several church traditions. Most of them have become accustomed to the traditions,

---

[365] Snaitang, *Ecumenism and Hill People* ..., 40.

[366] Downs, *Church Union: Theological and Non-Theological* ..., 1-2.

polities and practices which they inherited from their denominational churches. Each denomination remains loyal to its own ecclesiastical set up that they have inherited from their parents' churches, rather than being involved in a wider co-operation or fellowship with other churches that belong to other communities. The North East India Christian Council which is an ecumenical body for North East India is still not very active due to differences in culture, ecclesiastical structure, deep rooted denominationalism and conservative theology.

5.2.1.10. PREDISPOSITION TO THE LAXITY OF DISCIPLINE

There is also a predisposition to the laxity of discipline in such an inwardly heterogeneous but outwardly uniform-organic union. Discipline specifically means here the sense of harmony, mutual agreements and compatibility with each other in all matters of faith and practice. The age-long traditional beliefs and convictions of the teachings of the Scriptures are deeply rooted in their mind and have become a part and parcel of their life, which cannot be erased or compromised. Often they believe and do according to their own denominational convictions. Again their deep spiritual longings and needs are not met with proper spiritual nourishment and are left unsatisfied by their spiritual leaders.[367] Also their opinions are unheeded ignored or unnoticed and thereby developing in themselves a spirit of coldness and disharmony and even openly revolting against their church. It is natural that such laxity of discipline occurs in a big church or church union very often. In this connection the advocates of church union argue that the biggest church is the denominational church and not the union of a few churches in a small state. Yet in spite of the bigness of a denominational church they have practically no actions and disharmony as they have the same traditional beliefs and convictions which make them one in faith and practice.[368] The theological import with its contrary dual attitude of seeing one's own faith and institution as the only best way and others as false is another significant dimension of NEI Christianity.

5.2.1.11. VOICES AGAINST EPISCOPACY

The concept of Episcopacy is one of the greatest conflicting problems as relating to Church Union movement negotiation in NEI. There is tendency that Episcopacy a belief which teaches that a Bishop has sole authority to rule over the churches directly in all matters without any acknowledgment of laity. Baptists hold and teach that Jesus Christ alone is the Head of the Church and that without any human intervention or ritualistic ceremony. Therefore He is the sole authority in all matters of faith and conduct, in the life both of the Church and of the individual as well as community.[369] The Baptist Churches under the Council of

---

[367] Likok, *A Picture of an Organic Church Union* ..., 5.

[368] Snaitang, "Ecumenism and Hill People's Culture in North East India ..., 37.

[369] Lumpkin, Baptist Confession of Faith.....418.

Baptist Churches in NEI do not have bishops or Episcopal system. The Baptists maintain local church autonomy where each church is an autonomous unit in its own right. It grants power to local churches laity to administer discipline and decide their own business and not from associations or any other forms.[370]

When the Council accepted the revised Plan of Union and the Draft Constitution, which was revised by the drafting Committee, it was sent to all the affiliated bodies in July 1970.[371] During the second session of the Church union consultation at Guwahati in 1971, the Council of Baptist Churches in NEI (CBCNEI) found this Draft Constitution unacceptable and objected. One of the main reasons for the objection of the draft plan was the inclusion of the office and term of bishop.[372] Churches in North East India have both Episcopal and non-Episcopal administrative structures. As we have indicated, one of the reasons why the CBCNEI withdraw its commitment to the already approved union was on the displeasure with episcopacy or centrally administered organization.[373] The Baptist Churches in NEI had been critical about the draft constitution, which has a hierarchical set up in which the bishop became the supervisor and those below them have no power. The Baptists followed apparent democratic principles where the laity involved in all their administrations and deliberation relating to church matters. But in the plan of the united church, gradually, all administrative control and church programm of work would be placed in the hands of the bishop. The proposal of authoritarian centralization is a serious problem at the level of local churches.

5.2.1.12. AUTONOMY IN BAPTIST CONVICTIONS

The autonomy referred in Baptist convictions has to grant the power to local churches to administer the discipline of the church and decide their own business and not to associations or any higher authority. The several ecclesiastical structures developed by the Protestant missions were decentralized in nature, with the basic authority resting in units that corresponded by and large to a single tribe. Each of the existing denominations like Lutheran, Baptist, and Presbyterian had never allowed outsiders to control their churches.[374] This is really an issue of prestige to administer and control its own institution. This was certainly one of the main reasons people in this region were strongly opposed to church union plan. And a denominational church as judged from the Baptist's point of view is more desirable and comfortable for the Baptist.

---

370 Rao, *Baptist Distinctives …*, 109.

371 *North East India Christian Council, Minutes and Proceedings of the Annual Conference*, 6-10 May 1970.

372 Renthy Keitzar, *Church Ministry and Mission: Essay in Honor of K. I. Aier* (Panbazar, Guwahati: CBCNEI, 1988), 69.

373 Snaitang, *A History of Ecumenical Movement …*, 169.

374 Downs, *Christianity in North East India Vol. V Part 5 …*, 129.

Each Baptists Church in North East India follows the congregational pattern of church government where they claim the autonomy of each local congregation and the church is run by all members in a democratic type of management of church affairs.[375] Which means the total life of the congregation is in the hands of the individuals who are by their own choice members of the church. The congregation controls the church by the simple process of majority rule.[376] Not only do they make their own decisions about the church matters; all matters affecting the life and work of the church are decided by the congregation without respect to any outside authority.[377] Such statements as these should signal in advance that Baptists have not been advocates of organic union, merger with other communions or joining established ecumenical organizations.

The Baptist Churches of CBCNEI were completely autonomous of one another, conducted their own financial campaigns, appointed their own missionaries and agents, and maintained their own boards of directors and membership lists. Baptist churches are almost uniformly insistent upon retaining and exercising this local responsibility for discerning and following what they perceive to be the will of the Lord.[378] Therefore, the Baptist churches under the Council of Baptist Churches in NEI reacted unfavorably on merging with other churches in view of wider fellowship and wider power for witnessing in the name of organic church union. Baptists conceive of the local church as the highest tribunal of Christendom. They have an inborn fear of anything that resembles a super church or a hierarchical structure over the local church. So integration with other churches is a challenge for the Baptist churches in NEI.

5.2.1.13. THE QUESTION AGAINST CHURCH'S CREEDS AND TRADITIONS

There is also a contradiction between the Baptists Church and the union church on the question against church's creeds and traditions. The Baptist Churches do not accept creeds and traditions as a necessary standard of faith and practices. They believe that the addition of creeds or the tradition into the authority of the scriptures is inadequate for their faith and practice, just as in the act of justifying a repented sinner the merit of some good work is necessary on man's part to be added into the all sufficient grace of God to make the justification more effective, then it indicates that the all sufficient grace of God is not enough or the effective justification of the believing sinner.[379]

---

375 Rao, *Focus on North East India Christianity* ..., 17.

376 Claude U. Broach, "Introducing Southern Baptists," *Greek Orthodox Theological Review*, 22/4 (Winter, 1977), 367-375.

377 Hinson, "The Baptist World Alliance: Its Identity and Ecumenical Involvement ..., 412.

378 Patton, *Communicating Baptist History in a Local Church*..., 175-179.

379 Likok, *A Picture of an Organic Church Union*..., 15.

Henceforth, Baptists are willing to accord the supreme authority to the Holy Scriptures alone and are willing to accept the fact that the Holy Scripture alone is the supreme and decisive standard of their faith and practice. There is no necessity of accepting the tradition or creed as also a necessary article of faith and practices. The addition of creed and tradition into the authority of the scriptures, unknowingly leads the churches into errors.

5.2.1.14. CHRISTIAN LIFE

Baptists view on Christian life as one of personal faith and of serious dedication to live according to the highest Christian precepts. Each person is thus to be born again, converted into a new life, and gathered into the church community through adult baptism by immersion. The Baptist held that the way of salvation, from the very beginning, depended upon grace and is appropriated by faith. This is the decisive emphasis of the Baptists.

The focus on an individualistic concept of salvation is more prominent in Baptists life.[380] This emphasis upon the individual causes many Baptists to think of the Gospel of Christ in the narrow terms of individual salvation and grace. It is for this reason that Baptists in general and in particular the Baptist Christians in NEI, have stood apart in seeming indifference to the call of ecumenical concern. Emphasis upon individual responsibility has been allowed to create a mood of pre-occupation with individualistic concept. Therefore it does not require any kind of union movement.

5.2.1.15. ROLE OF LAITY

In spite of its importance and significance, objection to the scheme of union, was raised by the Baptist churches under the CBCNEI. Their objection was that they feared that the emphasis on the importance of the role of laity towards individual congregation and each church member would disappear swamped in a vast and complex organization. In practice, Baptists have manifested vast variety in the way they have allowed, assisted, or encouraged lay persons to assume leading roles in ministry.[381] They express their strong dissatisfaction over the view that any function of ministry performed by un-ordained members of the church could not have been performed properly and validly. They feared that if such views scuttled the importance of laity would disappear. Therefore they did not accept the function of higher authoritative system, but rather they insisted upon an individualistic principle, and the importance of the role of laity in church affairs.

---

380 Walter, *Spiritual authority in Baptist life ...*

381 E. Glenn Hinson, "Historical Patterns of Lay Leadership in Ministry in Local Baptist Churches," Baptist *History and Heritage*, 13/1 (January, 1978), 26-34.

5.2.1.16. THE BAPTIST CHURCH GOVERNANCE

The nature and structure of the church according to the Baptist concepts is a local body of baptized believers' who are associated by covenant in the faith and fellowship of the gospel. They observe the two ordinances of Christ, (Baptism and Lord's Supper) committed to His teachings, exercising the gifts, rights, and privileges invested in them by his Word, and seeking to extend the gospel to the ends of the earth. This church is an autonomous body, operating through democratic processes under the Lordship of Jesus Christ. In such a congregation, members are equally responsible.[382] Their idea of the nature of church is still a community of gathered individual believers, to lead a common life in witnessing the Lord and serving the brethren.[383] The Baptist understands of Church as local body of baptized believers, its structure and functions classified into various forms, which are challenges to the wider church union.

Christ is the only head of the church, and the early Baptist pioneers earnestly contended for what they called the crown rights of the redeemer. The local church is autonomous, and this principle of government is described as the 'congregational order of the churches.'[384] The Baptists belief is that the church is to be governed not by an order of priests, nor through higher or central councils, but through the voice of the Holy Spirit in the hearts of the members in each local assembly. Whereas in a strictly democratic order of church government there would be a government of the church by the church, the Baptists position makes recognition of Christ's rule in the church through the church.[385] The equality of status of every church member and the recognition of the diversity of gifts, acknowledge that each member has a right and duty in the government of the local church, but not the council or union.

5.2.1.17. DEMOCRATIC TENDENCIES

Still another aspect of this emphasis is found in the recurring stress upon democratic government in Baptist churches. In earlier chapter the Baptists Church is described as operating through democratic processes. Hence the stress is not upon ultimate authority but upon the way in which decisions are made, as is true with the use of the word 'autonomy.' So, here again Baptists would deny any suggestion that human wisdom should be the ultimate court of appeal in the church's life. Instead, it would be acknowledged that divine leadership

---

382 Robert T. Handy, "American Baptist Polity: What's Happening and Why?" Baptist *History and Heritage*, 12/3 (July, 1976), 176-179.

383 Mathew, *Christianity in Assam and Inter Faith Dialogue* ..., 184.

384 James Leo Garrett, Jr., *Baptist Church Discipline* (Nashville: Broadman Press, 1962), 51.

385 Hillyer H. Straton, "Where is our Authority: A Baptist View," *Anglican Theological Review*, 37/2 (April, 1955), 131ff.

must be sought and followed in every instance.[386] But, the democratic concept sums up the conviction that the leadership of the Lord is more reliably discerned when the responsibility for finding and implementing it is placed upon the entire community rather than in the hands of a few leaders.

The democratic tendencies in a Baptist churches are very different from all other forms of democracy where there are political parties. Rather the church comes together, to confer and consider in the atmosphere of prayer and respect or one another's opinion, and to bring every proposal to the test of the gospel. It is democratic where the will of the people may prevail and find expression through the corporate fellowship of the body of consecrated disciples.[387] Yet on the other hand the organic church union as existing today is governed by bishop or Episcopal forms. The advocates of the union church teach that the union church has the constitution and the supreme synod and the diocesan councils as a symbol of democracy. But fair representations of all local churches is impossible, which contradicts with the Baptists distinctive and the councils are liable to be used as instruments for exercising authority by the persons in authority in the different levels of the structure of an organization. T. Likok rightly stated that "the Baptist churches regarded the organic church union with its authoritative constitution as another form of hierarchy."[388]

The advocates of the organic church union say that the form of the government of the church union will not stick to any particular polity of any of its constituent member churches. But the negotiating body of North East India Christian Council has resolved that the plan of the church union will have an Episcopal form of church ministry. The very nature of an organic union does not create any place or diversity of forms of church government and ministries contradicting with one another. So, sooner or later gradually uniformity of government ministry and worship will be enforced upon them, therefore such kind of motive will be always contradictory to Baptists position and understanding of democracy.

5.2.1.18. CONGREGATIONAL PRINCIPLES

In church polity, the Baptists are congregational, which means each church enjoys absolute autonomy. In adopting the congregational principles of church government, with no formal creed, with no external authority and each member having equal rights and responsibility, the Baptists Church is largely dependent on the reality and vigor of the spiritual life of its individual members.[389] Therefore

---

[386] Kevin D. Dougherty and et al., "Religious Diversity in a Conservation Baptist Congregation," *Review of Religious Research*, 50/3 (March, 2009), 321ff.

[387] A. Dakin, *The Baptist View of the Church and Ministry* (Great Britain: Southampton Roe, 1945), 19ff.

[388] T. Likok, *A Picture of an Organic Church Union ….*, 7.

[389] William L. Lumpkin, *Baptist Confession of Faith…..* 419.

all gifts of different individuals are under God for the edification of His church. Here each member has full right to say in the management of the church to which he/she belongs, but at the same time the church members submit to duly appointed leaders of their church. The affairs of the church and everything to do with its life are settled at the church general meeting, the meeting of all the members of the church not only Pastors and Deacons. The members also can demand a church meeting through the church officers if they desire it and the church officers can not reject it.[390]

All the members of a Baptists church are eligible to vote in any matter that may come up for congregation decision. This does not mean, of course, that every decision in and for the church must be settled by vote of the congregation. Responsibility naturally and necessarily is delegated, to the minister, to church staff, to committees, or to deacons. It does mean, however, that the entire congregation claims the responsibility for delegating powers, and that any matter could, in practice, be called up specifically for congregational vote.[391] From the above statements it is clear that the government of the Baptists church is on the democratic lines and the authority in the fullest sense is vested in the congregation principles. At any rate of decisional matter the association or council will not decide without the approval of each local congregation. Therefore, having such principles of congregationalism, Baptists are not so favourable towards any greater unity or union discussion and this could be one of the factors that lead to the failure of church union negotiation in the NEI.

5.2.1.19. FREEDOM OF CONSCIENCE

Baptists have emphasis more on freedom of conscience and of personal belief, on the importance of Christian life and work rather than on ritual, on their distaste for creeds, dogmas, and ecclesiastical authority. Many Baptist churches are known for their independent and free style of worship and social attitudes. As a result, Baptists concern for freedom of speech and conscience and for freedom from interference by any civil or ecclesiastical authority that distinguishes the Baptists from other Protestant communions[392] and consequently from that point of view the Baptists do not desire for wider union movement at this juncture.

5.2.1.20. THE OFFICERS IN BAPTIST CHURCH

Generally, in Baptists church the officers are the pastors and the deacons. The pastor exercises the different pastoral functions and the deacon is his assistant in both spiritual and temporal concerns. The chief office bearers in Baptist churches

---

390 Likok, *A Picture of an Organic Church Union* ...., 6.

391 Richard D. Patton, "Communicating Baptist History in a Local Church," Baptist *History and Heritage*, 12/3 (July, 1977), 175-179.

392 Straton, "Where is Our Authority: A Baptist View,"..., 138.

are pastor or elder, who was to preach, teach, counsel, admonish and rule.[393] The primary function of the elder or Pastor in a Baptist church is to lead in public worship. Beyond the preaching and worship-leading task, the pastor also is expected to be a shepherd to the flock, manifesting this role through visitation of the sick, the bereaved and troubled members of the congregation and, upon request, others outside the congregation. Wedding ceremonies, funeral services, and the ordinances of baptism and the Lord's Supper are always included among the services a pastor is expected to perform.[394] Difference of church polity and ministerial functions was also another challenge that led to the rejection of the church union plan. As we have already indicated, one of the reasons why the Baptist churches under the Council of Baptist Churches in NEI withdrew its commitment to the already approved union was their displeasure with episcopacy or centralized administered organization.

In Baptist understanding of polity and ministry, every Baptist church will have a small group of individuals who make up a semi-official body known as the 'Board of Deacons,' or the 'diaconate.' They are chosen and elected by the congregation to serve in a variety of ways, but they cannot make decisions for the congregation, they can only make recommendations for the congregation's consideration. In many churches they serve for a specified term, and then retire until, perhaps, chosen again for a new term.[395] Some churches regard them as a kind of executive board, while others see them chiefly as an advisory council to a pastor who draws upon their combined judgment for his own guidance. In still other churches, they are a group of pastoral guides, sharing with the pastor such ministries as visiting the sick, pursuing the wayward, and being alert to both physical and spiritual needs within the congregation and the community.[396]

Deacons traditionally assist in the observance of the Lord's Supper, by serving the elements of bread and wine to the congregation. In the absence of a pastor, worship services, prayer meeting, or Bible study would usually be conducted by a deacon, though in most churches there is no rule requiring this; it is rather the obvious selection of one who has already been identified as a trusted servant of the church to fill still another place when needed.[397] Henceforth, Baptist accepts two forms of officers, the pastor and deacons in each local church for the proper

---

393 Norman H. Maring and Winthrop S. Hudson, *A Baptist Manual of Polity and Practice* (Valley Forge: Judson Press, 1063), 87.

394 Craig Van Gelder, "Defining the Issues Related to Power and Authority in Religious Leadership," *Journal of Religious* Leadership, 6/2 (Fall, 2007), 1-14.

395 Lynn E. May, "Baptist Deacons: A Story of Service," Baptist *History and Heritage*, 25/ 2 (April, 1990), 5ff.

396 Wilburn T. Stancil, "Recent Patterns and Contemporary Trends in Deacon Life," *Baptist History and Heritage*, 25/2 (April, 1990), 22.

397 Ken Smith, "The Local Baptist Congregation and the Laity," *Review & Expositor*, 85/4 (Fall, 1988), 645ff.

functioning of the church matter. But, the policy decisions in the Baptist Church must be made by the congregation. There are no official rules and regulations imposed by any agency or individual outside the church's own membership.

5.2.1.21. AUTHORITY IN BAPTIST LIFE

The definition of authority for this purpose is an object of allegiance and guidance in the religious pilgrimage. For Baptists, ultimate authority is to be found in Christ the Lord (Mt. 28:18; 1 Cor. 15:24-28). Baptists believe Jesus of Nazareth was the Christ, the incarnate manifestation of the Eternal God. To say, therefore, that 'Christ is Lord,' is to say that 'God is ultimate.' That is the Protestant Principle and the Baptists conviction. The goal, therefore, for Baptist people has been a Christocracy, the rule of Christ over their lives.[398]

In support of Baptists life, penultimate religious authority is to be found in the Canon, the sixty-six books of the Bible.[399] Baptists seek the rule of Christ over their lives by reading and obeying the Bible in the light of the actions, attitudes, and spirit of Jesus of Nazareth. Baptists have regarded the scriptures as either the sole or the supreme doctrinal authority under the Lordship of Christ or the sovereignty of God.[400]

The local church constituted, according to the Baptists, is an assembly of believers managing its own affairs and separated from the state, receiving no subsidy from the latter and being completely independent in religious matters from any and every authority serve that of Jesus Christ, the only Head of the universal church which is his body.[401] As for Baptists the rule of Christ is defined by the local Church as it seeks the mind of Christ through the examination of scripture and the leadership of God's Holy Spirit.[402] While the Baptist goal is a Christocracy, Baptists believe that the best means of achieving that goal is through the democracy of the local church, not through the autocracy of a single individual or the aristocracy of a few individuals. In the end, the local church, not the ecumenical church, the denomination, civil government, or the individual believer, is the final arbiter of Christ's will for the local body of believers.[403]

---

[398] Walter B. Shurden, "Spiritual Authority in Baptist life," Baptist *History and Heritage*, 39/1 (Winter, 2004), 6-7.

[399] Jeff B. Pool, "Christ, Conscience, Canon, Community: Web of Authority in the Baptist Vision," *Perspectives in Religious Studies*, 24/4 (Winter, 1997), 417ff.

[400] Garrett, *Sources of Authority in Baptist thought* ..., 41-49.

[401] Lumpkin, *Baptist Confession of Faith*..... 414.

[402] Straton, *Where is our Authority: a Baptist View* ..., 131-138.

[403] Shurden, *Spiritual Authority in Baptist life* ..., 7.

5.2.1.22. VOICE AGAINST INVOLVEMENT OF STATE IN CHURCH LIFE

Another aspect of authority for Baptists life is individual conscience.[404] This is a reference to personal experience as authority and the right of the individual to follow God's leadership for his or her life. The authority of individual conscience includes the freedom to submit one's soul to the authority of Christ, the freedom to interpret the Bible for oneself, and the freedom to speak one's conscience within the local congregation of believers.[405]

This above positions work together to constitute a constellation of authority in Baptist life and therefore it helps to guarantee that authority in Baptist life is dynamic and static. This survey has demonstrated that Baptists have regarded those authorities as either the sole or the supreme doctrinal authority under the Lordship of Christ or the sovereignty of God. Thus, Baptists authority is not found in big church or union church. This genuine unity is not contingent on a big visible organization but is rested on the organic union of each individual believer with his risen Lord Jesus Christ through the indwelling Holy Spirit. Being under the direct authority of Christ, the church can take no guidance from the state or union nor is there in the Baptist churches any control of bishop or synod or any other committee. This is directly contrary to the teaching of the Baptists life.

5.2.1.23. THE EMERGENCE OF INDEPENDENT CHURCHES

The existence of many independent churches in the region is another factor that hampered the church union discussions. Apart from the teaching of the mainstream church, different teachings was introduced among the christians in the region, which led to rise of independent churches in NEI. Most of these churches were more conservative and did not co-operate with the wider union, instead they concentrated on enlarging their own missions through evangelistic work in others' comity area.

Division in a Christian community and the establishment of independent churches are in certain areas regarded as a sign of Christian maturity.[406] But, a serious problem at the level of local leadership was the influence of Conservative Evangelism that equates church union of any kind with liberal ecumenical theology.[407] Perhaps this is another problem that most churches remained non-committal to any decision for union because they are serious about maintaining

---

[404] James W. McClendon, "The Concept of Authority: a Baptist view," *Perspectives in Religious Studies*, 16/2 (Summer, 1989), 101ff.

[405] Shurden, *Spiritual Authority in Baptist life* ... , 8.

[406] Fanai Hrangkhuma, "Why are there Many Christian Groups in Mizoram," *Indian Missological Review* (September, 1991), 23.

[407] Vanlalchuanawma, "*An Appraisal of Church Union Movement in Northeast India*," Presbyterian Review, IX/33 (January – March, 2003), 29.

their own independent church's integrity other than involvement in church union negotiation.

5.2.1.24. ORGANIC UNION AS DIRECT CONTRADICTION TO BAPTIST CHURCH POLITY

The proposed plan of Church Union Movement in Northeast region was a type of an organic church union model, whose structure is a sort of hierarchical setup and its nature of ministry is an Episcopal type, which was contrary to the Baptists polity. The organic church union is regarded as unsuited for the Baptists because it fails to provide a standard of democracy on which the form of government of the Baptist Churches, their polity and ministry are based.[408] And it also claims that the true head of the Church is the Lord himself and not the human authority. Thus T. Likok rightly pointed that "it is in direct conflict with, and contrary to the true Baptists conviction and thereby endangering the denominational unity and consequently weakening the witness the Baptist Churches have to make."[409] In Baptists structure and practice it finds the churches forming into associations, which in turn an organized into conventions and finally these into council but the sovereignty of the local churches is maintained decisively.

In the organic unity or Episcopalian form of government it has central administration set up and a uniform ministry whereas the Baptist Churches follow the process of transferring the authority of the members of the churches or the congregations. When the church is run on an independent policy the proposed system will take the place of democratic practices now followed, centralized and dictatorial type of administering things will prevail. Thus, for the Baptist it would surely be a depressing circumstance for the lay and ordinary people. According to Baptist polity, any ordinary member has the right to voice his opinion in any church conference or meeting. Local churches freely elect their Church Pastor and deacon but in the united church the appointment of the priest would be done by the Council, and the local churches would have very little chance to express their opinion. Thus, the organic church union is contradictory to Baptists beliefs and practices.

On the recommended union of the North East India Christian Council (NEICC), 'the organic church union,' where a reaction was made by T. Likok entitle 'A picture of an Organic Church Union' in 1970, which was published as a polemic against acceptance of the NEICC plan by an influential member of one of the CBCNEI associations. Downs made this response in his 'A Reply to A Picture of an Organic Church Union' in the same year, that the the term organic in the christian context simply means the visible manifestation of our unity in

[408] Likok, *A Picture of an Organic Church Union* ..., 5.

[409] Likok, *A Picture of an Organic Church Union* ..., 2.

the body (organ) of Christ.[410] The alternative to organic union of some sort is to say that each individual christian is a church by himself. It is understandable that serious attempt has been made but clearly there has been no noticeable effect so far as the result of it, which shows that organic union, is not viable model for the churches in NEI.

5.2.1.25. BAPTIST ASSOCIATION VIS-À-VIS CHURCH UNION

The first level of organization beyond the local church among Baptists was the association. In a study on associationalism among Baptist churches, Walter B. Shurden determined that the objectives of the early associations of Baptists were to (1) promote fellowship among the churches, (2) maintain uniformity in faith and practice among the churches, (3) give counsel and assistance to the churches, and (4) provide an organizational structure through which churches could cooperate in their broader ministries.[411] A Baptists historian, E. C. Watson himself later reaffirmed in a work entitled the Baptists Association;

> A Baptist association is a self-determining Baptist inter-church community, created and sustained by the churches affiliated with it and responsible to them through their messengers, in which the churches foster their fellowship, their unity in faith and practice, and give and receive assistance in achieving their purpose.[412]

The Baptist Association is only a voluntary and fraternal organization for promoting fellowship and cooperation among Baptists, not an administrative, legislative, judicial or authoritative body. It adheres to the Baptist principles of freedom, autonomy and fraternity and pursues moral and spiritual aims, seeking to express and promote unity and fellowship among the Baptists of the region or area; to secure and defend religious freedom; and to proclaim the great principles of our common faith. Therefore, Toby Druin pointed that "the Association is a creature of and a servant of the churches; it has no authority to exercise over any individual or other Baptist body."[413]

This is simply what the name implies an association of Baptist churches, working together on a voluntary basis, within a given area, for the mutual encouragement of one another, cooperation in evangelism. And also for the sharing of responsibility for community missions and service, cooperation in establishing new Baptist churches in areas where needs justify such a venture. However, from

---

[410] F. S. Downs, *A Reply to A Picture of An Organic Church Union* (Panbazar, Guwahati: CLC, 1970), 4 -5.

[411] Walter B. Shurden, *Associationalism Among Baptists in America: 1707-1807* (New York: Arno Press, 1980), 103.

[412] E. C. Watson, *The Baptist Association* (Nashville: Convention Press, 1975), 33.

[413] Toby Druin, "The Baptist Standard, Texas Baptists, and Southern Baptists," Baptist *History and Heritage*, 33/3 (August, 1998), 61ff.

the beginning of Baptist associational life, the autonomy of the local church has been guarded. The churches in an association should be in agreement in doctrine and practice while they are independent in their own authority and power. Baptists' conventions, associations and council play no greater role of authority, they are only coordinating various congregational works.[414] Benjamin Griffith mentions that;

> An Association is not a superior judicature, having such superior power over the churches concerned; but that each particular church has a complete power and authority from Jesus Christ...independent of any other church or assembly whatever.[415]

Though, Baptists implies an association, but they practice the system of autonomy of the local church for any decisive matter related to church affairs. On the other hand, having such kind of fellowship and cooperation within the Baptist churches, most of the members of a particular church were not prepared to do away with what had been introduced so far as church unity. As a result the members did not see any profit from the union.

5.2.1.26. FEAR OF DIVISIONS AMONG BAPTIST

In 1964, the North East India Christian Council started church union discussion of its own and after four meetings representatives of the majority of protestant churches published a plan of church union and draft constitution of the church of NEI, but the Council of Baptist Churches in North East India (CBCNEI) was unwilling to do so for fear that its own internal unity would be threatened. Council of Baptist Churches in North East India (CBCNEI) is a union of churches, associations and locals, who covenant together, and so each Baptists church has freedom to order its own life and ministry.

With regard to the church's sacraments or ordinances, each uniting church is permitted to observe them in their own denominational convictions and such a permit seems to satisfy their convictions so as to come into the union more readily.[416] But on the other hand, it is feared that the united church may adopt the form of the ministry of a particular member church such as the Episcopal type of system with its official ministry and the ordination of ministers after the formation of the union should adopt a common liturgy then such permission will become invalid. It follows from this feature of Baptist churches that practices, patterns of internal organization and involvement in the denomination's work will vary considerably from one congregation to another.

---

[414] Walter B. Shurden, The Authority of a Baptist Association," Baptist *History and Heritage*, 40/1 (Winter, 2005), 6-7.

[415] A. D. Gillette (ed.), *Minutes of the Philadelphia Baptist Association, from A.D. 1707 to A.D. 1807* (Philadelphia: American Baptist Publication Society, 1851), 25.

[416] Patton, *Communicating Baptist History in a Local Church* ..., 175-179.

Moreover, there are regional as well as local traditions that are the despair of an interpreter who would like to generalize about Baptist ways of life and ministry. One of the psychological fears was that of the loss of Baptist identity, the loss of cherished traditions and relationships. One of the problems then for some members of the uniting churches was breaking their relationship with their historical identity, ties with so-called parent churches. Having such kind of psychological fear among the Baptists, they felt that it will be no better union for the Baptist Churches in Northeast India and therefore they responded negatively towards the church union plan in the region.

5.2.1.27. UNAWARENESS OF MISSIONARIES

The ecumenical clarion call and movement of the 19th and the early 20th centuries appeared to have not touched Christian missionaries in Northeast India. Some of the reasons that had not promoted ecumenical awareness among the several protestant missions and missionaries in the region were the geographical locations, mission agencies' concentration on specific areas without much friction and conflict. They were apparently unaware to any ecumenical fellowship as such but there was none to initiate the move.[417] Due to such unawareness, when the foreign missionaries came to North East region they propagated the gospel on the bases of their denominational patterns.

The result was the establishment of a denominational divided church faced with the enormous task of proclaiming the gospel of reconciliation and wholeness in a religiously, culturally, linguistically and socio-culturally pluralistic society in the region, which was also torn apart by tribal divisions legitimized by religion. Therefore, it was not startling to observe that the most members of a particular church were not prepared to move forward for the Christian unity, because the pioneering missionaries were not unaware and did not teach them about the ecumenical movement. There still many local church congregations were unaware and unheard of word ecumenism, as a result the moved for Christian unity at local level might be still strange. Therefore Baptist members did not show any interest to join again another type of groups or union which they feel as challenges for them.

5.2.2. NON-THEOLOGICAL CHALLENGES

The non-theological factors that does not belong directly to theological basis, but which springs from some other cause like geographical isolation, socio-cultural and linguistic differences etc. Thus, the primary difference between Baptists and other denominations seems to be more cultural and sociological than theological basis. The following are some of the non-theological factors that are obstacles to the progress of church union discussion in the region.

---

[417] Snaitang, *A History of Ecumenical Movement* ..., 160.

5.2.2.1. GEOGRAPHICAL ISOLATION

Geographically, Northeast India has a distinctive character of being independent geographical areas and political entities from the beginning. Thus, geographically they are detached and uncommon with the surrounding villages or states. There have also been great communication barriers between the states because of rugged and dense forests where the people find it difficult to travel around or to make link with each other.

Such was the geographical area in to which different Protestant denominations from the West established their missions. They came and concentrated on a compact geographical area. There had been only a limited encounter with other communities of Christians like Lutheran, Anglican etc. As a matter of fact, they did not feel the necessity for wider union. Particularly there was little desire at the grass-root level for this type of union because the largest portion of the area is hilly or mountainous, and majority of the people live in such hilly areas. They are broadly scattered along the rugged mountains stretching from China down to Burma, inhabited by different tribes and sub-tribes.

Thus the geography of the Northeast India contributed to the inactiveness of the desire for any kind of union. Thus Downs writes, "Not only were the tribes separated from each other but also even village inhabited by the same tribe were often on terms far from friendly."[418] As a result the churches or groups of churches have existed over long periods separated by geographical, cultural or other factors. Thus they have developed differences in doctrine, church order and Christian discipline. At a certain point this divergence may have turned into a breach of communion. Thus, alienated nature of the country makes communication very poor and unfriendly. People were quite unaware of one another even within a short distance. And it is this reality that stand as the major obstacle to have a united church for the Christians in NEI.

5.2.2.2. ETHNOLOGICAL DIVERSITIES

Ethnological diversities may be a suitable term to explain diversities among the Northeast India. Terminologies are man-made and often liable to be inaccurate. But, it sometime becomes imperative to invent terms to explain contextual issues. That each of the numerous tribes in NEI has its distinctive cultural is real and indisputable. Yet the basic distinction is to be identified in terms of dialect and adopted dresses.[419] The people of Northeast India, including the plainsmen are by and large assumed to belong to the Mongoloid stock. This racial identity with its resultant geographical and cultural distinction often results in racial prejudice against people of Aryan or Dravidian stock. For good or for bad, the natural

---

418 F. S. Downs, "Tribal Ecumenism in North East India: The Christian Role in Solidarity Movements," in *Good News For North East India: A theological Reader*, edited by Renthy Keitzar (Panbazar, Guwahati: CLC, 1995), 10.

419 Vanlalchuanawma, *An Appraisal of Church Union Movement in Northeast India* ..., 28.

tendency of North East Indians is first to differ with their neighboring Indians in conceptualizing social, ecclesiastical and cultural ethos.[420] It, therefore, becomes natural for the christians in NEI initially to take a negative view of the church union negotiations elsewhere in India. Such distinction seems to be implicitly major obstacle for the development of church union negotiations.

5.2.2.3. THE CONCEPT OF TRIBALISM

The NEI consists of different tribes, which never had experienced any sense of common identity. Though they live in the same geographical milieu they seldom have interaction with outside world or among themselves. Each community has a strong tendency to maintain its own identity. There more than 160 tribal groups who assembled in this region with feelings of apprehension. Some of the major tribes of the region are the Assamese, Nagas, Mizos, Manipuris, Kukis, Khasis, Bodos and so on. Traditional political system, clan based religious beliefs and practices and social differences in each tribal group have been among the factors for cultural disunity.[421] In real sense anybody who does not belong to the particular group is an outsider. Therefore the tribal in NEI have variety of groups, who lived in isolation from one another for centuries. To talk about unity within one cultural group of people is one thing, but to talk about unity under one structure which includes people from other cultural groups is quite another thing due to the deeply rooted 'community feeling' in them. This explains how much the people are devoted to their own tribal affinity.

Even Christianity fostered, in one way or the other, the development of a sense of communalism with divisive potential.[422] Missionaries converted the tribals to Christianity in large numbers, yet it raised another wall between the hill tribes and the plainsmen, culture and religions.[423] It makes clear that the missionaries were not necessarily trying to isolate the tribal people, but such separation was the inevitable outcome of their contributions to the conscience of tribalism.

The identification of the ethnic groups on denominational line did not easily facilitate the ecumenical spirit of unity.[424] Each tribe has been strongly based on its own tribal values and culture, which often makes the people of a particular tribe filled with pride and hatred of another nationality or tribe, often repulsing the authority from other groups. An organic church union with an authoritative constitution and liturgy for all member churches may not equally

---

[420] Vanlalchuanawma, *An Appraisal of Church Union Movement in Northeast India ...*, 27.

[421] Sangma and Syiemlieh, *Essays on Christianity in North East India ...*, 185.

[422] Downs opines that even Christianity built up a sense of tribal identity through the introduction of comprehensive tribal institutions in the form of ecclesiastical structures, Downs, Christianity NEI... 167.

[423] Singh, *Tribal Situation in India ...*, 405.

[424] Snaitang, *A History of Ecumenical Movement ....*, 167.

satisfy such tribal feelings.[425]A sense of human relationship among the people is also difficult to develop in the traditional cultural milieu. Reminiscences of the past among the northeast people still keep the heinous acts of headhunting afresh. Such unfriendly cultural notion is apparently passed on from one generation to another generation. It is true that tribal division is difficult to do away with even in the church. Therefore, one of the primary factors that is working against towards the church union plan was tribalism.

5.2.2.4. EGALITARIANISM

A very significant fact about the people of NEI was the development of an autonomous thinking that was very obvious in the village setting. Each village is virtually an autonomous unit and each has its own distinct history, which is often quite different from that of other village. Consequently each has its own culture and social structure of republic in its own right.[426] The type of rule is varied from tribe to tribe and village to village. And there is no common system of government for the entire tribe. Most had some sort of a democratic village council. This democratic set up in its own right fitted well with the Baptists organizational set up brought in by the missionaries. Democratic system of administration was largely the more familiar system in the region.[427]

It was in such democratic structure that most hill peoples were nurtured. As the 'states' were independent, there was hardly record of people's willingness to be under the dictate of others. Thus, a spirit of democratic tendencies has become deeply rooted in mind of the people of every tribe. Any project creating an identifiable distinction between the leadership and the general public would antagonize the civic sentiment of Northeast people.[428] Setting the proposal of Episcopal system with a bishop as the supreme administrative head aside, the confinement of the plan of union leadership seems to have caused general suspicion.

5.2.2.5. LINGUISTIC BARRIER

Each state of NEI had lived in separation from one another that in course of a long process of time they developed distinct cultures and dialects of their own. Each village set up was an autonomous village-state, which tended to develop its own dialect or the standard of its own language.[429] The linguistic link was weak among the tribals due to dialectical differences. There are indeed about one hundred and sixty-six distinct tribal communities in this region and their languages and dialects

---

[425] Likok, An *Organic Church* ..., 11.

[426] Downs, *Christianity in North East India: Historical Perspectives* ..., 10.

[427] Vanlalchuanawma, *An Appraisal of Church Union Movement in Northeast India* ..., 29.

[428] Vanlalchuanawma, *An Appraisal of Church Union Movement in Northeast India* ..., 29.

[429] Downs, *Christianity in North east India* ..., 7.

total almost the same number.[430] The language of a one particular tribe, in many cases, was totally incomprehensible to those other tribes living in the neighboring areas around them. And each tribe had dissimilar idiom, which is neither related to the other tribes nor intelligible to other dialectical groups.

Even there was language diversity within the same tribes. Linguistic barriers within one major tribe also made the speech of those from one area a hurdle to some of the dialectical groups within the tribe itself. This happened so because each tribe has generally wanted to preserve and speak one's own language and they had grown up in a context of closed door worldview with strict dialectical identity.[431] So, due to linguistic problems each tribe tried to establish separate mission associations or synod and most of their members became used to the associations which they inherited from the missions.[432] Thus, not only the formation separate associations or synods but also the linguistic diversity creates a wide gap among the Protestant denominations in the region. With the multiplicities of a language the discussions about the formation of a church union were limited to only the educated people in the congregations and that too only among the leaders and this gave a lesser chance for exchanging their views and problems openly with others especially regarding the united church in NEI.

5.2.2.6. GAP BETWEEN THE TOP AND GRASSROOTS LEVEL

Since 1930s negotiations have been made within the Protestant Churches to have a kind of church union in NEI. But, it has been without much success because it had been initiated by the NEICC rather than by the local denominations themselves. There was a great gap between the top-level church leadership and local church leadership on the issue of church union because it was confined only to the former.[433] In one sense it was the interest of only a few leaders and there was no commitment to it by the churches at the grassroots level. The plan of union was not based upon a careful analysis of the historical and cultural context of the region itself. Therefore it is undeniable fact that the ecumenical influence of the NEICC has been confined to the top-level church workers.[434]

The approach to the plan of union did not prove effective because it came from the level of the council and not from the respective affiliated churches. Particularly, in the case of Baptist, each local church is based on the principle of autonomy, therefore it is an assembly of believers managing its own affairs, separated from the state, which is governed by the grassroots congregations. They are completely independent in religious matters of any and every authority.

---

430 Renthy Keitzar, "Tribal Cultural Ethos and Christianity in NEI," *ETC Journal*, 1/1 (1980), 48.

431 Snaitang, *Ecumenism and Hill People* ..., 37.

432 Jyrwa, "Church Union Movement in North East India: A Historical Perspective ..., 29.

433 Jyrwa, *Church Union Movement* in North East India: A Historical Perspective ..., 30.

434 Snaitng, *A History of Ecumenical movement* ..., 166.

Hence, the church union negotiation still remains with the top level without reaching the local churches. As such, when the church union plans does not reach the grassroots level, the union discussion could not moved further since it is done without the knowledge of the laity. It is highly suspected that the leaders were not aware of such local churches functions and practices.

While the North East India Christian Council has been a relatively active organization, its ecumenical influence was largely confined to some leaders in the Protestant Churches. This type of co-operation certainly did not represent a widespread interest in ending the existing ecclesiastical divisions through church union. Few were active participants in the Union negotiations.[435] The type of co-operation in it did not indicate a widespread interest in church union. The general public remained un-informed and un-aware of the Plan of Union, so hotly debated by their leaders only.[436] The role of lay persons in the churches of NEI is too big a matter to ignore. The laypersons play a major role in the formation and development of the Baptist churches in NEI. The laity involvement in the local church administration was very active and authoritative. As a matter of fact, the plan of church union started with the church leadership and ended with the same.

5.2.2.7. NO SENSE OF URGENCY

Looking back to history, it is believed that the Church Union Movement began very early in NEI. To an average Christian, ecumenical or church union was known. Even most of the local church leaders who were lay-workers and also who were having little theological knowledge did not have much idea of the Church Union Movement that takes place somewhere outside.

As shown elsewhere, the circumstances that led to the church union discussions were outside influence. There seem to be no serious commitment for forming a united church among the churches affiliated to the NEICC. There were by and large excellent working relationships among the denominations involved in Union discussions.[437] However, each association or Synod seemed to be so much devoted to the upliftment of their own ecclesial rather to work for the wider union. Such philosophy of vested interest constantly impeded the tribals to accept others belonging to different denominations in truth and spirit. And they were contented with the denominations to which they belonged. Thus, there was no sense of urgency among the member bodies of the NEICC to have united churches in NEI.

---

[435] Downs, *History of Christianity in India, Vol. V, part 5* ..., 128.

[436] Vanlalchuanawma, *An Appraisal of Church Union Movement in Northeast India* ..., 30.

[437] Vanlalchuanawma, *An Appraisal of Church Union Movement in Northeast India* ..., 30.

5.2.2.8. VOICE AGAINST CENTRALIZATION OF PROPERTY AND MONETARY

Another problem arises from the transfer of finance and properties of each uniting church and their church related institutions to the union church. Here the owner of properties, finance and institutions such as school, hospital, orphanage, rent house, etc. should be the union church and not the local or denomination church. Also funds from abroad and funds raised locally will be channeled through the synod or other appropriate boards according to the budget coordinated by the central Board. The available funds will be transmitted through the regional boards to the local churches and institutions according to the need of each church or institution.[438] The union church will be having financial and property control over the local churches and institution and thus promotion of each local church and institution is curtailed and church members may show an attitude of coldness in giving as a result.

5.2.2.9. ATTACHMENT TO THE ADOPTED DENOMINATION IS HARD TO CHANGE

The missionaries who had participated in the propagation of the faith the North East regions hailed from different national backgrounds. As such they brought the spirit of nationalism, for instance, British Baptist, American Baptist, Welsh Presbyterian etc. These missionaries did not share the same cultural roots. Their different nationalistic identities too became another volatile factor for maintaining a hard stand on any move or co-operative venture.[439] Therefore Downs wrote that:

> The question of Church Union is not just a matter of Presbyterians and Baptists getting together, it is a matter of churches established by Britishers and churches established by Americans getting together. It is not just a matter of Presbyterians and Anglicans getting together, it is also matter of churches established by Welshmen and churches established by Englishmen getting together, undoubtedly these biases will diminish with time. It would certainly be unfortunate if at this late date the missionaries in our midst sought to perpetuate them.[440]

Attachment to the adopted Western denomination is hard to change. There is a fear among the Baptist churches that the establishment of a church union may lead to the loss of the distinct characteristics of the particular denomination. It becomes an uphill task to persuade those Christians with ecclesiastical conservatism to come forward to any church union. Baptist felt that their in born denomination served the need of the people better as well as mission at the grass

---

[438] Likok, *A Picture of an Organic Church Union* ..., 16.

[439] Snaitang, *A History of Ecumenical Movement* ..., 168.

[440] Downs, *Theological and Non-Theological* ..., 4-5.

root level. Hence, people were hostile to church union. The root of the trouble lies with the denominational establishments. They have become self-centered power blocs, interested almost exclusively in the preservation and growth of their own institutions. Snaitang rightly mentions "therefore it was not surprising to observe that the more churches in the region were opened to the ecumenical movement, the firmer they adhered to their own denominational traditions."[441] Closely related to the adopted denomination from outside in many cases is hard to break with. It becomes an uphill task to persuade those Christians with ecclesiastical conservatism to enlarge their ecclesiastical relationship or partnership. This explains why even after almost one and a half centuries, churches in the region are still closer to their parents' churches in the West than to the other neighboring churches in the region.

5.2.2.10. BRAND OF COMMUNALISM

Another serious problem of disunity among the churches in Northeast India lies in an indigenous brand of communalism. Each community or state remains loyal to its own ecclesiastical set up rather than being involved in a wider co-operation with churches belonging to other communities or state. This is a reality within the Council of Baptist Church in North East India (CBCNEI) and Presbyterian Churches in NEI (PCNEI), where the CBCNEI may think, it is the largest council in Northeast India, and a same way the PCNEI may think that it is the most well established Synod. Each community thinks of its own people only. Even within the church set up this feeling existed and is a real problem for unity. Each association has its own polity and doctrine with sacramental practice and clear conscience of faith and practice based on the Scripture. This is why Downs put it this way, "… afraid that in union discussions some people would be more concerned with where the headquarters of the united church were to be located than in anything more profound."[442]

The mission put various tribal groups within a single denominational structure and most of them have become accustomed to the traditions and practices they inherited from the mission. This common inheritance became a strong bending force between them. But, when it look closely into the relation between different tribal groups within single denominations, i.e., PCNEI and CBCNEI, that their relationship were not as close as one would expect. This is due to the result of the brand of communalism. Thus, communalism seems to be one of the fundamental obstacles to the development of Church Union Movement in NEI.

---

[441] Snaitang, *A History of Ecumenical Movement …*, 168.

[442] Downs, *Church Union: Theological and Non-Theological …*, 5.

5.2.2.11. ISSUES ON ETHICAL STANDARDS

There is certain agreement among Christians upon central principles of conduct which do not preclude disagreement regarding the application of them to particular cases. Each church introduced certain rules for maintaining a distinctive identity in the community. Some churches did not encourage its members to use or continue some practices. For example, there is general agreement that gambling, eating betel nuts or smoking is a major social evil, but not upon what this means for Christians practice. There are churches particularly Baptist Churches in NEI, which are opposed to such practices in any form, there are others which would seem to take a less stringent view. Such differences undoubtedly help to keep the churches apart, especially when they are held to be justifiable on scriptural and doctrinal ground.

It must be remembered, however, that differing ethical standards divide not only the Christian communions but also groups within each communion. Within each church there can be noted the opposing views of people who regard each other as unduly puritanical and unduly lax. Forms of pleasure and recreation which some follow in good conscience may seem to other as to be wrong. Members of the same congregation, agreeing that the Lord's Day is to be honored, may yet differ about the kinds of activity permissible on Sunday or agreeing that drunkenness is a vice, hold contrary views about total abstinence. It would appear, therefore that such differences ought not to keep apart churches which earnestly desire union, and that the united body should be able to carry within itself the tensions between the more and the less puritanical attitudes. Nevertheless, the differences in fact exercise a subtle pressure which tends to divert those whom it affects from approaches to union.

5.2.2.12. TRADITIONAL CULTURAL BARRIERS

Traditional cultural factors may have played a greater part in creating tension between Baptists and other Christian communities in NEI. The people who occupied the province in Northeast India belonged to different cultural backgrounds. Though many of them might well be classified as hailing from the same larger Indo-Mongoloid stock, and are characteristically tribal, they are nevertheless people with uncommon history.[443] Their uncommon history of origins, the people's long settlement in the region resulted in the rise and development of autonomous and independent cultural strands even among the homogenous group of people.[444] These ethno linguistic and cultural groups came from different directions since time immemorial. The people in Northeast India are socially divided and this division may last for many years still. The churches,

---

[443] Mathew, *Christianity in Assam and Inter Faith Dialogue* ..., 181.

[444] Snaitang, "Development of the Ecumenical Movement in Northeast India ..., 42.

being religious agencies equipped with only spiritual means, are not in a position to remedy the socio-cultural disunity of the people.

5.2.2.13. SOCIO-POLITICAL TENSIONS

To establish the unity of the church, it needs stable socio-political settings. Looking at the context of North East India, this region may be the most unstable and underdeveloped part of India. The destabilizing factors are mostly of political nature and also the traditional social disunity. In spite of all the differences in identity of language, dress codes, culture and physical features, the Nagas consider themselves Nagas, Mizos consider themselves as Mizos etc., and added that it is more of sentimental feeling of oneness than any real unity. With such background various national political movement emerged which created the situation more critical and complicated even it constrain communication between the states.[445] They became more sensitive toward safeguarding their homeland, and since then, they became more aware of their common ethnic identity and they realized the importance of nationhood.[446] This tension hinders the growth of religious unity and also limits the contact between the churches in many cases.

The people of Northeast India are socially divided and this division may last for many years still. The churches, being religious agencies equipped with only spiritual means, are not in a position to remedy the social disunity of the people. To work among the divided people, there is feeling that the divided churches are more successful. The people in this part will not feel at home with the organization of the united church. Such kind of Socio-political instability and divisions always jeopardize the prospects of church union discussion among the people in North East region.

When the protestant denominational groups decided to come together and form NEICC a remarkable and largest number of Baptist Churches under the Council of Baptist Churches in North East India refused to join the union further. The representatives of the Baptist churches were hesitant to open their mind with the Church Union Movement because of certain theological as well as practical objections. In the initial period their approach towards the union became positive. However, the Baptist churches in NEI to preserve their congregational identity, differed and hesitated to participate in the formation of NEICC. The shift from leadership of the people to Episcopal order was the matter of dispute between the supporters and opponents of the union. Therefore it is an ongoing struggle between the Baptist churches in NEI and NEICC.

---

[445] *The Shepoumaramth in the Naga National Movements* (Kohima: Shepoumaramth Region Pub., 1995); Also see in L. Jeyaseelan, "Conflict Situation in North-East India: The Church's Response," *Vidyajyoti: Journal of Theological Reflection*, 63/6 (June, 1999), 439ff.

[446] Visier Sanyu, "The Nagas in the 1st half of the 20th Century," in *From Darkness to Light*, edited by Nagaland Baptist Church Council (Kohima, NBCC, 1997), 146-147.

It is obvious that Baptists have continuously sought to formulate and articulate their faith by means of brief doctrinal summaries. From the beginning of Baptists life, the autonomy of the local church has been guarded. At the other extreme in polity are the denominations and sects of congregational or independent government, in which each individual congregation exercises authority in matters of doctrine and discipline. In evaluating this position it may be considered that the serious concern for a church of committed believers and the resulting insistence on believers' baptism was one of the main causes for the rise of the Baptist movement. Here Baptists see their contribution to the church's search for a credible identity. It should not be forgotten that the Baptists movement, originating in the seventeenth century, was from its outset not simply a reform movement within the context of a larger Christian denomination, but more a church movement with a strong sense of Christian identity.

5.3. CONCLUSION

Many Baptists feel that it is their obligation to stand by and to maintain their traditional views, especially in the area of ecclesiology. Such legalistic understanding and traditional practice within the Baptist churches display a strong anti-Christian Unity attitude; consequently, unity with other denominations is discouraged. It has even affected Northeast India Christian Unity discussion. Nevertheless one must not give up the hope for the formation of a united church in NEI. The next chapter will be in search of possible solution against the challenges of Christain Unity in the region, for which, one important task is to find a church unity model relevant and accessible to the local church members and meaningful to today's context.

Chapter 6

Search for a Viable Model for Christian Unity

INTRODUCTION

This chapter will map out some steps or certain tangible goals of the Christian unity in Northeast India. Firstly, we shall mention some of the question why Christian unity desirability. It is mention that the desirability of Christian unity is dependent on our perception of the unity that is required of us. Later, we shall deal a few aspects of the unity we seek. This will be in search of that some of the existing church union model will be explore, to pick up a viable model of Christian unity, which would be helpful in giving acceptable church union structure to the churches in NEI. Therefore, the objective under taken in this chapter is to show how church unity could be more effectively achieved from a Baptist perspective and how diversity may be expressed within a scheme of church union discussion in NEI. Let me mention a few aspects of the Christian unity why we seek.

6.1. CHRISTIAN UNITY IS THEOLOGICAL MANDATE

The theological foundation of mission in unity is built on the *koinonia* of the triune God. Mission is based on the infinite love of God, who created out of nothing the whole of creation and humankind in God's image and likeness, so as to make us partakers of this ineffable love. The Father sends the Son (John 16:5) and the Father and Son sent Holy Spirit. This inner communion of the Holy Trinity is the source of the unity of the church and the aim of God's mission: to invite every human being to experience fellowship with God and with one another according to the inner unity of the One God in three Persons (John 17:21)[447]

It is supremely important to note that whenever we discuss the question of Christian unity we are not simply talking about a sociological convenience. In fact we are responding to the demand of a theological mandate: the Christian proclamation that God is *God* demands that we name the various idolatries that sway us away from our singular commitment to God. This means that the disunity of the church is a direct affront to the unity and singularity of God.[448] As Karl Barth writes:

> There is no justification, theological, spiritual, or biblical, for the existence of a plurality of churches genuinely separated in this way and mutually excluding one another internally or externally. A plurality of churches in this sense means a plurality of lords, a plurality of spirits, a plurality of gods. There is no doubt that to the extent that Christendom does consist of actually different and opposing churches, to that extent it denies practically what it confesses theoretically — the unity and the singularity of God.[449]

What model of Christian unity is the consultation to follow as its member churches consider covenanting toward church union? The proposed plan of church union was to follow the model of full organic union. The 'Draft of the Basis of Union' for the churches in Northeast India was formulated in November 1965, under the section III 'our Approach to Unity,' clause No. 1 read as, "The churches now in existence would join together in an organic body."[450] It included one identifiable system of government with the united ecclesial oversight of bishops. It was not formally voted on by the member churches, mainly from Baptist Churches under the Council of Baptist Churches in Northeast India (CBCNEI) because they are so much loyalties to its own denomination.

The history of our division bears ample witness to the way in which we have paid idolatrous allegiance to our denominational loyalties, our particular historical beginnings and our specific formulations of the Christian faith. All our divisions are expressions of our attempt to "domesticate" God into our own

---

[447] Cf Mission and Evangelism in Unity Today' 10—13. In: Jaques Matthey (ed.) *'You are the light of the World. . .* " pp. 65-66. Cited in Towards common witness to Christ today: mission and visible unity of the church By: World Council of Churches Commission on World Mission and Evangelism.. In *International Review of Mission*, 99 No. 390 Apr 2010, p. 86-106.

[448] Thangaraj, M Thomas Is Full Church Unity Possible or Desirable, *The Ecumenical Review*, 44 No. 1 Jan. 1992, p. 91-99.

[449] Karl Barth, *Church Dogmatics,* IV/1, Edinburgh, T. & T. Clark, 1956, p. 675. Cited in Thangaraj, M Thomas Is full church unity possible or desirable, *The Ecumenical Review*, 44 No. 1 Jan. 1992, p. 91-99.

[450] *The Plan of Church Union and Draft Constitution of the Church of North East India,* edited by the Convenor, Church Union Committee. Shillong: NEICC, 1970. 3.

histories and loyalties. Most of our divisions have resulted from absolutizing our relative truths and understandings, and thus a divided church stands under the judgment of God, the God of the whole universe. Thus the theology which as Christians we hold dear and precious invites us to mourn sincerely our divisions and seriously seek ways to express our Christian unity in a divided world.

6.2. CHRISTIAN UNITY IS CHRISTOLOGICAL MANDATE

Christian unity is grounded in our commitment to the Lordship of Jesus Christ. In Christ we seek this unity. No document on ecumenism in this century, it seems, has failed to refer to Jesus' high-priestly prayer in John's gospel. This Christological grounding of church unity is not simply a matter of conforming to the prayer of Jesus, but is deeply grounded in the person of Jesus Christ himself. This is so in two ways as M. Thomas Thangaraj mentioned in "Is full Church Unity Possible or Desirable? First, Jesus prays that his disciples may be one and united, even as he and God are one. It is this hypostatic union of God the Father and God the Son that we are invited to emulate in our church unity. This means that church unity cannot but be full unity in every sense of the word "full". Secondly, the incarnational element in our Christological commitment requires us to move far beyond a disembodied "spiritual" unity between churches. We are called upon to seek an incarnational unity which involves both invisible and visible forms of unity. The morphological element in church unity must never be underestimated. A form of unity which does not express itself in visible and morphological forms is not an incarnational unity, and thus fails to be grounded in its Christological base.[451]

An incarnational unity demands a visible expression of itself. As Michael Kinnamon writes:

> Unity needs to find some form of embodied, visible, structured expression. Genuine unity should never be confused with structural merger (an imitation of the business world), since true unity rests on shared faith. But, such faith is not simply an inward disposition; it seeks expression in common worship, common service, common witness and these demand some form of structure.[452]

It is our grateful response to the salvation that is available to us in the death and resurrection of Jesus Christ. This Christological grounding of Christian unity is not simply a matter of conforming to the prayer of Jesus, but is deeply grounded in the person of Jesus Christ himself. This is so in two ways. First, Jesus prays that his disciples may be one and united, even as he and God are

---

[451] Thangaraj, M Thomas Is Full Church Unity Possible or Desirable ...91-99.

[452] Michael Kinnamon, *Truth and Community: Diversity and its Limits in the Ecumenical Movement,* Geneva, WCC, 1988, p. 88. Cited by Thangaraj, M Thomas Is full Church Unity Possible or Desirable, *The Ecumenical Review*, 44 No. 1 Jan. 1992, p. 91-99.

one. It is this hypostatic union of God the Father and God the Son that we are invited to emulate in our Christian unity. Secondly, the incarnational element in our Christological commitment requires us to move far beyond a disembodied "spiritual" unity between churches. We are called upon to seek an incarnational unity which involves both invisible and visible forms of unity. The morphological element in church unity must never be underestimated. A form of unity which does not express itself in visible and morphological forms is not an incarnational unity, and thus fails to be grounded in its Christological base.[453]

6.3. CHRISTIAN UNITY IS MISSIOLOGICAL MANDATE

It is both interesting and enlightening to note that the worldwide ecumenical movement had its dramatic beginnings with the world missionary conference at Edinburgh in 1910. It was those who were actively involved in the missionary movement of the church who came to recognize, in a fresh way, the scandal and tragedy of division.[454] Thus, it was in the context of its missionary calling that the question of unity became a central concern of the church. As K. S. Latourette writes:

> Edinburgh 1910 did more than build on past achievements in evangelism and unity: it prepared for the turbulent years which lay ahead, blazed new trails in Christian fellowship and cooperation, and enlisted and inspired men (and women) who were to become outstanding leaders in the ecumenical movement in later years.[455]

For the first time in history, an attempt was made for a global gathering in order to facilitate cooperation across denominational barriers. Such a grounding of unity within the matrix of the mission of the church helps us to move away from two possible misunderstandings of church unity. First, unity perceived as a missiological task enables us to recognize the question of unity as intimately related to the very essence and being of the church. Mission is not an appendix to the life of the church; it is the very life breath of the church. But, if the church exists because of its mission then it ceases to be church when it is divided, because division violates its very being and denies its very essence. Second, the unfortunate division in the history of the ecumenical movement between doctrine and service can no longer be maintained and defended. The famous slogan of the Life and Work movement, "Doctrine divides; service unites", is simply not true. Service

[453] Thangaraj, M Thomas, "Is full Church Unity Possible or Desirable ... 91-99.

[454] Kenneth S. Latourette (1967) Ecumenical Bearings of the Missionary Movement and the International Missionary Council. In: Ruth Rouse and Steven c. Neill (eds), *A History of the Ecumenical Movement 1517—1948,* The Westminster Press, Philadelphia, p. 355.

[455] Bengt Sundkler, *Church of South India: The Movement Towards Union, 1900-1947,* London, Lutterworth, 1954, p. 101. Cited by Thangaraj, M Thomas Is Full Church Unity Possible or Desirable ...91-99.

demands that we unite ourselves in doctrine; and similarly doctrine demands that we unite ourselves in service.

What we have outlined so far is the desirability of Christian unity on the basis of the belief that the unity we seek is a unity in faith; faith in God and Christ, unity in mission, unity in form, unity in process and unity in praise. We need to recapture this grand vision of full church unity before we tackle the question of the possibility of such a unity. It is time for the Northeast Christian family to heal the pain of our divisions, because unity through healing and reconciliation is an integral part of God's mission.

If the North East India Christian Council reaffirm the church union committee which will seek ways and means to develop a clearer vision and understanding of the nature of unity. Also to develop models of church unity what shape church union might take, especially at the local level of church life and also recognizing each denomination settings in the context like Northeast India. The earlier church union plan of organic union with one identifiable system of church government is not presently even possible. Therefore this section has to deal with suitable model of church union which would be helpful to give an acceptable church union structure to the pledges of agreement to the churches in NEI.

6.4. NATURE OF UNITY

The ecumenical discussions and negotiations have been going on for so long that some ecumenically-minded Christians are becoming "tired" of ecumenism. Another important way is to bring back the mission focus of the issue of church unity. The twentieth-century ecumenical movement was rooted deeply in the missionary movement. It is in our being with and being in dialogue with those outside the institutional church that we discover our strength and inspiration for ecumenical action. Furthermore, Christians are today engaged in dialogue and conversation with people of other religious traditions and secular ideologies. Here the issue is not simply that of efficiency in mission but that of credibility. How credible is our Christian witness in the setting of a divided church.

Unity is God given reality. The Unity Concept is God given veracity designed to bring churches and people together, through acceptance and understanding of differences in their history and theology and celebration of united commonality. Each and every denominational setup on the planet is unique with their own divine tapestry, with their own doctrine and theologies. To really embrace equality and diversity we need to be acknowledging of each other traditions and belief systems. We can grow together through understanding how other work and tick. The Unity Concept invites every Christians to share their own culture, to be educated about other churches heritage. Only through mutual respect and understanding can we ever hope to achieve a world where we can all live in harmony. We can learn so much from each other if we communicate more and open our eyes to the diversity all around us. Through recognising the differences between us and learning from each other we can become more responsibility to accept the differences between us. Unity invites churches to showcase whatever aspects of herself that each feel is at their core. The message of unity is one love, one church, with different forms of self-expression. Through mutual respect and understanding we can be pioneers in shaping this world and truly reflecting equality and diversity in all we do.

Unity concept is both a gift and a calling. It is never lost, only obscured and broken. It must be rediscovered and renewed. Therefore, unity is a present and at the same time an eschatological reality; it must be constantly sought. Unity is not something that is achieved once and for all, but a living, unfolding process, not a goal that is reached but rather an ongoing reality that is constantly renewed. Unity by its very concept is invisible because it lies at the level of the faith and the mystery of the church. Nonetheless, it must manifest itself visibly in and through a fellowship becoming a concrete reality in history.

In fact, in the ecumenical movement and particularly in the World Council of Churches, unity has always been described as a visible reality. It always remains the ultimate goal of the ecumenical movement. The WCC, in the early period of its existence, did not define a particular understanding of unity. It became a forum for dynamic interaction between various concepts and models of unity. Even membership in the council did not imply the eventual acceptance of any particular model of unity. The first attempt to reach a common definition of unity was made by New Delhi assembly 1961.[456] It provided the framework for future study that the model of conciliar fellowship has gained considerable acceptance but it must be noted that the WCC has never confined itself to any particular concept or model of unity.

Currently there exist many views concerning the concept and model of unity. There are many ways in which different Christian confessional groups or denominations have come together under common ecclesial structures to express Christian unity. Among the various models that have emerged in the ecumenical movement, we shall briefly highlight some of the concepts of Christian unity, which are considered being the most important ones under this study.

6.4.1. ORGANIC UNION

The structure which was much sought after by denominations or churches negotiating for union is known as the organic union structure. Organic union is the long-favored model of the Faith and Order movement and still remains a viable option for many.[457] An organic union refers to a union of churches in which two or more uniting churches of the same confession or of different traditions

---

[456] Aram Keshishian, *Conciliar Fellowship: A Common Goal* (Geneva: WCC Publication, 1992), 63.

[457] Paul A. Crow, "Ecumenics as Reflections on Models of Christian Unity." *Ecumenical Review*, 39/4 (1987), 397.

become one living body, which lives and acts as one church, and which is therefore one church.[458] This type of union is much needed where there is overlapping of work of different church bodies in towns and cities, where the mission comity agreement cannot be put into operation effectively. The main emphasis in the organic union is the visible unity as expressed in the intercommunion. The heart of this unity is not an elaborate central organization but intercommunion.[459] There are at least fourteen largely recognized organic church unions in different parts of the world, such as England, the USA, Central Africa, Holland etc., and the best example is the United Church of Canada,[460] which was formed on 10 June 1925.[461]

Generally, the essence of organic union is described both as an act and a state of being, much like marriage, by which previously separated church entities come together in faith, worship and sacramental life, ministry and mission all the ingredients of a fully shared life as identified by the New Delhi-Nairobi vision.[462] The necessary conditions of organic union, as normally conceived, and laid out in 1970 by the conference of united and uniting churches at Limuru, Kenya, include:

> A common basis of faith; a common name; full commitment to one another, including the readiness to give up separate identity; the possibility of taking decisions together and of carrying out the missionary task as circumstances require.[463]

In addition there are characteristics which identify the nature of unity as offered through organic union. Firstly, it is a model which seeks to bring all aspects of the church's life and mission into 'one fully committed fellowship.' Secondly, Organic union is committed to the discovery of a form which represents unity-in-diversity, and to achieving a fellowship in which authentic diversity is honoured and encouraged and in which authentic unity and communion are experienced. Thirdly, While it in no sense proposes a political or business merger or the

---

458 A. Behera, "Theological Education and Church Union in North East India," *Presbyterian Review*, VIII/32 (Oct-Dec, 2002), 54.

459 Rao, *Focus on North East Indian Christianity* ..., 31; Also Cf. Behara, *Theological* Education..., 54; Cf. O. M. Rao, *Christian Unity; Guideline Study Material* (Panbazar, Guwahati: CBCNEI, 1985), 3.

460 The Congregational Churches of Canada, the Methodist Church, the Presbyterian Church in Canada, and the Local Union Churches in Western Canada came together to form 'United Church of Canada'.

461 Jaroslav Pelikan and Valerie Hotchkies, eds., *Creeds & Confessions of Faith in the Christian Traditions, Vol. III, Part Five: Statements of Faith in Modern Christianity* (New Haven, London: Yale University Press, 2003), 445.

462 Crow, "Ecumenics as Reflections on Models of Christian Unity," ..., 397.

463 "Notes from the Limuru (1970) Conference," *Mid-Stream: An Ecumenical Journal*, IX/2-3, (Winter-Spring, 1971), 13-33.

merger of all church organizations, organic union does assume the importance of common structure and order. This implies local and universal structures of common accountability and enrichment in teaching the faith and in fulfilling Christ's mission in the world. The unity of the people of God, especially as it would exist between churches within the same territory, could scarcely be realized without some expression in structures of ecclesial relationship and service.

Fourthly, Organic union is a costly act in that churches are asked to offer their confessional or denominational identities to the larger wholeness of the body. In the language of the New Delhi statement, which affirmed organic union as the goal, "The achievement of unity will involve nothing less than a death or rebirth of many forms of church life as we have known them. We believe that nothing less costly can finally suffice."[464] In this commitment organic union in no way denies the spiritual gifts that have come through these traditions; only a denial of their divisive nature is sought, while seeking to mingle them in a wider experience of catholicity. Finally, the shape of the church's unity attained through organic union is designed to be a visible sign of the unity of humankind in a particular place. Such a united church would creatively embody the distinctive religious experiences of minority groups and those Christians who have been marginalized by the traditional ecclesiological configurations.[465]

The often quote passage in support of this organic unity is St. Paul's metaphor of the body (I Cor. 12, Eph 4:16).[466] Though there are different members in a physical body yet all are coordinated in one single organism, so must the church be in given nation.[467] It is this kind of unity, which is described as an organic model. Under this form of union, different existing denominations are merged into a new centralized organizational structure. They do no longer remain autonomous or independent as they used to exist before. The merger does not imply accepting the organizational structure of a particular denominational church but a combination of different constituent models.[468] The Organic Union expresses the idea that different denominations or churches of different traditions come together in a mutual co-operation to form one organic church. The Church of South India (1947) and the Church of North India (1970) are good examples of what has been commonly described as organic union.[469] Such a union involves a complete merger of the uniting churches in which structural identities and names are surrendered to a single structure and name. The uniting churches organically become one church, though within that one church considerable diversity in

---

[464] Crow, "Ecumenics as Reflections on Models of Christian Unity…, 397.

[465] Crow, "Ecumenics as Reflections on Models of Christian Unity …, 397-398.

[466] Taken from Revised Standard Version.

[467] Rao, *Christian Unity* …, 3.

[468] Snaitang, *A History of Ecumenical Movement: An Introduction* …, 81.

[469] Pritam B. Santram, "Structures of Christian Unity," in *Experiment in Christian Unity* (Delhi: ISPCK, 1983), 43.

thought and practice continues within the frame work of commonly accepted doctrines and practices.

6.4.2. FEDERAL UNITY

The word "Federal" or "Federalism" derives from the Latin "*Foedus,*" meaning 'covenant,' 'alliance,' 'bond'. In modern ecumenical usage "federal" relationships have been established within a single country among denominations, which while maintaining their separate identities, desire or collaborate in certain limited areas.[470] The Federal Unity sought the co-operation between different church bodies or denominations often for a common task or mission. In this kind of union various denominations retain own identity while co-operating as parts of the wider platform.[471]

In other words, a federation of churches is a union based upon an agreement or contract between the churches regarding a common object or purpose in which these churches however remain independent, so far as the independence does not frustrate the object of the agreement.[472] In the federal setup, the distinctive expression of each denomination and its rich heritage are maintained and at the same time, unity is required for a common mission and fellowship, as confined to a particular region.

The federal model of church union believes in the form of unity in diversity. It recognizes the presence of numerous cultural identities, ecclesiastical differences, allows the continuance of distinctive characteristics and autonomy in each church group but maintains a general administrative body for the entire Christian churches. The federal type of church union preserves the special heritages and diversity of the member churches.[473] Thus, federal unity allows for a great measure of freedom, diversity and autonomy among federated churches and at the same time, is a recognizable structure of mutual fellowship, sharing of experience and working together in mission of the church. Hence, such 'Federal Unity' model is the suitable example for the church union movement in North East India.

6.4.3. CONCILIAR FELLOWSHIP

The concept of a Conciliar Fellowship holds that a general or ecumenical council is the supreme authority in a church.[474] The term usually is specifically applied

---

470 Geoffrey Wainwright, "Federalism," *Dictionary of the Ecumenical Movement*, edited by Nicholas Lossky et al., (Geneva: WCC Publication, 1991), 418.

471 Rao, *Christian Unity* ..., 3.

472 Behera, *Theological Education* ..., 54.

473 Snaitang, *A History of Ecumenical Movement*..., 80.

474 C. J. McNaspy, "Coiciliar Theory," *The Encyclopedia Americana International Edition*, Vol-7, (Danbury: Grolier Incorporated, 1996), 504.

to the western historical development of the 13th and 14th centuries.[475] As we have seen, 'conciliar fellowship' as a model of unity emerged as an elaboration of organic unity. It contains the essential elements recognized by most churches today as indispensable for visible church unity, the mutual recognition of the fullness of the catholicity of other churches, common witness to the same apostolic faith, mutual sharing of baptism and the Eucharist, recognition of each other's members and ministries, with common commitment of witness in the world and with a sustaining relationship in conciliar gatherings.[476]

At the centre of this model is the commitment to understand unity as a unity of 'local churches' which are 'truly united.' One of the characteristics of this model is its trans-confessional nature, i.e., it proposes a union of the previously divided congregations and local churches and a reconciling of rich diversity of the previously divided denominations or confessions.[477] Such a possibility often raises fears and concerns among those who believe confessional identities are the most vital expression of the church. In a united church of conciliar fellowship, however, the confessions or traditions would not be denied or abandoned. Nor would their particular witness to universality be swept away.[478] Such a visible unity would, however, reconcile the divisions which these confessions represent and which obscure their witness to Christ's mission to all humankind.

Since 1960 ecumenical reflection on conciliairty has been prompted by the event of Vatican II (1962-65) and by the need to clarify the significance of the WCC and the goal of unity which it is intended to serve. The Uppsala assembly 1968 suggested that the member churches should "work for the time when a genuinely universal council may once more speak for all Christians and lead

---

[475] During this period the western schism (137-1417) divided the Catholic Church into factions supporting different claimants to the papacy. The conciliar theory thus gained widespread popularity as the solution to the schism. The Catholic Church teaches, however that no council can be above or against the pope because without his presence or approval, a general, or ecumenical, council cannot be validly held. See in C.J. McNaspy, "Coiciliar Theory," in *The Encyclopedia Americana International Edition*, Vol-7, (Danbury: Grolier Incorporated, 1996), 504. The most radical forms of the conciliar theory in the Middle ages were found in the 14th century writings of Marsilius of Padua, an Italian political philosopher who rejected the divine origin of the papacy, and William of Ockham an English philosopher who taught that only the church as a whole, not an individual pope or even a council is preserved from error in faith. The 15th century saw serious attempts to put the conciliar theories into practice. See in"Conciliarism," *The New Encyclopedia Britannica* Vol-3, edited by Philip W Goetz (Chicago: Encyclopedia Britannica, Inc., 1815), 515.

[476] Faith and Order Paper, No 72, pp. 113; Cited by Kuncheria Pathil, *Ecumenism: Unity and Diversity* (Bangalore: Dharmaram Publication, 2006), 65.

[477] Crow, "Ecumenics as reflections on models of Christian unity," *Ecumenical Review ...*, 397.

[478] Crow, "Ecumenics as reflections on models of Christian unity," *Ecumenical Review ...*, 398-399.

the way into the future."[479] Faith and Order took up this suggestion at Louvain 1971 and started a study on conciliarity understood as "the coming together of Christians, locally, regionally and globally, for common prayer, counsel and decision, in brief that the Holy Spirit can use such meetings for his own purpose by reconciling, renewing and reforming the church by guiding it towards the fullness of truth and love."[480] The Salamanca consultation 1973 shows that "in this conciliar fellowship local churches possesses, in communion with the others, the fullness of catholicity, witnesses to the same apostolic faith, and therefore recognizes the others as belonging to the same church of Christ and guided by the same spirit."[481] This description has been further developed at different level of consultations and its continuing work on the nature and goal of unity of the different churches.

Furthermore the model of conciliar fellowship calls for representative conciliar gatherings, structures of common decision-making, which would be manifestations of visible unity. This has been described as 'a genuinely universal council,' much like the ancient ecumenical councils, through which the church in our time can make common decisions about its faith and mission. Conciliarity in this sense touches deeply the ways and various levels in which the churches relate to each other and respond together to their mission and their environment. Finally, the vision of the one church as a conciliar fellowship is an expression of the inclusive participation of the people of God from their many cultures, races, and nationalities.

6.4.4. RECONCILED DIVERSITY

This model of unity was developed in the mid-1970s amid the renaissance of the World Confessional Families or, as they are now known, Christian World Communions (CWC).[482] The Faith and Order Commission invited these bodies to reflect on their ecclesial identity and 'to clarify their understanding of the quest for unity.' The resultant model of 'reconciled diversity' emerged from the insights and experiences of the international bilateral dialogues and became one of the positions in the ecumenical discussion.[483]

This model, like conciliar fellowship and organic union, assumes the constitutive elements of full church unity and agrees on the one apostolic faith, fellowship in baptism and the Eucharist, and mutual recognition of ordained ministries. What is distinctive is its understanding of what constitutes church

---

[479] "Conciliarism," *The New Encyclopedia Britannica,* vol-3, edited by Philip W. Goetz (Chicago: Encyclopedia Britannica, Inc., 1815), 515.

[480] Emmanuel Lanne, "Concilirity," *Dictionary of the Ecumenical Movement,* edited by Nicholas Lossky et al., (Geneva: WCC Publication, 1991), 212.

[481] Lanne, "Concilirity," *Dictionary of the Ecumenical Movement* ..., 212.

[482] Crow, "Ecumenics as Reflections on Models of Christian Unity," ..., 399.

[483] Crow, "Ecumenics as Reflections on Models of Christian Unity," ..., 399.

division and what is the ecumenical role of denominational or confessional identities and heritages. Advocates of reconciled diversity accept confessional identity, e.g. Lutheran, Reformed, Roman Catholic, Anglican, Disciples, Methodist, Baptist, etc., as the primary legitimate forms and expressions of the diversity of the church of Christ. These confessions express diverse spiritual gifts, and are the essential components of the universal church. At the 1974 conference of secretaries of Christian World Communions, entitled 'The Role of the World Confessional Families in the One Ecumenical Movement', stated: 'We consider the variety of denominational heritages as legitimate insofar as the truth of the one faith explicates itself in history in a variety of expressions.'[484] At Lutheran World Federation (LWF) spoke: reconciled diversity 'is a way of living encounter, spiritual experience together, theological dialogue, and mutual correction, a way in which the distinctiveness of each partner is not lost sight of but is transformed and renewed, and in this way becomes visible and palpable to the other partners as a legitimate form of Christian existence and of the one Christian faith.'[485]

Accordingly, unity in no sense 'entails the surrender of confessional traditions and confessional identities.' These forms of the Christian faith have an abiding value in all their variety. As Harding Meyer claims, 'church unity in a full, unimpaired, and enriched form (can be achieved) even where these confessional traditions, identities and peculiarities are retained.'[486] In evaluating this model offer a key caveat, namely the assumption that 'the existing differences between churches will lose their divisive character' by being transformed, changed and renewed in the process of bilateral dialogue. In its boldest form, reconciled diversity assumes that the separate confessional churches could, indeed should, continue to exist side by side at local, national, and international levels; they can be reconciled but remain institutionally separate.[487]

As with all the models under discussion, reconciled diversity has a host of defenders and critics. Lutheran theologian Ulrich Duchrow believes it could 'lead the churches which employ it into perilous theological error,' mainly because rather than expressing faithfully the biblical concept of reconciliation it assumes the only witness to truth is the post-Reformation patterns of ecclesiological identity.[488] This raises the question as to whether denominations or confessions

[484] *WCC Exchange*, 3/2 (July 1977), cited by Crow, "Ecumenics as Reflections on Models of Christian Unity," ..., 399.

[485] Arne Sovik ed., *In Christ - a New Community: The Proceedings of the Sixth Assembly of the Lutheran World Federation, Dar-es-Salaam, Tanzania,* June 13-25, 1977, Geneva, LWF, 1977, cited by Crow, "Ecumenics as Reflections on Models of Christian Unity," ..., 399,

[486] Günther Gassmann and Harding Meyer, *The Unity of the Church: Requirements and Structure*, LWF report No. 15, (Geneva, Lutheran World Federation, 1983), 9, Cted by Crow, "Ecumenics as Reflections on Models of Christian Unity," ..., 399.

[487] Crow, "Ecumenics as reflections on models of Christian unity,"..., 400.

[488] WCC, *Conflict over the Ecumenical Movement: Confessing Christ Today in the Universal Church,* Geneva, WCC, (1981), 183, cited by Crow, "Ecumenics as Reflections on Models of

are the only ultimate ecclesial expression of the diversity which the gospel gives to the church.

In the early days when it was first proposed, reconciled diversity was so interpreted as to be perceived as an alternative to organic union and conciliar fellowship. This bias produced a polemical situation, which proved unhelpful to the creative search for models which express the commonly agreed upon goal. Some lessening of this tension was achieved at the first forum on bilateral conversations (1978), which brought together representatives of the international bilateral between Christian World Communions and of the multilateral conversations promoted by the Commission on Faith and Order of the World Council of Churches.[489] This forum's report set forth two methodological agreements which are important for our continuing discussion. First, the bilaterals and the multilaterals are understood to be 'complementary to one another within the one ecumenical movement,' while confessing that 'the closer fellowship or unity of two churches, or even of two world confessional families, still falls short of being the visible unity of all Christian people.' Second, the forum made clear that organic unity (conciliar fellowship) and reconciled diversity, while different in their focus, should each be considered reasonable, provisional forms of visible church unity.[490] Undoubtedly the dialogue between these particular models constitutes an important part of the future ecumenical agenda.

6.4.5. COMMUNION OF COMMUNIONS

In some ways this model is a slight variation of 'reconciled diversity,' but in other ways it may speak more forcefully about the depth of unity in Christ sought by organic union and conciliar fellowship. Its significance can also be attributed to the fact that it comes from the theological reflections of the Roman Catholic Church. On the eve of Vatican II, Fr Bernard Lambert proposed that future ecumenical ecclesiology concentrate on the 'typologies of the form of union,' which represent the different Christian traditions through which the one gospel of Jesus Christ has been received.[491]

Emmanuel Lanne, a long-time Faith and Order participant, expanded this model by describing the image of unity as 'a variety of typologies within the same ecclesial allegiance.' In a revealing sentence he declared: "It is clear that we must try to discover together in what manner and measure God intends the unity of his Church to express also diversity and pluralism in a single communion of faith and

Christian Unity," …, 397.

[489] Crow, "Ecumenics as Reflections on Models of Christian Unity," …, 400.

[490] "The Three Reports of the Forum on Bilateral Conversations," *Faith and Order Paper 107* (Geneva, WCC, 1981): 4-5, cited by Crow, "Ecumenics as Reflections on Models of Christian Unity," …, 400.

[491] Crow, "Ecumenics as Reflections on Models of Christian Unity," …, 400.

church life."[492] Building on these ideas, this model was publicly and officially put on the ecumenical agenda by Cardinal Willebrands in an address at Cambridge in 1970. He proposed that the church's visible unity might be expressed in varied 'types' living in communion. This unity is a 'plurality of types' Roman Catholic, Baptist, Orthodox, Reformed, Anglican, *et al.* within the communion of the one and only church of Christ. Each *typos* is distinguished by the following elements: a 'characteristic theological method and perspective,' a 'characteristic canonical discipline,' a 'tradition of spirituality and devotion,' a 'characteristic liturgical expression.' The signs of their communion would be common teaching in faith and morals, eucharist sharing, and agreements on ministry and papacy.[493]

This model is intriguing because of its sense of balance. It reveals sensitivity to the diversity of traditions and spiritualities. Yet it equally places communion, a deep relationship, at the centre. A communion of communions would certainly not be possible unless each tradition *(typos)* undergoes significant change and renewal and each becomes an integral part of the whole fellowship. Sister churches would move beyond their separate identities into a common identity.

One of the lesser known structures of unity is the Joint Council of the Church of North India, Church of South India and the Malankara Mar Thoma Syrian Church. It was established in July 1978 as a result of union negotiations between these three churches. In the process of these negotiations these three churches realized that there already existed among them a unity of ministry, the sacraments and the basic doctrines. They entered into a mutual relationship of full inter-communion, recognizing each other's members, ministry and sacraments.[494] The three churches continue to be autonomous churches but recognize themselves as belonging to the one church of Jesus Christ in India.

This unity implied in a mutual recognition and acceptance of each other's church members, ministries and sacraments, is not a conciliar fellowship but an organic oneness.[495] It is, in fact, an organic union minus the acceptance of a common polity or administrative structure and a common name. The three churches continue to have their respective synods which govern the inner life of each church as well as their relationship with others churches. The main purpose is to express the unity these three churches already have, to provide for an opportunity to seek together ever greater unity and to guide the constituent members in joint action in mission as well as undertake joint evangelistic and service programmes wherever possible.

---

[492] "Pluralism and Unity: the Possibility of a Variety of Typologies Within the Same Ecclesial Allegiance," *One in* Christ, VI/3 (1970), 435, cited by Crow, "Ecumenics as Reflections on Models of Christian Unity," ..., 400.

[493] Crow, "Ecumenics as reflections on models of Christian unity," *Ecumenical Review* ..., 401.

[494] Santram, "Structures of Christian Unity," in *Experiment in Christian Unity*..., 44.

[495] Santram, "Structures of Christian Unity," in *Experiment in Christian Unity*..., 44-45.

6.4.6. SPIRITUAL UNITY

Spiritual unity denotes the common participation of Christians and churches in the communion of God's own Trinitarian life. It affirms that already the churches live in communion with each other.[496] Spiritual unity, it means by this the unity that grows out of common relations to Christ as Saviour and Lord. The thing that constitutes of man a Christian is his acceptance of Jesus Christ as his Saviour and submission to Him as Lord. Without this nobody can be a Christian. Christian unity then is a unity that grows out of the fact that men and women are drawn together around Jesus Christ as a common Saviour and Lord. Person can never get together in spiritual unity until they get together in Christ. From a spiritual point of view sin is essentially divisive and the only thing that can overcome the dividing power of sin is the saving grace of God as manifested in Jesus Christ.[497] But, as person come to know Christ as Saviour and are drawn to Him as the great spiritual magnet they are drawn to each other in a bond of spiritual unity.

The spiritual unity arose during early 19th century, but it does not have any sorts of union structure. Rather it is a spontaneous response to the faith community that flows from the depth of one's love. Jesus Christ envisages a spiritual model of unity based on renewal, faith and love. He ministers to those who have passed through spiritual experiences and accepted Him as Lord and God.[498] In his highly priestly prayer, Jesus on the eve of his death prayed that his disciples might be one. But, this was not an end in itself. They had to be one, 'so that the world may believe' (John 17:21). Spiritual ecumenism consists in identifying with Jesus' prayer so that through the action of his Spirit he himself can raise up from within each people a reconciled church capable of proclaiming the good news to all. Historically, it takes the form of a refusal to identify the proclamation of the gospel with any one culture. On the contrary, the Christian life and message are to be incarnated in the various cultures, making use of elements belonging to those cultures. Thus, spiritual unity can be understood in practice as an effort of the separated Christians to create 'a new unity and communion not only within the cultures in question but also within the church universal.'[499]

Spiritual ecumenism as affirmed from 1910 onwards may thus be defined functionally as a gospel requirement which is prior to practical and theological ecumenism, as expressed in the conference of Life and Work 1925 and Faith and Order 1927. It is for this function the WCC was constituted in 1948. In the Roman Catholic Church spiritual ecumenism has been affirmed since 1930s,

---

[496] *Minutes of the Faith and Order Standing Commission, 9—16 January 2002, Gagyada, Utaly.* Faith and Order Paper No. l 91, WCC, Geneva, pp. 47-48.

[497] Walter Thomas Conner, "Walter Thomas Conner (1877-1952): The Essentials of Christian Union," *Southwestern Journal of Theology,* 51/1 (Fall, 2008), 24.

[498] Snaitang, *A History of Ecumenical Movement…*, 79.

[499] Regis Ladous, "Spiritual Ecumenism," *Dictionary of the Ecumenical Movement,* edited by Nicholas Lossky et al., (Geneva: WCC Publication, 1991), 948.

with some forerunners preparing the way for the changes made by Vatican II. Mention may be made, Paul Couturier a priest from Lyon, who organized the world week of prayer for Christian unity and Jean Monchnin, who went to India in 1938 and founded ashram, a place for prayer and encounter for Christian and Hindu forms of spirituality.[500] It is true that the spiritual unity makes possible to combine the duty of evangelism with respect for religious liberty and the diversity of culture.

6.5. FEDERAL UNITY: AN EFFECTIVE POSSIBLE MODEL

A survey in the form of interview was done in search for an affective possible church union model which would be relevant and accessible to local church members and meaningful for the churches in Northeast India. In the discussion with the existing ministers of Baptists and other groups of churches in NEI,[501] They were asked to classify the voices of their church attitude towards church union movement and also asked to identify the favourable and practicable union model for the Northeast churches. They were also asked to classify whether their community patterns do not allow or encourage much ecumenical involvement at the present context.

Majority of the respondents indicated that the model needed is of a union which is less than a unified system of church government, which provides more autonomy to local churches. The respondents were in favour of "Federal Unity" which they believe that would be the best possible model for the present Christian scenario in NEI. The federations in which an old denominational structure continues intact but works together and the churches retain their identities but function together as a single entity for certain purpose.

The study reveals that the possible model of Christian unity for the churches in Northeast India would be federal unity. One fact to be noted is that, counciliar unity already exists among the different Christian denominations in NEI, for example CBCNEI, PCNEI etc. Thus the Churches in North East India should give more prominence on federal form of Christian ecumenism. Because it is in fact undeniable that in Northeast India denominationalism is strong and it tends to cause much conflict and division in the community as well. In such a context, the ideal union would be federal unity that will have a new atmosphere of identity while retaining the existing denominational polity and practices without being affected. To achieve this, the churches need to educate the believers/congregation on Christian ecumenism, to may bring forth better unity among the Christians in NEI.

---

[500] Ladous, *Spiritual Ecumenism* ..., 948.

[501] Question that were asked to classify the voices of the church attitude towards church union movement are as follows; Is church union needed? What type of union is viable model; what would be the ways or means to make them understand? Any suggestion? What should churches do; Interview with K.I. Aier, Former CBCNEI Secretary, 8 June 2010.

The research intended to elucidate federal union as an effective model, which would be a possible solution towards the success of Christian Unity in Northeast India. However, it is clear in the Baptists' vision of church unity, that they reject the vision of organic unity and are doubtful of any move towards organic union of churches. But, they understand that ecumenical cooperation does not require acceptance of organic union as the only option for expressing the unity of the church. Perhaps, what is needed is a model of union which is less than a unified system of church government but which provides more freedom to the local churches.

6.5.1. Federal Unity: Measure of Freedom and Autonomy

When we speak of the church union activities in NEI, first it deals with the socio-cultural and political context where the churches are located. It is very true that Northeast India is politically divided, socio-culturally diverse people and religiously exists different Christian denominations developed where the churches preserve their ecclesiastical unity within the geographical section of NEI. Consequently each tribe has its own culture and language and social structure. Each of the many small tribes has traditionally lived in isolation from the others and each has its own distinct history, which is often quite different from that of other tribes, even between hills and plains people. The situation was further complicated by the fact that among most tribes the village was an autonomous unit, a kind of village-state, which was often in conflict with neighbouring villages of the same tribe.[502]

The churches, being religious agencies that initiated with denominational pattern of missionary work in the region, led to the establishment of a Christian community divided into several different church bodies. As such each denomination has its own distinctiveness and autonomous principle, which is hard to change and accept any structural form of union in the region. In line with the denominational pattern, indigenous factors, like linguistic, tribal and socio-cultural differences have often placed strains upon the unity of even these denominations. Therefore, the idea that different denominations or churches of different traditions coming together in a mutual co-operation to form one organic church is not practicable in Northeast context.

The possible model to enhance the success of church union discussion in the region of NEI churches would be therefore, a federal set up. A Federal unity would create a new church identity while retaining old identities.[503] Federal union is not merger into one unified organizational structure. Federal allows the churches to retain a good deal of their traditional identity and power.

---

[502] Downs, *Christianity in North East India: Historical Perspective* ..., 10.

[503] E. Stanley Jones, *The Reconstruction of the Church-On What Pattern?* (Nashville: Abingdon Press, 1970); Cited by Stuart G. Leyden, "An Appeal for Federal Union: An American Model of Church Union with Ecumenical Horizons," *Journal of Ecumenical Studies*, 20/2 (Spring, 1983), 278.

Union demands a sense of common identity.[504] The churches or communities in a federal union would recognize one another's members and ministries and create a national administrative unit for agreed-upon program and mission. No participating church would be expected to sacrifice its present identity or radically modify its internal discipline.[505]

Such a scheme of Federal Unity would preserve the number of ecclesiastic options available to both clergy and laity. The autonomous traditions of each church would be preserved and, in a sense, guaranteed. At the same time, the increase of communication among the churches would spur new forms of ecumenical worship and mission. Such would be able to celebrate the special gift of God to churches, pluralism within the Christian family and, at the same time, move toward a wider unity.[506] Thus, the North East India Christian Council (NEICC), church union committee need to re-affirm the type of federal unity seriously to guide its member churches for the wider ecumenism in NEI.

Furthermore, federal union provides the framework within which the various denominations and churches evolve their distinctiveness.[507] It is in this perspective that one has to look at the following peculiar features that federal unity display. First, it describes an intrinsic quality and an integral aspect of the life of undivided church at all levels. Secondly, it expresses the co-operation and fellowship of the local churches that are separated by geography, time, culture and theology. Third, it provides similar confessions and practices have often become a part of a larger structure without surrendering their autonomy or identity. Fourthly, it manifests the unity of the church through common federated procedures, acts and decisions. Federal unity stands for a great measure of autonomy, multiplicities and fellowship among the federated churches and as well, a recognizable structure of mutual unity and serving cooperatively in mission of the church.

6.5.2. Federal Unity: A Unity in Diversity

The unity of the church has, from the very beginning, existed at the very heart of diversity. Diversity is an essential aspect of true unity. It is the indispensible mark of the church at every level. Unity and diversity belong to the very nature of the church as *Koinonia*. Unity cannot be equated with uniformity which is alien to

---

[504] Stuart G. Leyden, "An Appeal for Federal Union: An American Model of Church Union with Ecumenical Horizons," ..., 278. Also ref. in William D. Carpe, "Unity of the Church: Another Model," *Lexington Theological Quarterly*, 11/2 (April, 1976), 49ff.

[505] Jones, *The Reconstruction of the Church-On What Pattern?...*, 278.

[506] Leyden, "An Appeal for Federal Union: An American Model of Church Union with Ecumenical Horizons," ..., 278.

[507] "The Federal Idea," *Christian Century*, 82/34 (Aug. 25 1965), 1028-1029.

the nature of the church. As Nairobi affirmed, "true unity is not monolithic."[508] For the church, "diversity is just as essential as unity."[509]

Even if the churches are not yet of a common mind on the form of visible unity, they all agree that the unity towards which they strive is not one of uniformity, but a unity in diversity. This clearly means that in a federal unity the local churches will maintain their proper distinctiveness. Federal unity will not become a homogeneous fellowship. It is a kind of fellowship through which local churches will be able to express their specificities and, at the same time their unity expresses between the various traditions and identities. It is vitally important to note that federal set up is never merger but a communion of local churches through their deepening understanding of and growth in certain common missions and projects. Therefore, diversity is a constitutive element in federal unity which requires different expressions at different levels and in different contexts. The one church needs that kind of diversity which does not tear us apart from one another and that kind of unity which does not impose uniformity upon desirable diversity. In fact, federal set up maintains a healthy and creative balance between unity and diversity affirms and safeguards diversity without weakening and enhances unity without endangering diversity.

The church unity has been instrumental in breaking down the walls of separation among the churches. Sharing with others, working together and discussing issues with one another gave birth to a new phenomenon in the life of the church. The federal unity model will provide the churches with wider opportunities to work and witness together. While the goal of church unity is always a process and much more than a particular structural model, this federal unity model may possess the best possible way of facilitating the process for North East India Christian Council. Federal unity commends itself because it draws upon ecumenical theology and is more compatible with Northeast India ethos.[510]

6.6. CONCLUSION

What Christian unity? What steps must be taken if progress is to be made in the years ahead? Progress along the road to Christian unity depends of course ultimately on our spiritual readiness for it. Only when we are driving by the reconciling, uniting power of Christ shall we be drawn together. But, on the other hand this drive can only operate effectively if we can see clearly and together what is required of us today. We must concentrate our thinking much more vigorously on the concrete problems of achieving unity. The actual initiative or unity has to come from the church at ground level. It is the member churches and congregations, even individual Christians, who must take the necessary steps.

---

[508] David M. Paton, ed., *Breaking Barriers: Nairobi 1975*, Official Report of the fifth Assembly of the WCC (Nairobi, 1975, London, SPCK and Grand Rapids, Eerdman, 1976), 60.

[509] John Macquaries, *Christian Unity and Christian Diversity* (London: SCM, 1975), preface.

[510] For details see section 6.3. in the same chapter.

Chapter 7

Challenges to the Life and Witness of the Baptist Church

During the week of prayer for Christian unity in 2014, Pope Francis said,

> *"Unity will not come about as a miracle at the very end. Rather unity comes about in journeying. To journey together is already to be making unity...If we do not walk together, if we do not pray for one another, if we do not collaborate in the many ways that we can in this world for the people of God, then unity will not come about."*

INTRODUCTION

At this point we will focus on the issues and challenges to the life and witness of the churches, particularly to the Baptist church in Northeast region. The discussion is set against the background of the survey done in the previous sections. Here the aim is to provide a general understanding of the present state of the debate of integral Christian unity and the ensuing influence of the said debate over the Baptist distinctiveness in Northeast India. The Baptist churches under the Council of Baptist Churches in North East India have probably displayed greater reluctance than other communions to engage with other Christians or denominations in serious efforts to effect Christian unity. Behind their hesitancy lies a potent corporate fear of ecclesiastical structures which might exert control and coerce either individuals or congregations in matters of religion and thus circumscribe freedom of the word of God. Therefore, to develop new and broader channels of communication with other Christian groups in region, it would suggest to establishment certain common project with the spirit of understanding and cooperation. The most realistic hope of working towards greater understanding and cooperation lies in the commitment of the North East India Christian Council (NEICC). The NEICC and the Baptist church in Northeast India should begin by joining in co-operate ecumenical ventures in some common projects before embarking on the viable model of church unity in the region.

7.1. CONFRONTING COMMON PROGRAMME AND PROJECT

The churches are called to identify ways of witnessing in unity, of partnership and cooperation, and of responsible relationships in evangelism. The common program like the week of prayer for Christian unity, spiritual awakening program, peace initiative project, relief camp project and seminars should prepare jointly by NEICC and Churches in NEI. Such kind of united work will enhance be great significant indications towards the beginning to unite the churches for mission and removes the isms. It is general feelings that more must first be done in active cooperation in Christian service before the various views of the churches can be sufficiently harmonized to make such union possible. The cooperation would prepare the way for some kind of federation to begin with and ultimately for the greater unity of all Christians which would seem to be the mind of Christ, and to which each communion has its contribution to make.[511]

Such would provide common ground between Baptists and other Christians to give a sense of understanding and cooperation among different denominations. Also it would seek out and develop areas of common concern, common commitment, common cooperation, and common action with other denominations. Therefore, it is believed that the establishment of confronting common program and project would be a practical and an effective starting point and a constructive step forward in broadening the relationships between Baptists and other denomination in NEI. Significant steps have been taken towards the goal of Christian unity over the last century, but there have also been many setbacks along the way. While recognizing the intransigent nature of the many sources of their division, churches need to recommit themselves both to the ongoing struggle to overcome their divisions and also to engage in "common witness" whenever and wherever it is possible to do so.

7.2. JOINT MISSION ENTERPRISE

Historically, Christian mission in North East India are mission oriented churches. But, they had tendency to stress a dichotomy between each denominational set up or foundation from which they are adopted to do mission activities. They find that ecclesiastical differences are deeper than Christian unity negotiation in NEI. Limatula Longkumer rightly pointed out that "Inter-denominational churches'

[511] J. H. Rushbrooke, (ed.) (1939) *Sixth Baptist World Congress*, report, Atlanta, Georgia, U.S.A., July 22–28, 1939, 123.

fellowship or union is still a far off in NEI,"[512] which is very true in the present scenario of Christians in Northeast region. In such a way the Christian community in NEI was divided into several church traditions. There is a fear that the establishment of a united church may lead to the loss of the distinct characteristics and mission projects of the particular denomination. Thus, it is encouraging to see how each Association, Synods, Presbyteries, Councils and Churches in NEI, including some individuals, are so enthusiastic in mission and evangelization task. But, our understanding of mission work is still dominated by church plantation, conversion and evangelism process of 19th and 20th century missionary model. Hence, mission is understood as an expansion of the denominational churches.[513] Many of them have started their own mission projects, which occasionally results in undesirable conflicts and misunderstandings among the missionaries from different associations and churches working in the same area.[514]

It may be noted that the two largest ecumenical structures, viz. the PCNEI and the CBCNEI have made efforts, but in their own ways, to bring Christians together at large. As such the way of doing mission in the North East region creates more denominationalism than unity of the churches. Therefore, the constituent members of NEICC, representing the largest body of Christians union body in NEI, it is important for them to realize that the Christians in NEI normally take course of action in accordance with the steps they have taken and the examples they have set. It would however be found that attempt has been made to refer, in one way or another, to the contributions of the member bodies of the NEICC in the project for unity and co-operation of the Christians in NEI.[515] It becomes urgent for the churches affiliated to the NEICC to maintain the fundamental ecumenical concept in its structural organization and its evangelical conviction to its mission.

For an effective Christian unity in NEI, they should develop and venture common mission projects. The churches and associations are to recognize a united missionary motive in terms of both structure and sponsorship. In order to promote common project, it is proposed that the units be encouraged to undertake common project of mission. If the different denominations come under one umbrella and work together in mission project, they will do great work for God. And such united enterprises in missions will not only bind all the Christians but it will bring the sense of oneness to the minds of the people.

---

512 Limatula Longkumer, "Wider Ecumenism and Ecclesiology," in *Ecumenism in India Today*, ed. James Massey (Bangalore: BTESSC/SATHRI, 2008), 47.

513 Longkumer, Wider Ecumenism and Ecclesiology…, 47.

514 J. L. Roy, "Primal Vision and Hermeneutics in North East India: Protestant Tribal View," in *Good News for North East India: A Theological Reader* …, 173.

515 Vanlalchhuanawma, "An Appraisal of Church Union Movement in Northeast India," (A Paper presented at the Consultation on Church Union Organized by NEICC at CBCNEI, Guwahati, January 23-25, 2003).

Therefore it is necessary that NEICC need to explore possibilities of joint mission and evangelism projects in which all the churches can participate. If all the churches cooperate, the evangelistic outreach mission could be more effective. Several mission projects in different places in which various missions, associations, synods, councils and churches are involved, now can also be strengthened if they started joint projects. The purpose is not just a joint project but participation in such project will improve the sense of understanding and cooperation among the churches in NEI.

7.3. DIALOGUE

The word dialogue is used in various senses, ranging from the general dialogical existence of man with his neighbouring to technical discussion among experts on highly specialized questions. Ecumenical dialogue however refers to warmest and prayerful conversations among Christians of various churches, whether officially delegated or meeting informally, with a view to promote greater mutual understanding and more intimate fellowship among the Christians of differing traditions.[516]

Ecumenical dialogue requires mutual respect and the willingness to listen sympathetically to other points of view is essential. Criticism of each other as well as response to it should be made with chastity and sincerity. Each should seek to put the best construction rather than the worst on position held by others. Every partner, however, has the obligation to reinterpret the tradition of his own church to meet the issue of the day in an ecumenical spirit. The impact of dialogue cannot always be predicted. Yet the desire to recover the unity of the church and in the meantime to live and work together in a fellowship seem to be necessary for fruitful ecumenical dialogue.

The technique of ecumenical dialogue is discovering and correcting our terrible misconceptions of one another. By doing this it may create some understanding of the situations and an atmosphere of good well. It also may help the churches to understand each other better, and more easily enter into one another's views by two or three hours of conversation than by two or three years epistolary correspondence. Most Christians remain in agreement that dialogue helps in making clear what forms of cooperation may be entered into without compromise, and what forms must be for a future date, if ever. For ecumenical, bilateral dialogues are not merely about finding ways to recognize other churches as expressions of the one church of the triune God.

They are primarily about seeking mutual understanding and following the ground in search of a basis for common witness to the glory of God.[517] The dialogue explicitly states as the goal of the conversations. As long as we are

---

[516] Paulos Mar Gregories, *On Ecumenism*, edited by Jacob Kurian (Delhi: ISPCK & MGF Kottayam, 2006), 65.

[517] Callam, *Baptists and **Church Unity*** ..., 304-314.

unwilling to "address one another meaningfully and directly according to Jesus' instruction in Matthew 18," we cannot grow in our common understanding of the one apostolic faith. It is also easy to settle with the different perspectives that tend to be divisive, for example, on church, mission, religious freedom, the concept of the true Christian and others, accepting these as facts of life, without making real and renewed efforts to enter into deeper dialogue. In an attempt to probe convergence and divergence in the churches' self-understanding and teaching, the dialogue is to focus on the Word of God in the life of the church.

It need far more creative dialogue about the shape of the church and dedicated pursuit of the unity God wills for the churches in NEI. Also involves far wider participation by ministers and lay people in the process, especially the participation of theological students and professors in the theological seminaries where ecumenism has been woefully eclipsed. It also requires greater understanding of models of church unity in the local context of North East India where there is the struggle for unity and renewal in the human community. In the multi-culture and multi-denominational context of NEI, a dialogue which can provide an enriching experience that enhances the theology, life and witness to the life of the people. With these perspectives the search for an effective model of unity will become less of a faith and order debate and more of a faith pilgrimage.

7.4. NEEDS FOR CONSCIENTIZATION

In the context of North East Christians the word 'Ecumenism' or 'Christian Unity' has not been a familiar word till recently. Though the churches came together under the banner of North East India Christian Council (NEICC) to build and to work together for the Kingdom of God, it needs further discussions and education on church union which is important at the grass root level. It appears that most of the Christians in region are still not aware of the movement of union. Although, people at the higher circle of church organizations are well informed about the church union movement, the larger number of people is not yet awakened to what is going on. If proper education on church union is imparted it is hoped that the people will respond favorably to it. Also let the local church committee have its members involve in the discussions so that it will not end with the leaders only.

At a random interview with the people of Mokokchung district in Nagaland, where 100% of Baptist Christians, many of them responded that they did not know and heard about the church union movement in NEI.[518] Therefore, it should not be a regional council, but the local churches themselves that should initiate discussions on church union negotiations. The local churches should desire for it. But this process will certainly take time. Even at present, there is much ignorance about other denominations among the common Christians in the region that

[518] Interview with Rev. Luen Jamir, Ex-Pastor, Mokokchung Baptist Church, Nagaland, 12 April 2012.

gives rise to misunderstandings and divisions. Many of the Christians with whom the researcher discussed have the desire to have united church in NEI, whereas many more others ruled out the urgent need of having such unity. The reason for their negative responses is that most of the Christians have blind adherence to the denominational structure of the church to which they belong. In most of the areas denominational exclusiveness has blinded the eyes of Christians and prevents them from making real and true commitment to the movement. Unity is lost when a community is badly divided on denominational allegiance. And unity is possible when Christian fellowship is sought above denominational parochialism.[519] Thus by giving a careful education on ecumenism and its discussions, people may begin to accept, respect and understand one another. Only in the context of mutual respect and understanding of one another will any plan of church union be successful and prospects in NEI.

7.5. THEOLOGICAL INSTITUTION

Apart from the formation of comprehensive ecclesiastical structures, the ecumenical gesture in the region was to be perceived in the establishment of theological institutions. In NEI, the first theological seminary was founded by the Welsh Mission at Cherrapunji in 1887, which became affiliated to Senate of Serampore College in 1937. The same mission started in 1907 a theological school at Aizawl, which was affiliated to Serampore College in 1965. The CBCNEI also established a Eastern Theological College at Jorhat in 1950. Ao Baptist Church Association also started Clark Memorial Theological College at Aolichen, Mokokchung much later. These pioneering seminaries were efforts within church denominations. Limatula Longkumer stated in this regards that;

> Most of the theological colleges in North East India are sponsored by denominational and tribal group based churches. Often these colleges have to abide by the governing principles and policies of their churches. Hence, theological education serves to promote more denominationalism and its theology rather than wider ecumenism.[520]

At present NEI have more theological colleges and seminaries of which only 8 are affiliated[521] to the Senate of Serampore College (University). The rapid growth of theological colleges in NEI has weakened theological education as well as created theological differences in the churches. Majority of the teachers,

---

[519] Nicholas K. Apostola, "How Much Unity? How Much Diversity?" *Greek Orthodox Theological Review*, 50/1-4 (Spring-Winter, 2005), 119 ff.

[520] Longkumer, *Wider Ecumenism and Ecclesiology* ..., 47.

[521] Academy of Integrated Christian Studies, Aizawl; Aizawl Theological College, Aizwal; Baptist Theological College, Pfutsero; Clark Theological College, Aolichen; Eastern Theological College, Jorhat; John Robert Theological Seminary, Shillong; Trinity Theiological College, Dimapur and Trulock Theological Seminary, Imphal.

lecturers and students are connected with their respective denominational bodies that support these institutions.[522] Because of this, most of the seminaries are oriented to their particular church traditions and lack a free interdenominational and cross-cultural environment. As such, the teachers and students do not have a basis or interest for a common joint program in the region. Despite this, it is imperative that all theological colleges and seminaries should see that they formulate plans to create an ecumenical and interdenominational academic as well as practical atmosphere.[523]

Subsequently talking about unity in action, the Council discussed the proposal of closer co-operation in higher theological education with the definite aim of having united theological colleges, but unfortunately the plan was not materialized.[524] It is quite understandable that each denomination or ethnic groups would want to maintain its distinct identity in theological education. The rapidly increasing theological institution in Northeast region creates more problems than profit to local churches. At the same time many of these institutions have separatist tendencies and to negotiate church union with leaders who are graduates of some of these institutions is difficult.[525]

Therefore, it needs to suggest that those theological seminaries in NEI should develop a kind of federated program, with such kind of joint program it can facilitate to make the faculty exchange with the objective of unity. Such would be a kind of beginning to open the ways for the further achievement of church union movement in the region. There is a great need for common planning, inter-seminary meetings, and seminars to bring those seminaries nearer to each other to create an atmosphere of cordiality.

7.6. EDUCATION AND LITERATURE

Considering the educational institutions in NEI, the government has generously established various schools colleges and universities at different area for the purpose of higher studies.[526] The problem is that there is no real moral instruction in many of those schools and colleges. The students spend a lot of time at schools and colleges but there is not much Christian environment provided for them there. Therefore it is an urgent need to establish a good Christian oriented institution in the region.

In 1947 at the Assam Christian Council annual session resolved to start united Protestant college. With great hope a united Protestant college had taken

---

522 Behera, *Theological Education* ..., 53.

523 Interview with C. Walu Walling, Literature Secretary, ABAM, Impur, June 2010; K.C. Vangliaka, Bawngkawn, Presbyterian Church Aizawl, 10 May 2011.

524 *Assam Christian Council, Minutes and Proceedings*, 1947 ..., 11.

525 Behera, *Theological Education* ..., 53.

526 Nuklu Longkumer, *The Growth of Baptist Churches Among the Ao's of Nagaland* (Nagaland: Changtongya Baptist Church, 1988), 83.

shape in the form of Union Christian College (UCC), founded in 1952 at Barapani,[527] near Shillong, the capital of Meghalaya. The Council has been trying different projects in order to promote its objectives of unity, but the UCC seems to be the only project that has been successful so far. Today youngsters are turning away from their faith because of an unbalanced education in many government run institutions. Even then many mission schools are declining due to the lack of unity and co-operation to sponsor and support it. Therefore the churches and church union committee should give more importance to and also concentrate on creating an educational program with true Christian commitment.

It is true that literary works bring a great change to every culture and society. The pioneering missionaries had published few books and periodicals in various languages in NEI. Now there are some contemporary writers who publish books and journals that enrich christian literature in the region. There are few periodicals like, Journal of Tribal Studies, Tribal Study Series and Women Study Series etc., which are the publications of Eastern Theological College, Jorhat and also Aizawl Theological College publications like, Mizoram Theological Journal, Presbyterian Review etc., are profitable yet these are far from sufficient as they are mainly based and confined to seminaries. As such, the Council (NEICC) should produce more literary works to improve the influence on different communities or tribes. The Council should take the initiation to publish common periodical books, as well as the lunching of common endeavors such as new translations of the Bible, an ecumenical and comprehensive history of Christianity in NEI and ecumenical published periodicals. It will facilitate a platform to work collectively to create a new sense of cultural community among all the members of the churches as well as associations.

7.7. NORTHEAST INDIA BIBLE SOCIETY

Bible Society of India (BSI) has contributed substantially to enrich the Christians in Northeast region. The first Auxiliary of the Bible Society of India for the Northeast was established at Shillong in 1957. It is a measure of the expansion of BSI activity in the region that there are now two other Auxiliaries based at Aizawl (1982) and Dimapur (1986) with Rev. C. Ronghinga and Rev. M. Savino as the respective secretaries.[528] The BSI provides the necessary aid for Bible translation in each and every dialect in the NEI. At present the BSI accomplished many translation projects of the whole Bible, and some selected portions of the Bible in different languages in NEI. BSI is also one of the constituent members of the NEICC. But, the main problem is that the BSI headquarters has its base in Bangalore, from which it provides consultancy service for the translators which

[527] Assam Christian Council, Minutes and Proceedings of the 15th Annual Conference, 1952.

[528] John Philipose, "The Bible Society and North East India," in *Good News for North East India* ..., 63.

makes things more expensive and more inconvenient for the churches in North East India.

Following are some of the reasons why independent Bible Society is essential for Northeast India: All the churches are very much enthusiastic about taking the good news or gospel to all the people, so bible society should be the means through which the gospel will reach different tribe, culture, people and languages. Having such means the churches in NEI collectively work in bible society to carry the gospel to unreached people and tribes. Such non-profit organization Bible Society, provide the platform where all the Christian denominations in NEI can actively involved in the ministry to propagate the gospel message to the whole North East region without any bias and prejudice. There are many dialect/language in North East India into which bible is not translated yet. And in some of the cases only a portion of the bible, like New Testament or only Old Testament or even only a smaller portion are available. In some case the version that are used need to be revised with proper version. There is urgent need among the people in the Northeast to make the accurate version of bible in different respective languages, and it is a great challenge for the bible society. So, if there can be separate bible society of Northeast India that particular organization will take coverage of the entire Northeastern region. And it will be a kind of platform where all the churches can come together more closely than before. Furthermore, it will enhance the unity of the church as this will open more space where church leaders, pastors can come together and interact in the form of communities and other program under the bible society. It will also enhance the relationship of the churches toward forming more intimate *koinonia* among the churches in the region for the unity of the churches.

North East India is geographically and ethnically different from the rest of the mainline India. So most of the Christian in Northeast India now belong to India and sometime at the ecumenical level. So who have joint program or joint venture with the people of mainline India, there are certain disadvantage because of geographical distances and also difference in socio-cultural background. Sometime it is difficult to fully identify with the Christian brothers and sisters with the rest of India. But if we have separate bible society in North East India, under that umbrella the people who have identical socio-cultural background could jointly work and share sources, also it would be easier to take decision for common concern in a meaningful and relevant manner. But, the bible society monitored from the mainline India seems to fail in recognising this, hence making it more difficult to understand the needs of North East people. Looking at the real situation of Northeast India there still exist issues like tribalism and ethnic clashes, conflicts that hampered the co-existence of people of Northeast India. In order to address to these issues, platform like bible society of Northeast India can play a very significant role.

Bible society is not only engaging in bible translation and distribution of the biblical text, but they also engage in peace making process, particularly Bible as word of God that need to address to all people, culture and race without strife. Bible society should involve and create a kind of ministry of peace building. There some social, ecumenical and ethical problem which the Bible society based in Bangalore hardly sees. It also fails to take into account the sources, experience of the people. So if Bible society in Northeast India can function independently within Northeast India then it will really address the economical, social and other dimension of the community in Northeast India. Therefore NEI needs to have its own independent Bible Society whereby all the churches and communities in the region could come together in the spirit of unity that would enhance their support to the organization through fervent prayers, liberal contributions and vigorous participation in the Bible translation as well as distribution of projects.

7.8. ROLE OF THE CHURCH IN SOCIO-POLITICO-ECONOMIC ISSUES

In spite of Christian majority where politicians, government officers and the people as a whole are Christians, NEI is rampant with corruptions, injustice, violence, etc. in every walk of life.[529] For decades violence and conflicts in the region have disturbed normal life both in the rural and urban. Though the cease-fire and peace process dialogue between the Indian government and different insurgency groups in the region is on course there are still untold bitter experiences among the people. Factional fights against the insurgency groups add fuel to the fire of hardships of the people.[530]

Competitively and comparatively with other parts of the nation, NEI is still lacking behind in terms of several development areas. And due to socio-political disorders, developmental projects and other empowerment agencies are being stalled. Again, development works and schemes from government and Non-governmental Organizations (NGOs) are either delayed or stuck due to trust deficit between public and developmental agencies. In the meantime, corruption has become one of the biggest obstacles to fair and equitable economic development and social justice. It is no longer a problem that is infesting in the so called "secular world" as chided by the Christians, but it has also affected Christian missions and churches. For instance, relief organizations, missions and churches are themselves part of both the problem and its solution. It is so because today's judges, customs officers, military and law enforcement officials and all concerned

---

[529] J. Thungjamo Lotha, *Christian Approach to Politics: A Case Study of Nagaland* (Kohima, Nagaland: NBCC, Youth Dept., 1987), 47.

[530] Mayang Imsong, "A Better Tomorrow: Hope for the North East India Tribals Suffering in Indo-Naga Conflict," *Journal of Tribal* Studies, VII/1 (January – June, 2003), 232.

personnel who maintain our societal structures are corrupted. Theologically, corruption is deeply rooted in the nature of man as it is corollary of original sin.[531]

Therefore, corruption is sinful and a moral failure, which is utterly detrimental to the hope of a free Christian society now and in the days to come too. This conflict has rendered their world a very complex, dangerous and insecure one, a life of pain and sorrow. At this juncture, the people are at loss and worried about their future. The hope to answer the long struggles become a distant reality for the tribal, though the cease-fire is extended and peace talk held several times.[532] In order to give guidelines to the people for more effective Christian participation, it is advisable for the churches to execute joint social programs in the region.

The churches in NEI will have to engage themselves in more activities concerning social transformation along with their regular mission of preaching, evangelism and social action planting churches. Christian life cannot be limited to oral witness. It has to creatively respond to the call of the poor, the oppressed and the marginalized.[533] Though there is a peace effort within denominationalism it is not in wider scope. Therefore it is high time for the church leaders in NEI to put their heads together once again and go for a change and solidarity of the Northeast people.

7.9. A HOLISTIC YOUTH PROGRAM

In many Churches in NEI, there are unthinkable problems among the youth. Today many youths are addicted to drugs, indulge in gambling and others of that sort. Many young people spent money without any source of income. Society is disturbed by their activities. Parents have heavy hearts because of their uncontrolled children.[534] Taking seriously the situation and the needs of youth, the Council should regard this as one of the most urgent matter in the present society.

There is a crying need for a holistic youth development program. The churches should come with a vital vision and plan to generate the potential of the Northeast youth. Instead, one can see most youth falling under one of the following characteristics; Inwardness, which leads to anti-authoritarianism, Fatherless, which leads to a turning away from existing structures and leading to

---

[531] *Baptist News CBCNEI, July to September 2016*, Report o the General Secretary May 27 to October 17, 2014, Edited by Solomon Rongpi, Guwahati, Assam: CBCNEI, 2017.

[532] Rui de Menezes, "Insurgency in Northeast: A Christian Response," *Journal of Tribal Studies*, VII/1 (January–June, 2003), 198.

[533] K. Lung Muana, "North East India and Ecumenical Trends," *Presbyterian Review*, IX/34 (April-June, 2003), 24.

[534] Nazarine V. Marbaniang, "Youth Participation in Socio-Political Awareness in the North-East," in *Society and Culture in North-East India: A Christian Perspective*, edited by Saral K. Chatterji (Delhi: ISPCK, 1996), 36.

destruction and violence.[535] The Council has to begin for holistic youth programs like; youth camp, youth rallies, workshop, seminars and youth awakening program in different regions. Such program should take into consideration the young person as he/she grows and develops through various stages of life. This holistic youth program will consider the young person in his/her relationship to an absolute God, in relationship to society and in relationship to a positively constructive personal future for unity.[536]

It has been said that leadership is largely a matter of nurture and training. Therefore apart from the efforts of the local churches, the Council needs to extend its ministry to reach out these youths to nurture the spiritual as well as mental needs. As such the churches should join together with the NEICC to develop certain program to heal those wounded youth by providing facilities like educational, vocational guidance, which will progress the church union movement in the region.

7.10. STRENGTHEN COMMON FRONT MINISTRY

In order to overcome the scandal of proselytism, we are called to practice common witness as an act of ecumenical evangelism. Common front ministry is the witness that the churches, even while separated, bear together, especially through joint efforts, by manifesting whatever divine gifts of truth and life they already share and experience in common. The Northeast Christians are often conscious of one's own denomination, community and tribe. They give their best to their local church program and association ministry. But, when it come to common front program there is a tendency to contribute less. This weakens the Church Union Movement. If we look at the present trend, many Christian organizations recognize the North East India Christian Council (NEICC), but our participation is often inadequate. Therefore, NEICC should call upon all its constituent members to give equal attention to common front ministry.[537] The collaboration with Roman Catholic Church, Orthodox Church, Salvation Army as well as other organizations is another area into which NEICC should need to engage itself. The models created by these churches and the regional Christian councils constituted by these churches can always provide direction for the churches in NEI also.[538]

Relation to people of other faiths is another area in which Northeast Christians needs to gain expertise. Most of the Northeast churches live in the context of tribal homogeneity and they did not have occasions to confront religious

---

[535] Aier, *From Darkness to Light ...*, 183.

[536] Dominic Jala, "Youth and the Challenges of the Twenty-First Century," in *Society and Culture in North-East India: A Christian Perspective*, edited by Saral K. Chatterji (Delhi: ISPCK, 1996), 65.

[537] Interview with Vanlalnghaka Ralte, Lecturer, Aizawl Theological College, Mizoram, 6 June 2010.

[538] Muana, *Ecumenical Trends ...*, 25.

diversity. As a result, the churches are inward looking and self-complacent. For the remaining part of the country, religious diversity is a reality to reckon with. Slowly religious diversity is creeping into the Northeast region also. The needs of other faiths, recognizing them as human beings and to enter into a dialogue with them are urgent needs.[539] These items are to be added to the regular agenda of the Northeast churches with the initiative of NEICC. It is vital requirement that the NEICC should see the ecumenical forum, where all the religious leaders could come together in one platform with the spirit of unity to express each ideology and to serve as the vehicle for unification of the isolated communities into a larger entity.

7.11. UNITED CHRISTIAN FORUM

The united Christian forum is meant to be an open meeting place for Christians of different denominations and traditions. It would be an ecumenical forum where people from different denominational and cultural backgrounds come together to have fellowship without any formal authority or structures. As such it will bring informal get-together between other Christians and Baptist will help to know, understand and appreciate each other and also to grow in Christian love towards each other.[540] It will also serve to eliminate sources of tension and misunderstanding created by distrust and prejudice. United Forum can be seen as a process of creating a fellowship for the widest possible range of Christians by building more relationships between the churches to promote a fuller cooperation and unity. The idea here is to create a forum that would reflect and discuss the kind of witness and that should be given to the society by the churches. It is to be hoped that the united Christian forum will lead to greater mutual understanding and improved relationships among the different Christian groups.

The united forum continues to be an important ecumenical expression of different churches in Northeast region, where it will have sharing and exchange of pulpit without any reservations among the ministers. The aim is to explore the present relationships of the churches and also continue to work for the wider unity of Christ's church. Such forum is to seek better ways of serving pastoral and administrative needs of the fellowship and continue to develop ecumenical agencies for co-operation, evangelism and service. Such kind of forum will help to reduce the prejudices and hostilities between the Baptists and other denominations in the region.

7.12. TOWARDS COMMON WITNESS

The churches are called to identify ways of witnessing in unity, of partnership and co-operation, and of responsible relationships in evangelism. In order to reach such a mutually enriching missionary ethos, the churches must repent

[539] Muana, *Ecumenical Trends* ..., 25.

[540] Interview with Toshi Aier, Lecturer, CTC, Aolijen, Mokokchung.

of past failures and reflect more self-critically on their ways of relating to one another and their methods of evangelizing. Churches must renounce all forms of denominational competition and rivalry and the temptation to proselytize members of other Christian traditions and avoid establishing parallel ecclesial structures, but rather stimulate, help and cooperate with the existing local churches in their evangelistic work. Condemn any manipulation of humanitarian assistance to individual Christians or churches to induce people into changing their denominational allegiance or to further the missionary goals of one church at the expense of another. Churches are called to help people who are in process of changing their church allegiance to discern whether they are being guided by worthy or unworthy motives and learn to "speak the truth in love to one another when they consider others to be proselytizing or engaging in dishonest practices in evangelism.

7.13. CONCLUSION

To sum up the above discussion, it is vital task for the churches and Christians to come together with mutual trust and be acceptable among the different denominations, which might ultimately lead to form a possible church union in the region. The Christian churches in NEI should face these new challenges with courage and determination. The challenges are an invitation for further growth and maturity to identify the kind of union that has been anticipated. A search for new way for closer co-operation and other alternative forms of union that would best suit to present Christian churches and position in NEI should be explored and considered. Looking at the existing churches tradition in the region, the unity of the churches in Northeast India is a necessity. It is possible to have inter-communion, however in a federal set up. Therefore, it is suggested that the federal unity model would be the most possible solution for the success of the Church Union Movement in Northeast India.

Chapter 8

Paradigm Shifts in Baptist Thinking and Understanding of Christian Unity

INTRODUCTION

The Christian Unity has become an important principle in the life of the church in this present generation. Since 20th century onwards ecumenical movement has called for a wider understanding of the meaning of Christian unity with regards to the church and in relation to humankind and in with whole creation. Paradigms have shifted. They have shifted from the side of the people the oppressed, the marginalized, the alienated, the poor and the whole creation. The future of ecumenism lies, humanly speaking, in how seriously we take the challenges, how we understand the context and how we are in solidarity with the people. This, we believe that will shape the new ecumenical calling of the Baptist/Christian churches in Northeast India.

The basic focus in this chapter is to analyzed that our understanding of the nature of the unity we seek have shifted in recent years moving from an emphasis upon structural and institutional unity to one that finds its focus in relationships and cooperation centered in Jesus Christ. Henceforth, the analysis our Christian unity discussions and involvements is that our unity is in Jesus Christ, not in structures or institutions or theological agreement but in the grace and love of God offered to us and to the world in Jesus Christ. As such Christian unity is not for its own sake, but for the sake of the world and its salvation for whole creation. Therefore, Baptist churches in the region need to make revision and think from the earlier understanding of Christian unity to our present very concept of

Christian unity. Responding to the basic concern to the question of what kind of unity are we seeking to the Christians in Northeast region is that the unity should not be coming from theological argument or agreement, but from the practice of love and trust centered in Jesus Christ. The model of unity should seek to witness to the interrelatedness of unity, mission, and identity.

8.1. UNDERSTATING OF CHRISTIAN UNITY

The realities and challenges of the present century have forced many Christians to embrace the original meaning of Unity. While seeking unity among Christians remains important to the nature and mission of the church, it has become clear that God's call to the church is to serve the unity of all creation. As we are grappling with, among other things, the effects of globalization, changing demographics of religion, climate change, poverty, marginality and inequality etc. it is clear that the ecumenical co-operations need to be broadened and all encompassing.

This paradigm shift for understanding Christian unity is to recovery of the biblical concept of unity since, in effect, unity is faithful to the teaching of Scripture to the extent that it is placed at the service of the Kingdom of God and his justice. Consequently, it is focused on crossing the frontier between faith and no faith, not only in geographical terms, but in cultural, ethnic, social, economical and political terms, for the purpose of transforming life in all its dimensions, according to God's plan, so that all people and human communities may experience the abundant life and unity that Christ offers.

Unity does not mean uniformity neither in belief, nor in practice. We are seeking oneness in Christ, not sameness in our theology, or worship, or work practices. Unity is more relational than institutional. (This is a new insight for the ecumenical movement.) Christian unity finds its life and reality in relationships as we serve together, as we engage in mission together, Unity does not begin with plans of union or major statements of theological consensus. Rather unity is known as we engage in deepening relationships with other Christians and other churches in the lived experience of worship, confessing the faith, addressing issues of social justice and peace together.

Many of us who speak often, even glibly, about "wider ecumenism", "macro-ecumenism" or "new ecumenism" are unaware or not sufficiently conscious of the passion, courage, commitment and daring that went into the challenge placed before the churches to enter into an ecumenical commitment and to strive towards visible unity.[541] The Common Understanding and Vision of WCC[542] document rightly and clearly states that despite ambiguities there is reasonable clarity on what the ecumenical movement is about:

---

[541] Ariarajah, S Wesley, "Wider Ecumenism: A Threat or a Promise?" In *The Ecumenical Review, 50 no 3* Jul (1998), p. 321-329.

[542] https://www.oikoumene.org/en/resources/documents/assembly/2006-porto-alegre/3-preparatory-and-background-documents/common-understanding-and-vision-of-the-wcc-cuv.

> Among the churches and ecumenical organizations uncertainty, ambiguity, and even confusion prevail about what is meant by the "ecumenical movement". There is (however) agreement that the term "ecumenical" embraces the quest for Christian unity, common witness in the worldwide task of mission and evangelism, and the commitment to diakonia and to the promotion of justice and peace (para. 2.2).

And the document picks up the comprehensive understanding of "ecumenism" that was present in the thinking of the pioneers and reformulated by the central committee in 1951:

> It is important to insist that the word [ecumenical], which comes from the Greek word for the whole inhabited earth *[oikoumene],* is properly used to describe everything that relates to the whole task of the whole church to bring the gospel to the whole world (para. 2.3).

The word "ecumenical", therefore, has hitherto been used quite unapologetically to mean primarily a movement of and within the churches, even though there is also increasing ambiguity in the use of the phrase within the churches themselves.

At the global level, there is an increasing recognition that the world's problems are not Christian problems requiring Christian answers, but human problems that must be addressed together by all human beings. We know today that whether it is the issue of justice, peace, human rights or the destruction of the environment, we need to work across boundaries of religions, nations and cultures. There are calls for global movements and for a "global ethic" that would govern our life together.[543]

There is still an urgent need to make re-visioning of Christian unity we have in Christ. Christians still need to find ways to speak, act and engage together to fulfill their common calling to be in witness and service to the world. There still needs to be an ecumenical body in which the churches can engage one another in mutual learning, correction and solidarity. Unfortunately the unity that is there in Northeast region today among Christians is one of an apologetic nature, a defensive mechanism. The unity that is required today is or the liberation of humankind and the whole creation.[544]

It is a movement for the unity of the church and of humankind to explore the shape of unity not only in relation to our many experiences and efforts in manifesting our oneness in Christ with other Christians, but also within the broader understanding of the vision of unity that comes to us from our involvements in the co-creation and their struggles. It is a movement in which

---

[543] Ariarajah, Wider Ecumenism: A Threat or a Promise ....321-329.

[544] Geeorge Mathew Nalunnakkal, "Search for Unity in the Changing Cultural Context," in *Discerning Mission Today* , Edited by Y Moses (Delhi: ISPCK, 2004), 82.

churches are engaged together in dealing with ethical issues. The search for unity follows the path of justice. Ecumenism is a dialogue among cultures. It is an inclusive movement, not only of all sectors in the church but of all their aspirations and struggles towards one ecumenical vision. It is concerned about all the people in the household of God and the sustainability of the earth for their habitation.

The re-visioning of Christian unity with justice for all and of unity of all Gods people is the imperative of the ecumenical movement. The movement is a project of hope propelled by prophecy. This paradigm shift calls for a renewed ecumenical commitment, the commitment to put into practice the unity that has always been in Christ, at the Lord's Table as well as in marching for visible unity, in the struggle for a more just society. The Baptist churches in Northeast region should reanalyze that it has always been a commonly accepted belief that the Christian unity as the goal of the ecumenical movement is not a goal for its own sake. Unity must result in witness and service in the world.

8.1.1. CHRISTIAN UNITY AS SOLIDARITY

A new model of unity has lately come to the ecumenical scene primarily from the experience of theologians and churches in third world nations. The heart of this model is not the relationship between the different confessions, but rather their common solidarity, suffering with the poor and marginalize. The fundamental division in humankind, according to this model, is the alienation between the rich and the poor, between the oppressed and oppressors. The deepest divisive boundary line among Christians is, therefore, not between different confessional families. The scandal of the divided church is no longer in the division between churches or types of traditions, but between different ways of living the faith in a Christian and ecclesial manner, and this division runs through the diverse confessions.[545] The essence of this division is not the contrast between formulations of the faith or orders of ministry. The scandalous division is between those who live and those who die; the deepest reality of brokenness is those situations where the unity of the human race which God promised and gives to all persons in Jesus Christ is denied.

God's as well as Christ's way of doing mission is the way of solidarity, solidarity with those among whom mission has to be carried out. In this sense the concept of solidarity has always been as element of Christian's unity. The incarnation of God in Christ is the concrete expression of God's solidarity with the suffering humanity. The sacrificial death of Christ on the cross is the sign of that God's solidarity with the suffering people. It affirms the fact that God step in for the salvation of those who stay dehumanized and threatened.

---

[545] Jon Sobrino and Juan Hernandes Pico, *Theology of Christian Solidarity* (Maryknoll, NY: Orbis Books, 1985), 45.

What this model implies for the traditional pursuit of models of unity is rather traumatic in North East context. It says that unless models of unity are committed to solidarity with the poor and oppressed, they will create a unity which is, at best, marginal in expressing the fellowship of believers. Only as the churches together face the fundamental division and overcome the primary scandal will they discover their legitimate unity; a unity in solidarity and suffering. Inter-confessional unity without prior solidarity with the poor of this world "is out of touch with reality, anti-Christian, and difficult to achieve in real history."[546]

Again the teaching and practice of Jesus furnish our clues. He cared without limits for the outcasts, the poor, the untouchables, those whom others rejected. Unity which is modeled on Jesus' ministry will be inclusive of the least of these. No confession of faith, no Eucharistic fellowship, no ministry or strategies for common mission which do not embrace the faithful, full participation of those who have lived on the periphery of power and privilege will bring authentic unity. When our unity conversations include, in this sense, the marginalized among the people of God, the churches in Northeast India will discover its wholeness and be able to function as a sign, instrument and foretaste of God's intention of reconciliation for a desperately divided human race.

8.1.2. CHRISTIAN UNITY AS NETWORKING

The internet access through Internet service is now such a powerful research tool that it has done away with lots of the old methods like learning and getting information by visiting offices or making correspondence. Life has become interesting and easier in the age of internet service as with the click of a button you can find information of any and every subject that you can think of. It is hard to believe that some few years ago many of us did not have the Internet access for Internet service nor did we care to know about it. Today, this technological advancement has propelled our society into the age of instant knowledge. In fact, today, most of us would be entirely lost without our Internet service. We do our banking, shopping and our homework and even dating on-line. No arena has felt a greater impact of the Internet service than education. We are now so dependent on Internet service that it will be intolerable in modern time to live without this new technology. Internet Service has changed the way of life from slow moving activities to the modern tracks where things move fast.

Ecumenical Network sites have brought enormous changes in interaction and social patterns. It is essential to engage in the internet to network people organization and churches who share different interest. There are varied roles to play and make church as the stage where we enact these roles. In the case of church net, it engage in various church activities through networking sites and it brings

546 "The Basis and the Forms of Unity", In *Mid-Stream: an Ecumenical Journal,* Vol. XXIII, No. 1, (January 1984), pp. 1-12. Cited in Crow, Paul A Jr, "Ecumenics as Reflections on Models of Christian Unity," *The Ecumenical Review*, 39 no 4 Oct 1987, p 389-403.

together the churches ecumenically. Mission is to network between the churches and also to initiate an ecumenical dialogue among the churches. Establishing the churches websites will also help a lot to provide information about the churches, programs, ministry, membership and other activities. As in the case of North East India, they have been great communication barriers between the states because of rugged and dense forests where the people find it difficult to travel around or to make link with each other.

Net provide a platform and also the space for people of different walk of life to express themselves openly in a way which might not be possible otherwise. Even many ecumenical issues can be discussed and freely express the concept and share best concept from one denomination to others. This could also help us to transcend our borders and establish relationship with each other. Networking can also help the churches to work together in the internet and to learn from each other the way to do the home mission as well as Outreach mission by the Northeast churches. Even constructing a website together with another church needs courage and a radical step. The churches should also be encouraged to recognize the importance of using the net in their mission and ministry. When the net helps people to break their barriers of language and broader, then it can also help to eliminate the denominational barriers and others types of blocks that could hinder the churches unity discussion in Northeast India from coming closer to one another.

8.1.3. CHRISTIAN UNITY AS HOSPITALITY

The online Oxford Dictionary defines hospitality as "the friendly and generous reception and entertainment of guests, visitors, or strangers,"[547] which is a good definition as it already implies friendship, generosity and attentiveness to the other whether they are friend or stranger. The practice of hospitality enables to see the other and therefore to establish a relationship which has profound consequences for how we live together in the world. Generous hospitality can lead to reconciliation and genuine embrace of the other. The practice of hospitality allows for creating space, space that allows room for both host and guest or stranger. Look at the Israel experienced God as a God of hospitality. Stories of hospitality are foundational to Israel's very existence and identity. Just as God created Israel as a nation, delivered them from slavery in Egypt and fed them in the wilderness, so their hospitality in turn serves as a reminder of and witness to God's hospitality towards them. And always they have the stories in their tradition that guests and strangers might be angels, bringing divine promises and provision.

Jesus takes this even further in the two great texts of Luke 14 and Matt. 25 where he distinguishes between conventional and Christian hospitality. In Luke 14 (vv12-14) Jesus says,

---

[547] http://oxforddictionaries.com/definition/americanenglisl1/hospitalitv accessed 23 May 2018.

When you give a dinner or a banquet, do not invite you friends or your brothers or your kinsmen or rich neighbours, lest they also invite you in return, and you be repaid. But when you give a feast, invite the poor, the maimed, the lame, the blind, and you will be blessed, because they cannot repay you. This is, of course, the prelude to the parable of the Great Banquet, a powerful metaphor for the Kingdom of God, where all are universally welcomed. When the expected guests turn down the invitation to the banquet, the same four groups are to be invited 'the poor, the maimed, the lame, the blind' and then everyone else from the highways and byways. Jesus was celebrating the messianic banquet but with all the wrong people. Even goes so far as to state that 'this table fellowship with sinners, and the reconfiguring of Israel's purity boundaries which this hospitality represents signifies the heart of Jesus' mission.'[548]

The Greek word for hospitality in the New Testament, *philoxenia,* refers not so much to love of strangers but to a delight in the whole guest-host relationship and in the surprises that may occur. Jesus is portrayed as a gracious host, welcoming children, tax collectors, prostitutes and sinners into his presence and therefore offending those who would prefer such guests not to be at his gatherings. But, Jesus is also portrayed as vulnerable guest and needy stranger who came to his own but his own did not receive him. (John 1:11).[549]

This transforming hospitality begins with seeing the other person with the act of recognition a powerful act indeed. It requires looking the other in the eye to the establishment of the relationship, which is a fundamental act of hospitality because it acknowledges people's humanity, accords them dignity and denies their invisibility. As Pohl says,

> Hospitality resists boundaries that endanger persons by denying their humanness. It saves others from the invisibility that comes from social abandonment. Sometimes, by the very act of welcome, a vision for a whole society is offered, a small evidence that transformed relations are possible.[550]

Christian hospitality and Christian mission require that we actively see the guest and stranger in our worlds. This means that we will see the other as authentically 'other' and allow them the space to be who they are created to be in Christ. Hospitality from the margins reminds us of the paradoxical power of vulnerability and the importance of compassion.

---

548 Bretherton, Luke. *Hospitality as Holiness: Christian Witness Amid Moral Diversity*, Ashgate (2006); Cited in Cathy Ross, "Creating Space: Hospitality as a Metaphor for Mission," Cited in *ANVIL Volume 25 No 3,* 2008.

549 Cathy Ross, "Creating Space: Hospitality as a Metaphor for Mission," Cited in *ANVIL Volume 25 No 3* (2008), 96.

550 Pohl, Christine. *Making Room: Recovering Hospitality as a Christian Tradition*, (Grand Rapids: Eerdmans, 1999), 64.

Hospitality involves paying attention. Paying attention and the gift of attentiveness are worked out so much more easily and fruitfully in community as well as in individual life. To be a part of the Christian community, we must open up a wider vision of the Kingdom of God, a broader and more challenging apprehension of the gospel, a larger understanding of God's world and a renewed vision to create more unity. Hospitality as presence may be practiced more authentically in community. This is why our faith communities or churches are so important. The church as the household of God is where God is, where we can find God, where we can live with God.[551] This metaphor resonates with the theme of hospitality, for surely the church, as foe household of God and foe body of Christ, is foe institution par excellence, which exemplifies and lives out hospitality as its mission and its purpose to bring and unite whole God's creation. Therefore believers are encouraged to establish inter-dependent relationships with fellow Christians as they grow into Christ. As a community it is aware that it is incomplete without inter-dependent relationships with other Christian denominations and communities in Northeast India.

Church or community is sustained by a way of life that acknowledges that our lives and our ways of knowing are inherently relational, enhanced by our life together. Hospitality as faithful presence might well involve challenge or resistance, even conflict, with certain ideas, particularly those that would undercut the very practice itself This hind of presence and attentiveness might lead us to the margins, to the outsiders, to the poor and to the rejected one in whom God has such a special interest and with whom Jesus spent so much time. Hospitality from the margins reminds us of the paradoxical power of vulnerability and the importance of compassion to have Christian unity. To make oneself vulnerable reminds us that both hospitality and engagement in Christian unity, which require authentic compassion and genuine love.

Generally, the Christians in Northeast churches are generous and hospitality in various way, but when it come to the discussion of Christian unity, there are still walls of denominationalism and other issues. We must create space and welcome the stranger, seeing the other, nourishing the other, attentiveness, presence, marginality, and creating Christian unity in diversity. May we never forget that we were once strangers until God welcomed us and may the stranger be always a person of promise, surprise and grace. We must never lose the ability to see the different denominations coming together as a foreshadowing of the heavenly feast where, with the whole company of Christ, we will sit and eat in His Kingdom. This attentiveness to the world church and presence in our own communities is hallmarks of our discipleship. Furthermore, in the divine act of the creation of humanity, this wonderful act of generosity, we have the privilege of participating in the divine nature, the nature that created space and allows not only for relationship, but also for unity and diversity.

---

[551] Cathy Ross, "Creating Space: Hospitality as a Metaphor for Mission ......97.

8.1.4. CHRISTIAN UNITY AS COMMON WITNESS

Christian Unity as common witness aspires to cover 'the whole inhabited earth,' not only across the barriers of ecclesial and mission structures, but also across boundaries of geography, region, nation, ethnicity and language. Those engaged in mission as common witness no longer talk in terms of a Christendom separate from the non-Christian world but of world Christianity. Thanks to the faithful witness of previous generations, the faith Christians share is widespread and rooted locally in almost every part of the world. Today one can easily notice and see that common witness is a much broader concept than just being in cooperation with each other or just our joint efforts together. It is broader, since it needs the acknowledgement, respect and appreciation of the shared gifts of grace, truth and love in our denominations and also the frank rejoicing and joy in their exercise. The spirit of common witness does not come from some strategy but from the personal and community experience of Jesus Christ.[552]

This common witness is an essential element in the shaping of mission for the future. In this reciprocal process, there has been a growing discovery from different gatherings and experiences of common ground from which Christians proclaim the good news of Jesus Christ to the world. It invites the individual Christians as well as the churches to fully devote themselves to live out mission in unity. There is a growing awareness tendency that common witness of the life and teaching of Jesus Christ is an authentic way of participating in God's mission. The Church cannot be the Church apart from its unity, and unity always happens in the horizon of the Church.[553] Thus, efforts to come to a greater common understanding and vision of their role in contemporary Christians and reaching out together in Christ's way to new frontiers of mission in listening, accompanying, walking with, resourcing, receiving from one another. Common witness is the witness that the churches, even while separated, bear together, especially through joint efforts, by manifesting whatever divine gifts of truth and life they share and experience in common search for unity among Christians.

Despite the many barriers which keep the churches apart, the NEICC member churches have been able to recognize a certain degree of ecclesial communion among themselves in various activities. Mutual recognition of each member churches is the foundation for Christian unity and common witness. On this basis, other grounds for common witness to the whole world can be affirmed together. Authentic common witness presupposes respect and understanding for other traditions and confessions. What should be emphasized is that which is common and can be done together, rather than the barriers which separate. Even when apparently irreconcilable differences remain on certain issues, the truth

---

[552] "Towards Common Witness to Christ Today: Mission and Visible Unity of the Church" By: World Council of Churches Commission on World Mission and Evangelism. In *International Review of Mission, 99 no 390* (Apr 2010), p. 86-106.

[553] Towards common witness to Christ today ....86-106.

should be spoken in love (Eph. 4:15), for the building up of the church (Eph. 4:12), rather than for giving prominence to one's position over against that of others. There is more that unites the churches than separates them. These unifying elements should be looked for in building up witness in unity.[554]

The Baptist churches in Northeast region are called to identify ways of witnessing in unity, of partnership and Cooperation, and of responsible relationships in evangelism and in order to reach such a mutually enriching unity ethos. The churches must rethink all forms of denominational competition and rivalry and the temptation to proselytize members of other Christian traditions. Perhaps, avoid establishing parallel ecclesial structures, but rather stimulate, help and cooperate with the existing local churches in their evangelistic work. Furthermore, help people who are in process of changing their church allegiance to discern to speak the truth in love to one another with understanding and common witnessing of God's love. In order to overcome the obstacles, we are called to practice common witness as an act of ecumenical evangelism. Common witness is the witness that the different denominational churches, even while separated, bear together, especially through joint efforts, by manifesting whatever divine gifts of truth and life they already share and experience in common call.

8.1.5. CHRISTIAN UNITY AS HEALING AND RECONCILIATION

Since the late 1980s, mission has been increasingly connected with healing and reconciliation. Furthermore, the language of healing and reconciliation has come to the form in many different contexts, and catches the imagination of people both inside and outside the churches. This is certainly also an invitation to the Christian church to promote in this broken world the concept of healing and conciliation in word and deeds.[555]

The Old Testament addresses the estrangement between God and God's people, and also God's work for the healing, reconciliation and restoration of a broken relationship with the God of life and justice. Similarly, in the New Testament, Paul is greatly concerned that those whom Christ has reconciled in his body should not be divided, and that community life should be the first expression of God's plan to reconcile all things. He envisages the unity in Christ of not only Jew and Gentile, but also of slave and free, male and female (Galatians 3:28).

Over the past years, reconciliation has become the emerging new paradigm that defines the unity of the Christian church in today's context. Catholic, Orthodox, Protestant and Pentecostal voices from all over the area increasingly are speaking one and the same language.[556] This should not only be voicing against healing and reconciliation towards injustice in our society, but also participating

---

[554] Towards common witness to Christ today … 86-106.

[555] Towards common witness to Christ today … 86-106.

[556] International Conferences of the International Association of Mission Studies (IAMS) in Malaysia, 2004 and in Hungary, 2008.

in the struggles of the oppressed, which may lead to loss of power, prestige, privilege, and even to death. The majority of the people in Northeast region are in a state of suffering being jobless, sick, oppressed as tribal, exploited, persecuted, rape, hungry and dying. Thus, healing and reconciliation means to steps in on their behalf sand to share in their shames and sufferings. These churches need to adjust and come together as one towards the healing and reconciliation work in evangelization by integrating social responsibility by re-visioning their commitment.

8.1.6. CHRISTIAN UNITY AS CARING FOR CREATION

God made all things good and has entrusted humankind with the responsibility to care for creation (Gen. 2:4b-9). The exploitation of the natural world and the misuse of its finite resources disclose a pattern of violence that often benefits some people at the expense of many. We know that all creation groans to be set free, not least from the abusive actions of humans (Romans 8:22). As people of faith, we acknowledge our guilt for the damage we have done to creation and all living things, through action and our inaction. The vision of Just Peace is much more than the restoration of right relationships in community; it also compels human beings to care for the earth as our home. We must trust in God's promise and strive for an equitable and just sharing of the earth's resources.

The Church in its visible manifestations is a sign, as well as an instrument, of communion with God and of the unity of all. This communion has a triple relational dimension: communion with the triune God, the communion of the Church, and the communion among human beings, and indeed, with the whole created world. [557] Thus, the Church's mission to the world in community becomes a testimony to Christ. In the dynamics of the reconciliation and healing process, truth, memory, justice and forgiveness are understood as essential aspects required within both the church and society at large. Healing and reconciliation as the restoration of right relations with God is the source of healing and reconciliation with oneself, with people of our own faith and other faiths, and with the whole of creation. [558] Therefore we pray, "Come Holy Spirit, heal and reconcile!" Called in Christ to be reconciling and healing communities, we pray that the Holy Spirit will breathe healing power into our knees, and that together we may move forward into the blessed peace of the new creation. It is time for the worldwide Christian family to heal the pain of our divisions, because unity through healing and reconciliation is an integral part of God's mission. This continuous reconciliation, in and through God's love in Christ Jesus, Christian witness becomes an expression

---

[557] Matthey, Jacques (ed.) *Come Holy spirit, Heal and Reconcile! Called in Christ to be Reconciling and Healing Communities. Report of the WCC Conference of World Mission and evangelism, Athens, Greece, May 9-16,* 2005. (Geneva: WCC, 2008).

[558] Geevarghese Mor Coorilos, "New Method of Evangelism and mission," In *International Review of Mission*, 101 No. 395 (Nov 2012), 299-308.

of visible unity in Christ. This witness is manifested by communities that are vibrant in themselves, and where work for peace, justice, reconciliation, and love for the poor cannot but be noticed by the wider world.[559]

The mission of the Church in the power of the spirit is to call people into communion with God, with one another and with creation. In so doing, the Church must honor the intrinsic and inseparable relationship between mission and unity. The Church has the responsibility to live out the unity for which Jesus prayed for his people.[560] As Jesus prayed for the unity of all, not exclusively for Christians and churches, the unity of human community and society and its relationship with creation are also important parts of mission. The Church in mission is thus to witness to the life-giving power of God as it is manifested by the work of the Holy Spirit liberating women and men and communities from all kinds of evils that are countering the fullness of life. As the subject of Christian unity in the triune God, we are the servants of God, who has given us the mission of proclaiming the good news to all suffering humanity and creation longing for a new hope in their lives. In this new vision, creation is not simply deemed an object of human concern, but also as an agent of God's mission where creation becomes a channel of divine grace and blessing for Christian unity.

8.1.7. CHRISTIAN UNITY AS MISSIO DEI

At the Willingen world mission conference in 1952, the rediscovery and reinterpretation of the ancient Trinitarian concept of the *Missio Dei* led the way out of the crisis of the concept of mission. *Missio Dei* became a frame of reference for defining mission. According to this notion, God's mission is directly related to the world, and the church is defined as the instrument a privileged instrument of God's mission of redemption and recreation of humanity and of the cosmos. This theological paradigm shift in the interpretation of mission has far-reaching ecclesiological consequences. In this concept, it is impossible to separate mission and Christian unity.[561]

In this sense doing mission and the Christian unity has deeply interrelated. At the Rolle 1951 meeting of the Central Committee of the WCC, this conviction was already powerfully articulated in its theological reflections on the relationship of the concepts of ecumenism and Christian unity:

> It is important to insist that this word ecumenical, which comes from the Greek word for the whole inhabited earth, is properly used to describe everything that relates to the whole task of the whole church

[559] Athanasios N. Papathanasiou, "Mission a Consequence of the Catholicity of the Church? An Orthodox Perspective," *International Review of Mission* 90:359 (2001), 409-416.

[560] Towards common witness to Christ today ... 86-106.

[561] Oliphant, Anderson and Ferrier, "The Central Place of Missions in the life of the Church." In: *World Missionary Conference 1910,* Edinburgh and London, s.d., Vol IX; cited in Towards common witness to Christ today ... 86-106.

to bring the Gospel to the whole world. It therefore covers equally the missionary movement and the movement towards unity, and must not be used to describe the latter in contradistinction to the former. We believe that a real service will be rendered to true thinking on these subjects in the Churches if we so use this word that it covers both Unity and Mission in the context of the whole world.[562]

The sad realities that there are parallel traditional Christian structures in North East region and that there is still much distrust, and sometimes even animosity, challenge our generation with a heavy responsibility as we seek the visible unity of the church of the Lord Jesus Christ today. There is, at the same time, an ever growing diversity of all kinds of interdenominational cooperation in mission. A growing communication in the area of unity can be recognized overarching denominational borders in Baptist and other denominational circles.

Thus the quest for the visible unity of the church has always been, and still is, its primary goal, especially in the context of, and for the sake of, the authenticity of participation in God's mission, painful experiences of divisions and disunity remain in the life of the church, hindering churches in putting the missionary nature of the church into practice.[563]

The theological foundation of mission in unity is built on the fellowship of the triune God. Christian unity is based on the infinite love of God, who created the whole world out of nothing and then proceeded to create all humankind in his image and likeness, so as to make us partakers of this ineffable love. The Father then sent the Son (John 16:5) to fulfill the plan of God's salvific work. The Word of God became incarnate by the Holy Spirit and became human. At Pentecost the Holy Spirit was sent to enlighten the apostles and to empower them for their missionary ministry. This inner communion of the Holy Trinity is the source of the unity of the Church. The aim of God's mission is to invite every human being to experience fellowship with God and with one another according to the inner unity of the One God in three persons.

The mission of God is the source of and basis for the mission of the church, the body of Christ. Through Christ in the Holy Spirit, God indwells the church, empowering and energizing its members. Thus mission becomes for Christians an urgent inner compulsion, even a powerful test and criterion for authentic life in Christ, rooted in the profound demands of Christ's love, to invite others to share in the fullness of life Jesus came to bring (John 10:10). The Christians in Northeast

---

562 WCC *Minutes and Reports of the Fourth Meeting of the Central Committee, Rolle (Switzerland), August 4 -11, 1951*, p. 65. cited in Towards common witness to Christ today … 86-106.

563 Norman Good, ed., Missions under the Cross: Addresses Delivered at the Enlarged Meeting of the International Missionary Council at Willingen, Germany, 1952, with Statements Issued by the Meeting (London: Edinburg House press,1953), 189. Cited in Towards common witness to Christ today … 86-106.

should realize the important of participating in God's mission, therefore, should be natural for all Christians and all churches, not only for particular individuals or specialized groups.

8.1.8. CHRISTIAN UNITY AS WITNESSING HOPE IN CHRIST

The mission of Jesus Christ is to proclaim and demonstrate the kingdom of God to the world. The salvific work of Christ starts with the proclamation ('k*erygma*) of conversion (*metanoia*) because "the kingdom of God has come near" Mark 1:15). Thus, the world will believe and find the way to reconciliation with God and one another and be saved. Jesus Christ, through his obedience to the Father, is led to the ultimate humiliation. He undergoes insults, suffers on the cross, dies as a human, and is raised from the dead to offer new life to human beings mired in sin. After the Ascension and the event of Pentecost, the mission of Jesus Christ is carried forth by the sending of the Holy Spirit upon the Church for the salvation of all until he comes again.[564]

We believe in Christ, who "made himself nothing" (Phil 2:7) through incarnation up to the consequences of suffering death on the cross, as well as in the resurrected Lord who was raised from the dead. Jesus became our Christ not through power (or money) but through his *kenosis.* Therefore the disciples who have been sent by Christ to proclaim his good news have to follow in his footsteps by witnessing to his humility and humbleness in their own practice of mission. This *kenotic* understanding of mission does not merely shape our methods, but is the very nature and essence of our faith in Christ. The missionary Church serves the glorifying of God in a doxology of *kenotic* love.

8.1.9. CHRISTIAN UNITY AS WITNESSING IN HOLY SPIRIT

Humanity, as God's creation, is blessed with a great variety of diverse and complementary gifts that are expressed in a multiplicity of cultural and historical contexts. It is God's design that such diversity does not lead to separation and division, to opposition and hostility but to interdependence and harmony. When considering the ministry of the Holy Spirit as a ministry of unity it is essential to see the work of the spirit as equipping the Church to experience unity in diversity both proactively and constructively. The spirit becomes the helper who transforms the problem of difference into the promise of diversity.[565]

The Spirit is also the teacher who provides both the dynamic context and resources needed for people to explore differences in a safe, positive, nurturing environment. Individuals from a variety of backgrounds, and with ideas and concepts new to their experience, need an appropriate educational framework in which to understand each other and to move beyond simple tolerance to embrace

---

[564] Towards common witness to Christ today ... 86-106.

[565] Towards common witness to Christ today ... 86-106.

and celebrate the rich dimensions of diversity that are contained within each individual and community.

Every church is called by the Holy Spirit to be a healing, reconciling community in full fellowship the Church across time and space, through proclamation and witness according to the scriptures. In affirmation of the Church's attributes one, holy, catholic and apostolic our witness to Christ is both catholic and apostolic. Hence, Christian witness expresses the apostolic faith across centuries through worship and diakonia in communion with Christ, in succession to the witness of the apostles, as it was lived out by the first Christian communities.

When considering the ministry of the Holy Spirit as a ministry of unity it is essential to see the work of the spirit as equipping the Church to experience unity in diversity both proactively and constructively. The spirit becomes the helper who transforms the problem of difference into the promise of diversity. It is essential for the Church to acknowledge its brokenness and repent of its present shortcomings. Striving for good health within the body of Christ needs to be seen as an integral part of the Church's mission. Therefore the Christians in Northeast India Baptist churches should undertake significant strategies and initiatives needs to be taken in order to ensure that responding to the Spirit's work will allow such recovery and restoration of unsuccessful attempt of Christian unity in the region.

8.1.10. CHRISTIAN UNITY AS UNIVERSAL ASPECT OF THE GOSPEL

In NEI, one of the major hindrances to unity among missions and churches is because of lack of understanding in Christian gospel. Instead of complimenting each other's denominational set up, we want to outrun others. However, let me be clear here, we are not competing in Christian denominationalism at least not for the sake of reports and funding. Yes, there can be room for competitiveness with the right perspective and that is to excel in the task God has given to the churches where we need to give our best effort to accomplish it. So, let us be reminded that we need to learn to complement each other's church traditions. Togetherness with love and understanding should, therefore, become the common platform for the Christian unity in NEI where every church, mission and Christian organization can come together to fulfill the Great Commission of Jesus Christ both in social and spiritual realms.

Christian Unity in reconciled diversity is evident on a wide scale at local level. Christ really has broken down the wall that divides and effected reconciliation reaching far beyond. Christians bear witness to their oneness in all the ways that matter: working together, worshipping together, weeping together, eating together, praying together, sharing the same facilities, rejoicing together and doing dozens of other tasks together. The challenge to ecumenical enthusiasts is to see this vision transmitted upward or, perhaps more to the point, to get out of the way and let it happen. There is an issue which is quietly tormenting the consultation on church union movement in NEI.

In the days ahead we need far more creative approach about the shape of the church and dedicated pursuit of the unity God wills for the church. We need far wider participation by ministers and lay people in the process, especially the participation of students and professors in the theological seminaries where ecumenism has been woefully eclipsed. We need far greater understanding of models of church unity in the Northeast context of the struggle for unity and renewal in the human community. With these perspectives the search for visible unity will become less of a doctrinal debate and more of a faith pilgrimage. The challenge therefore at all times is to engage in an effort to clarify, re-energies and reaffirm the ecumenical vision taking care to discover where its inner dynamic lies embedded, so as to give it the space to grow in the love of Christ. As a congregation of believers, witnessing to the gospel is inseparable from the daily witness we as Christians are called to live in unity and co-operation.

8.2. RE-VISIONING OF VISIBLE CHRISTIAN UNITY

Looking back the history there developed in subsequent years a wide spectrum of new ecumenical activities and at least initially, there was a positive expectation that leaving aside all ecclesiological difficulties, it would be possible to build up close cooperation the North East India Christian Council and the Baptist Churches in Northeast region. It might seem that the idea of unity would be distant to Baptist's, having given their strong views on independence and their doctrine of the autonomy of the church, but such is not the case. It all depends on what is meant by unity.

Baptists are not all of one mind about the Christian unity in the region. There are number of Baptist Associations and Conventions have been prominently identified and working with their own tribes. Some have participated in certain activities and on some occasions, but not on others.

At the present time Baptist groups who took membership with the CBCNEI are; The Council comprises Assam Baptist Convention, Arunachal Baptist Church Council, Garo Baptist Convention, Karbi Anglong Baptist Convention, Manipur Baptist Convention and Nagaland Baptist Church Council. They (Baptist) are moreover, a heterogeneous community, with considerable differences in theological outlook, polity and church practice and, though characterised by a strong sense of fellowship and brotherhood, have no central church authority. Each associations and convention determines its own' attitudes and standards.

For Baptist organic union is generally looked on unfavourably but federal set up or cooperation with other denominations would be possible. Baptist organizations are largely voluntary, cooperative ventures that have no legal binding force over their members. This is part of the Baptists ethos, allowing for freedom and concerted action to exist at the same time. Hence, the denominations do not exist as units, but are simply collections of individual Baptist churches. Thus, organic union with other denominations, if it requires giving up Baptist distinctives, is not favourable for them.

At the same time, Baptists approach to church union will undoubtedly be rooted in the recognition that it is insufficient for Baptists to be alone. The language of covenant is central to Baptists life and thought. It is the conviction that Baptists are bound together in covenant relationship with God and with one another, and this conviction is one that must be extended to include the wider Christian family. The commitment to seeking unity is an affirmation that all Christians already exist in covenant relationship, whether they like it or not, and so Baptists ecumenical horizon calls us to engage in shared worship, learning and serving. They are incomplete when they are left on their own. With the humble trust and openness that marks true covenant relationships.[566] Baptists must recognize that they cannot see only to themselves as part of the church, rather they also part of other denominations. Perhaps they are also in need of others in order to continue the ecumenical journey.

It might be said that each denomination has a distinctive calling, within the life of the wider church. For Baptists the commitment to the local will, perhaps, always be an important contribution, both to ecumenical life and to the way in which ecumenism is done. Therefore a proposal for any unity should not aim at structural unity but instead it should be primarily at developing a greater sense of understanding and cooperation among Christians. The present-day churches need not only a spiritual unity but now they need an effective church unity to witness the one Lord among the people.[567] But, the question is what kind of church unity could be an acceptable and viable model to the churches in North East India, particularly to Baptist churches. However, this study among the Baptist and other churches in North East region show that although the Baptists may raise the above and other objections, they would allow more exceptions and alternatives for the sake of unity in the church. The contemporary Baptists theologians and Christians are becoming more and more open to the tradition of other churches in NEI. This could be seen as a sign of hope to achieve an affective church union movement in NEI as CBCNEI did with WCC.

Once again, the hope for a larger realization of necessity for Christian unity still kept springing up in some Baptist hearts. One sign of hope is a renewed consciousness among Baptist Christians in NEI that the Holy Spirit who has placed in the human heart the desire for communion is also guiding the churches in living more profoundly the mystery of communion, so that they may become

---

566 Wayne Dehoney, "Southern Baptists and Ecumenism: Options for the Future," *Review & Expositor*, 66/3 (Summer, 1969), 314.

567 Nikos A. Nissiotis, "Towards a New Ecumenical Era," *Ecumenical Review*, 37/3 (July, 1985), 326ff.

more credible signs of this unity and more capable of responding together to the urgent need for unity among humankind.

Today many churches in NEI have made efforts to offer a deeper re-visioning of Christian unity, especially to those being trained for theological and pastoral ministries in their church. Re-thinking in such basic attitudes as sensitivity to the presence and action of God in the lives of other Christians, respect for the integrity of other Christian churches, openness to what is lived in them and willingness to learn from them, honesty about what needs to be renewed in our own church, humility to enter into dialogue, will help prepare a future that conforms better to the will of Christ for his church.

In search for the re-visioning of visible unity of the Church has always been and still is its primary goal for the Baptist churches in Northeast India, especially in the context of and for the sake of the authenticity of its participation in God's mission. There are still painful experiences of divisions and disunity present in the life of the Church, which hinder churches in putting the missionary nature of the Church into practice. In Christian understanding, unity has its foundation outside itself, in the unity of the triune God and in our being sent by Christ. This underlying, already existing, unity is the inward side of our being Church in a missionary way. How can this inner unity be understood? Is it necessarily identical with ecclesial or even structural unity? While we experience that cultural and linguistic diversity significantly challenges ecclesial unity today in NEI, and has challenged it throughout the ages, we do recognize that the visions of unity are contextual, too. Unity must be understood contextually, just as Christians in NEI understood its very core of mission and church are.

8.3. CONCLUSION

The Christian unity provides the churches with wider opportunities to work and witness together unity in service proved to be one of the most concrete and tangible manifestation of the churches. It tried to enumerate some of the means like education, social action and partnership in mission etc. to show a possible avenue where churches could work together to reduce the hostility and to create an atmosphere of Christian unity and solidarity with others. So while not many Baptists would hold to a vision of structural unity, one's need to accept the challenge of offering its own contribution to shaping and re-visioning what it means to live together and serve together in the future.

Conclusion

This book has been mainly meant to determine the challenges of Church Union Movement before the Baptist churches, which have been working against the formation and further development of Christian Unity in Northeast India. The research is based on the historical analysis of the pattern of church union discussion among the Protestant churches in Northeast India. The North East India Christian Council is only Christian Unity outfit in the region so far, yet the attempt has been a failure, due to the negative attitude shown from the Baptist, who constitutes one of the largest single denominations in the region.

It is identified that the Northeast India refers to the easternmost region of India consisting of eight States. They are composed of many diverse kind of people, culture, social, language and political structural system. Yet each group had developed its own worldview and had lived an independent life, isolated from that of the other community. In such background, in which different Christian missionaries (form American Baptist, Welsh Presbyterian, Lutheran, Anglican, British Baptist, Roman Catholic etc.) brought Christianity to this region. This led to establishment of different denominational church in the region. Most of them have become familiar to traditions and practices, which they inherited from their mother churches. This led to have more loyalty to its own church discipline rather than being involved in a wider Christian Unity.

The twentieth century has been a time when the presence of the modern ecumenical movement became evident in the Christian awareness. The world missionary conference that took place in Edinburgh in June, 1910 perceived 'the evangelization of the world in this generation' as a great challenge. Beginning from the World Missionary Conference the idea of Christian Unity, became the common discussion in many churches and the churches began to show interest in the church union movement. The form and structures of church union, which was carried out by the various organizations and churches were different forms of church unity. However, the wave of church unity started to spread across the world, which was also felt even among the protestant churches in Northeast India.

The impacts of the world ecumenical movements were more visible in other parts of India than in the Northeast India, those upshots were the Church of South India and the Church of North India. Although, some churches in the North East India participated in the talk for North India Union, but later they decided not to join the union because of geographical difficulties. On the other hand, they worked out a plan for a separate church union for Northeast India, but the church union has not yet been successful. Thus, a major task of the churches is that the unity of the Christian in the region believing in Christ remains unfulfilled.

The fact is that though the efforts of various Christian activities in NEI, brought the differences in church doctrine and discipline often lead to unfounded suspicion among the people. These frequently inflict severe strains upon the internal unity of the Christians in NEI. As such many church leaders have felt the need for church unity in the region. The effort was made under the name, Assam Christian Council formed in 1926, with the idea of having unity and co-operation by common counsel among the various Christian bodies in NEI. Since 1964 there were two Northeast Faith and Order and two Church Union Conferences under the auspices of NEICC. The basis of church union plan and the draft constitution were formulated and distributed to constituent members for study and response. But the Council of Baptist Churches in North East India, the largest Baptist body in the region had rejected the plan of union and draft constitution and refused to participate further in church union negotiations. Thus, the whole church union discussion lost its original momentum and for a certain period of time the church union discussions came to a halt.

The reasons given for this failure being matters related to baptism, power and terms of Episcopacy and the centralized form of church government in the draft constitution. Besides, denominational identities, different rituals and an uncommon history of origins also contributed to the unfruitful nature of the negotiation. It is significant to note that the theological issues as well as non-theological factors are main obstacles to the church union discussions in NEI.

Henceforth, there is challenge that Christian Unity could play an important part in uniting those separated ideology of tribalism, socio-cultural differences and the divisions between the hills tribes and plainsmen and, it fostered the development of a new sense of unity and fellowship with divisive potential to work against such isolation. Thus, Christian Unity as a stage in the realization of the Kingdom of God is construed as the bringing of the whole tribes into the union. But, the question stand still, where do Baptist churches under the Council of Baptist Churches in NEI (CBCNEI) stand in the Northeast India ecumenical stream? They have refused participation in the North East India Christian Council since 1970s. Though, church union movement lost its momentum, it is not a dead issue as some would like to think. But the question is what type of unity should we look for that would best suit our particular context of the Northeast India and which can be of help in the common witness and service.

Whether this kind of thinking propels the CBCNEI into the mainstream of ecumenism depends upon attitudes at the grass roots level, not in the upper echelons of leadership. Baptist churches in NEI profess to be strong advocates of the democratic form of government, they definitely are strong Congregationalists. As such most Baptists feared that organic incorporation would ultimately impair the truths for which Baptist stand. However, there is considerable difference of opinion among Baptists on some structural relation to other Christian churches. Meanwhile, there no lack of recognition of the value of practical cooperation in Christian work and witness with other churches and some pointed out the value of personal contacts with members of other churches as preparing for the larger realization of unity in the future. Once again, the desire for collaboration in Christian witness was expressed. Yet, the hope for a larger realization of unity still keeps springing up in Baptist hearts.

Perhaps what is needed is a model of union which is less than a unified system of church government but which provides more fellowship and co-operation, which does not require the demise of present church identities. A federal set up of churches would create a new church identity while retaining old identities. The churches or communities in a federal union model give organizational expression to all the affiliated churches which live in one communion with a mutual recognition of members, ministry, and shared sacraments. No participating church would be expected to sacrifice its present identity or radically modify its internal discipline. Therefore, such a scheme of unity which exhibits Christian unity and diversity is to be created within the scheme of union.

The Christian churches in NEI should face the new challenges with courage and determination. Challenges are an invitation for further growth and maturity. The Baptist contribution to Christian unity posed the question, to what extent are Baptists prepared for closer incorporation with other branches of the Christian church, in order to give expression to the church unity. Baptists desire to see more fellowship, dialogue and cooperation across denominational lines, without any hostile and prejudice. Which need to consider one another honestly with mutual respect, appreciation and recognition. The vital task for all the churches and Christians is to come together with mutual trust and acceptability among the different denominations, which might ultimately lead to form a possible church union in the region.

Finally, in Christian Unity journey there is always a hope for future that even Northeast India churches can enter into unity by mutual co-operation and common understanding of God's mission. The North East India Christian Council needs always to promote itself to the imperative need for a healthier union and it should strive humble seeking God's will for churches in region. If the ecumenical movement is to be understood as a process of conversation into which

God is leading His people then each part of the church must show its readiness to listen as well as to speak. This advance towards church unity will demonstrate that difficulty in a manner all too obvious, but it is being written in the hoped that it will be an indication of some readiness among Baptist to engage in this difficulty aspect of the church union conversation. There needs to be a constant reaffirmation and recognition of what ecumenism is all about. It is not just about re-organizing the church, or even about enabling the churches to witness to their own unity. It is about the unity and cooperation of all Christians that finds its life in God. It is important to affirm the signs of hope, in places where energy is allowing new ecumenical ventures to flourish. Look forward to a reality that transcends every human borderline that stands in the way of realisation of God's ultimate plan to sum up all things in Christ.

Common witness is the shared experience arising from our encountering with the risen Christ. This experiential testimony flows out in the proclamation of the good news in word and deed. We are human as we are Christians. This means that in the mediation of God's love, we listen to others by affirming our common humanity, just as God in Christ shared in our humanity, and through that process redeemed us from the power of sin. Baptist Christians in region invites to recognize our common divine heritage and to extend the love of Christ as revealed in him to others in a spirit of humility.

The missionary unity of the Church is the basis of the structural unity of the churches. Therefore, the structures must be related to the unity of the Church and thus to the unity of the churches. This is the reason to strive for more structural unity while at the same time holding that the visible unity is not restricted to structural visibility. Seeking unity in mission together is not an impossible task. Indeed, it is one of the most authentic ways of participating in God's mission. Witnessing to the gospel is inseparable from the daily witness, we as Christians are called to give in solidarity for the common good.

The sin and brokenness of our world is a reality that can be neither ignored nor minimized. It results in the alienation of humanity from God and from the person, the family, the churches, communities, nations, and creation, and leads to structural injustice as well. The sin of individual human beings contributes to the wider disorder and evil that affect the whole of creation. Paul expresses this graphically when he writes that "the whole creation has been groaning" (Rom. 8:22). This cry for help seeks healing and reconciliation. In response, the Church is called to be a healing and reconciling community. The answer is found in the healing and reconciling ministry of Jesus Christ as a model for the Church to follow today. Healing and reconciliation include the transformation of life made possible by crossing cultural and religious boundaries. In this connection, it becomes important for the Church to realize that her calling is a response to the gifts of healing and reconciliation, which equip and enable her to fulfill that role. The healing and reconciling ministry of Jesus Christ has always been an integral part of his mission. A closer look at the experience of various churches will show a consistent link between both salvation and healing and salvation and reconciliation. A rediscovery of the work of the Holy spirit in healing and reconciliation, which is at the heart of today's mission theology, has significant ecumenical implications.

It was a very ambitious plan to bring churches in NEI to bring together; however, it is still a not yet accomplished task. We have to continue this journey with a fresh attempt today, so that the Church becomes truly missionary church. At the same time, we need to open up our failure on Christian Unity discussion and bringing into a new paradigm hope to a wider understanding of Christian Unity, the unity with the poor and needy, and even the cosmic unity of the whole of God's creation. The Christian Unity that is grounded in our commitment to the Lordship of Jesus Christ while he pled for unity just before the Atonement, "That they may all be One, as thou Father, are in me and I am in you, so that the world may believe that you have sent me." (John 17:21).

APPENDIX-1

The Plan of Church Union and Draft Constitution of North East India, 1970. Compiled and Edited by the Convenor, Church Union Committee and Published by the North East India Christian Council.

I. THE PLAN OF UNION

I. Historical Statement

Since 1963 there have been two Faith and Order Conferences and two Church Union Conferences apart from general discussions in the Council itself for a number of years on the question of church union. The original plan was whether the affiliated churches of Northeast India (NEI) should form apart of the church of North India then in the negotiating stage. In view of certain objections and the practical difficulties involved in relating the churches of our area to such a union with the church of North India, the affiliated churches of this Council felt that in the circumstances now obtaining in India, it would be wiser to work towards a union within NEI itself in the first instance. Even the two churches namely, the Eastern Himalayan Church Council (UCNI) and the Assam Diocese of the CIPBC which have been effectively represented in the CNI negotiations expressed their preference for joining the Church of NEI, if it comes into being. The working committee of the Negotiating Committee of the CNI which met in Calcutta in July 1969 also expressed its appreciation of the view of the NEICC and the consensus of opinion was that the two units of the CNI in this region would be allowed to join the church of NEI if and when it comes into being.

The second draft of the Basis of union for the churches in NEI was formulated in November 1965 by delegates representing eight six percent of the non-Roman Catholic Christians in NEI as well as by observers representing another seven percent totaling 93% of the non-Roman Catholic Christians of NEI most of whom are either Baptist or Presbyterians. The second draft as well as Dr Downs paper entitled "Church Union: Theological and Non-theological Factors," were printed and circulated to all the affiliated churches. Many churches had translated the above two papers into the local languages either as booklet or as publications of the NEICC many of whom have accepted the second Draft as the Basis of union. Some units, most notable among which is the CBCNEI, have by and large accepted it at the higher levels but they have yet to carry all the associations and local congregations with them. This is understandable in the context of the organizations of each affiliated church as well as in view of the variegated nature of our multi-ethnic and multi-lingual community with different social background and heritage. But, the wind of charge has been blowing and circumstances have compelled us to draw closer to each other. Above all, the Holy Spirit is silently but surely working towards unity in spite of obstacles.

In the last Church Union Conference held in Shillong on September 19 and 20, 1969 we have gone one step ahead in deciding to set up this drafting Committee which will prepare the plan of Union and the Draft Constitution of the Church of NEI. Such a Plan of union and Draft Constitution will enable the affiliated churches to study more closely and concretely what would be the implications of Church Union thereby enabling them to grapple with and come to decisions on the basic issues of union.

II. Statement of Intention

At the level of the leadership, it was generally felt that the Churches should first unite in mutual trust, leaving the settlement of their smaller differences to be worked out in the context of the larger fellowship. In this context it may be noted that the CSI will be inaugurated in Nov. 1970. We in NEI have been moving slow because of several factors. Social changes are taking place at a very rapid pace in this world, and we in NEI have to catch up or else be swamped by undesirable ideologies. The churches cannot afford to be self-centered any longer. If we are not dynamic and live in a vacuum other forces will fill up the void with all undesirable consequences. Even while attempting to draw up a scheme that would be more relevant to our own region we cannot lose sight that we are part of a larger church even within India and so we should maintain a larger ecumenical perspective.

We Christian of NEI still belong to different denominations which have names like Baptist, Presbyterian, Lutheran, Anglican etc. If such names separate Christians from each other, then they are contrary to the teaching of the Bible. In this draft it is purpose that the now separated churches in our region unite because it has the will of God and to give a stronger witness different denominations will be formed, but the existing churches need to have larger their fellowship to include all the other Christians in the regions into one church representing all the protestant Christians instead of the more than fifteen separated denominations that now exist.

In former times that need for this kind of united church organization was not so great because there was some communications between the different parts of our areas. Today with the rapid progress of our peoples, the situations are very different. Government officers move from place to place and young people travel outside their own areas to study. In the towns and the cities, Christians from many different denominations live together but cannot have a congregation of their own together. Some of them are always guest of the denominations in that place-guest when they should be equally full members of that local church. Because of improved communications non-Christians are also becoming more aware of the divisions among Christians. This becomes a stumbling block for them. When they are asked to accept Christ as their Savior they ask, 'to which church shall I belong?" Because they receive many different answers they turn away, Christ said, that His disciples must be united so that all men are one in Christ. The presence of many different denominations denies this truth. Christians who condemn each other and do not have fellowship with each other bear false witness. Christians themselves are confused about the differences between the denominations. If Christians are confused, how much more confused must the non Christian be. For the sake of Christ kingdom, the stumbling block must be removed.

III Our Approach to Unity

The kind of united church that is proposed will not solve certain problem but it will give us greater strength towards the problem. The following are the few points on which a great measure of unanimity has been reached in past conferences and discussions:

a) The churches now in existence would join wider in an one organic body.
   No immediate changes will be imposed at the level of the local congregations on in the organizations such as Associations, Presbyteries or similar Councils which bring the congregation in one language area together.
b) The forms of worship and witness that now exist may continue until the uniting churches feel the need for a common form of worship.
c) There would be about ten Councils or more above the level of the Associations or similar authorities which would bring the associations or presbyteries within a region together.

d) There would be a central Assembly which would bring the Councils together.
e) There would be greater sharing of leadership and resources.
f) It is recognized that there are certain traditional differences among the denominations that would be coming together in the united church. These differences are important. It is not proposed that Christians should compromise or deny what they believe to be the truth. But, the best way to witness to the truth as we understand it is to witness within one fellowship. Even within the denominations are they now exit there are difference of opinion and theology, but that does not prevent each other as fellow members of the church, because God has given His own blessing to the work of each of the denominations in our area.

The Draft Constitution of the Church of North East India

I. The Name of the Church

1. The name of this Church of (sic) is the Church of North-East India.
2. The Church of North-East India is constituted by the Union of the following Churches:-

(a) The CBCNEI
(b) The Presbyterian Church of NEI
(c) The Diocese of Assam (CIPBC)
(d) The Eastern Himalayan Church Council
(e) The Baptist Church of Mizo District
(f) The North Bank Baptist Association
(g) The Tripura Baptist Christian Union
(h) The Northern Evangelical
(i) Luteran Church
(j) The Lakher Independent Evangelical Church
(k) The Church of God
(l) The Church of God (Ka Turoi Gospel)
(m) The Christ National Church
(n) Salvation Army (?)
(o) Goalpara Baptist Church
(p) Other Churches which may join at a leter (sic) stage

II. The Church and its Membership

The CNEI acknowledges that the Church is the Body of Christ in which members are knit together in the fellowship of the Holy Spirit. It agrees that those are member according to the will and purpose of God who are born again by the grace into the name of the Father and of the Son and of the Holy Spirit. It agrees that members of the Church maintain their vital union with the Head of the Body through the various means of grace which He has provided in His Church, and glorify His name by such good works as He has prepared for them to walk in.

The Church is the People of God, the Community of the Holy Spirit, the Body of Christ through which He continues His reconciling work in the world;

The Church is one because it is one family under one Father, whose purpose is to unite all men in Jesus Christ our Lord;

The Church is holy because it is set apart by God for Himself through the Holy Spirit to be His people in the world;

The Church is Catholic (universal) because it is for all people and for all times holding the Christian faith in its fullness;

The Church is apostolic because it is sent to preach the Gospel in the world and to proclaim the Lordship of Christ over the world, receiving its divine authority and teaching from Jesus Christ.

III. The Faith of the Church

1. The CNEI holds the faith in Jesus Christ, the Redeemer of the world, in whom alone is salvation by grace through faith, and in accordance with the revelation of God which He made being Himself God incarnate, we worship one God Father, Son and Holy.
2. It accepts the Holy Scriptures of the Old and New Testament as the Word of God, as containing all things necessary, to salvation, and as the supreme and decisive standard of faith and acknowledges that it must always be ready to correct and reform itself in accordance with the teaching of those Scriptures under the guidance of the Holy Spirit.
3. It accepts the creed commonly called the Apostles' Creed as witnessing to and safeguarding that faith which is continuously confirmed by the Holy Spirit in the experience of the Church.

IV. The Sacraments of the Church

1. The CNEI believes that the Sacraments of Baptism and Supper of the Lord (Holy Communion) as ordained by Christ are means of grace through which God works in us and by which we are united to God. It also believes that while the mercy of God to all mankind cannot be limited, there is in the teaching of Christ the plain command that men should follow His appointed way of salvation by a definite act of reception in the family of God (Baptism), and by continued acts of fellowship with Him in that family (Holy Communion), and this teaching is made explicit in the two sacraments which He has given us. It agrees that the sacraments should administered in the CNEI with the use always of Christ's word of institution and with the appropriate elements.

A. BAPTISM

2. The Sacrament of Baptism is a sign and seal of the Covenant of grace, of union with Christ in His Body, of forgiveness of sins in his Blood, of death to sin and rebirth to eternal life through Him. By this sacrament we are solemnly admitted into the household of faith for the lifelong service of Jesus Christ.
3. The Church of North-East India allows both Infant Baptism and Believers' Baptism but not both on the same person and shall receive as communicant members all those who have been baptized or confirmed. It assures freedom of expression for the particular convictions of different traditions.
4. All ministers of the Church shall be free to administer either or both forms of Baptism. A minister who, for conscientious reasons, is unable to administer Baptism to infants shall be free to invite some other minister of the Church to perform the rite.

B. HOLY COMMUNION OR LORD'S SUPPER

1. The Sacrament of the Lord's Supper (Holy Communion), as a showing forth of the Word of God, is the supreme set of Christian worship and the sign and seal of the covenant of redemption. It is the Thanksgiving or the Eucharist in which the Church members join with the incarnation of God in Christ and His perfect life on earth, His sufferings, death, resurrection, reign, words and action, shows forth His death until he comes, and pleads His sacrifice proclaims His victory over evil, and in Him shares together in life with God. Partaking in faith we receive Him sacramentally to our nourishment and growth in grace, presenting ourselves in Him a living sacrifice to God. In Him and also with these gathered in faith at the Lord's Table and with all God's company in heaven and on earth. Christ thus restores the penitent, assures them of God's steadfast love and draws them closer to Himself and to the whole Church.
2. In the service of Holy Communion, bread and wine shall be set apart with the unfailing use of Christ's words of institution.
3. Subject to para 2 above, and until an agreed liturgy in one or more forms have been formulated by the CNEI, any form of service of Holy Communion which before the Union was in use in the uniting Churches may be used.
4. The celebration of the Holy Communion shall be performed only by those who have by ordination received authority thereto.
5. Only those who have received full membership through Baptism and some form of Entry or Confirmation service and who are not under discipline are eligible to partake of the Holy Communion as communicants.

V. The Ministry of the Church

A. *The Ministry of the Whole Church*

The NEIC believes that the Church is a royal priesthood through which the risen and ascended Christ continues His High Priestly work. All its members are called, by virtue of their union with Christ, to a priestly ministry; both Godward, in the offering of spiritual sacrifices, gifts and prayers for mankind; and manward, in the showing forth by life and word of the glory of the redeeming power of God. No individual and no one order in the Church can claim exclusive possession of this priesthood.

It recognizes that it is the duty and privileges of every member to share in that service of God which is the ministry of the whole Church. This ministry includes both the laity and the clergy, each exercising its own ministry. Within this ministry, it recognizes and welcome a rich diversity of gifts both in men and women. It will be the prime concern of the Church that all its members should contribute fully to its life of worship, witness and service.

B. *The Special Ministry*

1. The CNEI believes that within this ministry of the whole Church, Christ has given a special ministry of the Word and the Sacraments. To this ministry some are set apart, receiving authority not simply from the Church but from Christ the Head of the Church. The special ministry is one of the organs of the Body through which Christ the Head acts by the Holy Spirit to build up the Body and to equip its members for their part in the ministry of the whole Church.

   It believes that the special ministry is a gift of God to His Church through Christ, who gave to His Apostles a commission which He perpetuates in the Church. It believes that God Himself calls men into the ministry of the Word and the Sacraments; and that He sets apart for the ministry, in answer to the prayers of His Church, those whom He has called and His Church has accepted. He perpetuates in the Church. It believes that God Himself calls men into the ministry of the Word and the Sacraments; and that He sets apart for the ministry, in answer to the prayers of His Church, those whom He has called and His Church has accepted. He thus bestows on and assures to them a commission which His grace enables to fulfill. It believes that the Church has the right and duty to test the vocation of those who believe themselves to be called by God into the special ministry. it believes that the member of the special ministry have a special responsibility in the proclamation of the Word of God to all men; in the administration of the Sacraments; in the offering of worship to God; in the building up of the Body of Christ; in pastoral care; and in the exercise of Church disciple.

2. The special ministry of the CNEI shall consist of Elders or Deacons, Pastors or Priests and Bishop.

3. *Elders or Deacons*

The CNEI agrees that there shall be recognized in the Church the office of Elder or Deacon. In each congregation men and women shall be elected by the congregation after prayer and careful consideration as persons who are recognized as having the appropriate spiritual gifts (Acts 6:3) for this office and shall be set apart in a solemn public service of the Church. Elders or Deacons shall share with ministers in the spiritual care, nurture and government of the Church, in evangelism and Christian service, in the conduct of public worship and in the preaching of the Word. Insofar as possible it is expected that Elders or Deacons shall undertake a course of Bible Study and Doctrine as arranged by the Church. All Elders or Deacons of a congregation will be members of the governing body of the congregation. Elders or Deacons shall be represented in the higher councils or assemblies of the Church in accordance with the Constitution.

4. *Pastors or Priests*

In any particular place or community, the Ministry of the Word and the Sacraments will be exercised by the Pastors. A Pastor will normally be posted by the Association or Presbytery to minister in a particular town, village(s) or district called a "pastorate". As the Church in any place has from Christ a mission to all the people of that place, so the Pastor as a minister of the Word and the sacraments will have a concern for all who live within the pastorate and especially for proclaiming God's Word to the whole community. It will be the duty of the Pastor as the ordained servant of the gospel by which the Church lives to strive to keep the life of the Church and of every member thereof in obedience to the Word and under the grace of God. He will do this interceding for the people committed to his charge, by preaching the Word of God, by administering the Sacraments, the Faith, by pastoral care, guidance, warning and encourage forgiveness. His relation to his people will be that of servant of Christ and shepherd of the flock.

5. *Bishops*

The Bishop will be a servant of Christ and for Christ's sake a servant of His flock in a Church Council's area.

The Bishop will be the shepherd under Christ of His flock in a Church Council's area, and their father in God. Under the guidance of the Holy Spirit and in Christ's name he will have a concern for all who live in the Council's area, whether Christians or not; and within the Christian community he will care particularly for the other ministers in the area. He will strive both personally and in the name of the Church Council, to ensure that the worship, preaching and teaching of the Church are pure, that its evangelism is zealous and effective, and that discipline is administered with a view to the welfare of both the whole body and the member who becomes subject to it Bishops will be elected by the Church Council concerned subject to the approval of the Assembly. The Bishops shall be chosen form among the ordained ministers.

6. The ordained ministers of all the uniting Churches shall be accepted as fully ordained ministers of the CNEI.
7. Future ordination of ministers shall be evolved as the Churches grow together. So also will be the form of ordination.
8. The selection for training of Ministers shall be done by the Association or Presbytery and approved by the Church Council.
9. The appointment of the Ministers shall be done by the Church Council.

VI. The Polity of the Church

1. The CNEI affirms that the Lord Jesus Christ is the only Lord and Head of the Church.
2. The CNEI accepts the Episcopal presbyteral and congregational elements in the Church order as the means through which the lordship of Christ in His Church may be realized.

VII. The Organization of the Church

1. The Organization of the Church of North-East India will consist of the Local Church, the Association or Presbytery, the Church Council or Synod or Diocese, and the Assembly.
2. *The Local Church*
   The Local Church is a congregation of believers organized for regular public worship and also for mutual aid and fellowship, and for witness and service to those outside its life. A local church may have its own Pastor, and therefore itself be a pastorate, or may be grouped with other local churches in a pastorate. Some local churches may also be grouped together in an intermediary unit next below the Presbytery or Association with as sub-district and the like.
3. *The Association or Presbytery*
   A number of local churches or pastorates within a suitable and convenient area will form an Association or Presbytery which shall be responsible for the spiritual welfare of the Churches and the supervision of their workers within its area. If considered desirable the Association or Presbytery may organize the local Churches into smaller units such as Sub districts etc.
4. *Church Council or Synod or Diocese*
   A number of Associations or Presbyteries within a larger geographical area will form a Church Council or Synod or Diocese and will also constitute the area of responsibility of the Bishop. The Bishop will preside over the Church Council or Synod, but will not have power to suspend any of its decisions.

5. *The Assembly*

All the Church Councils of the Church will together form the Assembly\, which will under God be the supreme governing body of the Church. It will have such authority as is necessary to enable it to maintain the life of the Church in loyalty to its Constitution, and to care for institutions or other expressions of the life of the Church which of necessity require an authority wider than that of a Church Council.

VIII. Forms of Worship

1. Forms of worship which before union were generally accepted and used in any of the uniting Churches shall be permitted in the CNEI. No forms of worship or ritual to which any congregation conscientiously objects shall be imposed on any congregation in the Church.
2. The CNEI will, however, gradually seek to adopt and develop more uniform forms of service adapted to the needs and experience of the region. it is expected that in due time, the Church will have a common Service Book, which will express the unity and breadth of its faith and life, and which will result naturally from fellowship in the united church. This will include a variety of forms, liturgical and non-liturgical, to meet the needs of various congregations, and to preserve the distinctive values in the various traditions of worship.

IX. Properties and Assets

The Properties and Assets of the uniting Churches will continue to remain with their Trust Association until with common consent, certain properties and assets may be transferred to the Trust of the CNEI when it is formed.

X. Interim Arrangements

Existing Church Organizations

As the basis of this union is that the existing Churches will join together in a democratic structure and as no immediate changes are proposed at the level of local congregations or Associations and Presbyteries, the existing Church organizations and their Constitutions, if any, will be retained during the interim period and will not be altered except with common consent or through voluntary adaptations of the units. It is however realized that though certain groups may more or less retain their traditional character during the period of transition, there will be certain limitations of their functions and powers in accordance with the provinces of this Constitution.[1]

[1] *The Plan of Church Union and Draft Constitution of the Church of North East India.* Edited by the Convenor, Church Union Committee. Shillong: NEICC, 1970.

APPENDIX-2

Second (Revised) Draft Constitution of the Church of the North East India

I. The Church and its Membership

We acknowledge that the Church is the Body of Christ in which members are knit together in the fellowship of the Holy Spirit. We agree that those are communicant members according to the will and purpose of God who are born again by the grace of God though faith, and who have been baptized with water into the name of the Father and of the Son and of the Holy Spirit. We agree that members of the Church maintain their vital union with the Head of the Body through the various means of grace which He has provided in His Church, and glorify His name by such good works as He has prepared for them to walk in.

The Church is the People of God, the Community of the Holy Spirit, the Body of Christ through which He continues His reconciling work in the world;

The Church is one because it is one family under one Father, whose purpose is to unite all men in Jesus Christ our Lord;

The Church is holy because it is set apart by God for Himself through the Holy Spirit to be His people in the world;

The Church is Catholic (universal) because it is for all people and for all times holding the Christian faith in its fullness;

The Church is apostolic because it is sent to preach the Gospel in the world and to proclaim the Lordship of Christ over the world, receiving its divine authority and teaching from Jesus Christ.

II. The Faith of the Church

We are united in our faith in Jesus Christ, the Redeemer of the world, in whom alone is salvation by grace through faith, and in accordance with the revelation of God which He made being Himself God incarnate, we worship one God Father, Son and Holy.

We accept the Holy Scriptures of the Old and New Testament as the Word of God, as containing all things necessary, to salvation, and as the supreme and decisive standard of faith. We acknowledge that the Church must always be ready to correct and reform itself in accordance with the teaching of those Scriptures under the guidance of the Holy Spirit.

We accept the creed commonly called the Apostles' Creed as witnessing to and safeguarding that faith which is continuously confirmed by the Holy Spirit in the experience of the Church.

The Apostle Creed

I believe in God the Father Almighty, maker of heaven and earth:

And in Jesus Christ His only son our lord, who was conceived by the Holy Ghost, born of the Virgin Mary, Suffered under Pontius Pilate, was crucified, dead and buried, He descended into hell; the third day He rose again from the dead, he ascended into heaven and sitteth in the right hand of God the Father Almighty; from thence he shall come to judge the quick and the dead.

I believe in the Holy Ghost; the holy Catholic Church; The communion of Saints; The forgiveness of sins; The resurrection of the body; and the life everlasting. Amen.

III. The Sacraments of the Church

We believe that the Sacraments of Baptism and Supper of the Lord (Holy Communion) as ordained by Christ, are means of grace through which God works in us and by which we are united to God. We also believes that while the mercy of God to all mankind cannot be limited, there is in the teaching of Christ the plain command that men should follow His appointed way of salvation by a definite act of reception in the family of God (Baptism), and by continued acts of fellowship with Him in that family (Holy Communion), and that this teaching is made explicit in the two Sacraments which He has given us. We agree that the Sacraments should be administered in the united church with the use always of Christ's word of institution and with the appropriate elements.

A. The Sacrament of Baptism

The Sacrament of Baptism is a sign and seal of the Covenant of grace, of union with Christ in His Body, of forgiveness of sins in his Blood, of death to sin and rebirth to eternal life through Him. By this sacrament we are solemnly admitted into the household of faith for the lifelong service of Jesus Christ.

As some of our churches practice Infant Baptism and believe that the practice should be continued and that others practice Believers' Baptism and likewise believe that it should be continued, the Church of North East India shall allow the practice of both forms of Baptism, and shall receive as communicant members all those who have been baptized and who have made a personal and public confession of faith in Christ. The Church shall assure freedom of expression for the particular convictions of different traditions.

There shall be a mutual acceptance of communicant (i.e., full) members of all the uniting churches.

If for deeply-held reasons of conscience any member of the Church of North east India, who has been baptized as an infant, feels convinced of the necessary for believers' baptism he/she shall be free to seek it; and likewise parents, guardians or sponsors who are communicant members of the Church and who feel convinced of the necessary of Infant baptism shall be free to seek it for their children.

All ministers of the Church shall be free to administer either or both forms of Baptism. A minister who, for conscientious reasons, is unable to administer Baptism to infants shall be free to invite some other minister of the Church to perform the rite.

B. The Sacraments of the Lord's Supper (Holy Communion)

The Sacrament of the Lord's Supper (Holy Communion), as a showing forth of the Word of God, is the supreme set of Christian worship and the sign and seal of the covenant of redemption. It is the Thanksgiving or the Eucharist in which the Church members join with the incarnation of God in Christ, His perfect life on earth, His sufferings, death, resurrection, reign and presence. In this liturgy the Church repeating Christ's word and action, shows forth His death until he comes, and pleads His sacrifice proclaims His victory over evil, and in Him shares together in life with God. Partaking in faith we receive Him sacramentally to our nourishment and growth in grace, presenting ourselves in Him a living sacrifice to God. In response to grace, we renew our covenant and communion with Him and also with these gathered in faith at the Lord's Table and with all God's company in heaven and on earth. Christ thus restores the penitent, assures them of God's steadfast love and draws them closer to Himself and to the whole Church.

IV. The Ministry of the Church

A. The Ministry of the Whole Church

We believe that the Church is a royal priesthood through which the risen and ascended Christ continues His High Priestly work. All its members are called, by virtue of their union with Christ, to a priestly ministry; both Godward, in the offering of spiritual sacrifices, gifts and prayers for mankind; and manward, in the showing forth by life and word of the glory of the redeeming power of God. No individual and no one order in the Church can claim exclusive possession of this priesthood.

We recognize that it is the duty and privileges of every member to share in that service of God which is the ministry of the whole Church. This ministry includes both in private and in public, the offering of daily life and work to God, Christian loving service both in the family of the Church and in the community at large and faithful witness to the gospel of Jesus Christ by life and word. This includes both the laity and the clergy, each exercising its own ministry. Within this ministry, it recognizes and welcomes a rich diversity of gifts both in men and women. It will be the prime concern of the Church that all its members should contribute fully to its life of worship, witness and service.

B. The Special Ministry

We believe that within this ministry of the whole Church, Christ has given a special ministry of the Word and the Sacraments. To this ministry some are set apart, receiving authority not simply from the Church but from Christ the Head of the Church. The special ministry is one of the organs of the Body through which Christ the Head acts by the Holy Spirit to build up the Body and to equip its members for their part in the ministry of the whole Church.

We believe that the special ministry is a gift of God to His Church through Christ, who gave to His Apostles a commission which He perpetuates in the Church. It believes that God Himself calls men into the ministry of the Word and the Sacraments; and that He sets apart for the ministry, in answer to the prayers of His Church, those whom He has called and His Church has accepted. He thus bestows on and assures to them a commission which His grace enables to fulfill. We believe that the Church has the right and duty to test the vocation of those who believe themselves to be called by God into the special ministry. We believe that the member of the special ministry have a special responsibility in the proclamation of the Word of God to all men; in the administration of the Sacraments; in the offering of worship to God; in the building up of the Body of Christ; in pastoral care; and in the exercise of Church disciple.

We agree that in the special ministry of the united church there should be the three officers of Elders or Deacons, Pastors or Priests and Bishop.

1. Elders or Deacons

We agree that there shall be recognized in the Church the office of Elder or Deacon. In each congregation men and women shall be elected by the congregation after prayer and careful consideration as persons who are recognized as having the appropriate spiritual gifts (Acts 6:3) for this office and shall be set apart in a solemn public service of the Church. Elders or Deacons shall share with ministers in the spiritual care, nurture and government of the Church, in evangelism and Christian service, in the conduct of public worship and in the preaching of the

Word. Insofar as possible it is expected that Elders or Deacons shall undertake a course of Bible Study and Doctrine as arranged by the Church. As general rule, only Elders or Deacons apart from pastors and bishops will conduct services. All elders or deacon of a congregation will be members of the governing body of the congregation. Elders or Deacons shall be represented in the higher councils or assemblies of the Church in accordance with the Constitution.

2. Pastors

In any particular place or community, the Ministry of the Word and the Sacraments will be exercised by the Pastors. A Pastor will normally be posted by the Association or Presbytery to minister in a particular town, village(s) or district called a "pastorate". As the Church in any place has from Christ a mission to all the people of that place, so the Pastor as a minister of the Word and the sacraments will have a concern for all who live within the pastorate and especially for proclaiming God's Word to the whole community. It will be the duty of the Pastor as the ordained servant of the gospel by which the Church lives to strive to keep the life of the Church and of every member thereof in obedience to the Word and under the grace of God. He will do this interceding for the people committed to his charge, by preaching the Word of God, by administering the Sacraments, by leading the church worshp by teaching and training in the Faith, by pastoral care, guidance, warning and encouragement and assuring the penitent of the reality of God's forgiveness. His relation to his people will be that of servant of Christ and shepherd of the flock.

3. Bishops

The Bishop will be a servant of Christ and for Christ's sake a servant of His flock in a Church Council's area.

The Bishop will be the shepherd under Christ of His flock in a Church Council's area, and their father in God. Under the guidance of the Holy Spirit and in Christ's name he will have a concern for all who live in the Council's area, whether Christians or not; and within the Christian community he will care particularly for the other ministers in the area. He will strive both personally and in the name of the Church Council, to ensure that the worship, preaching and teaching of the Church are pure, that its evangelism is zealous and effective, and that discipline is administered with a view to the welfare of both the whole body and the member who becomes subject to it Bishops will be elected by the Church Council concerned subject to the approval of the Assembly. The Bishops shall be chosen from among the ordained ministers.

C. Acceptance of Ministries

The ordained ministers of all the uniting Churches shall be accepted as fully ordained ministers of the Church of NEI.

V. The Organization of the Church

The Local Church

The Local Church is a congregation of believers organized for regular public worship and also for mutual aid and fellowship, and for witness and service to those outside its life. A local church may have its own Pastor, and therefore itself be a pastorate, or may be grouped with other local churches in a pastorate.

The Association

A number of local churches within a suitable and convenient area will form an Association, which shall be responsible for the spiritual welfare of the Churches and the supervision of their workers within its area. If considered desirable the Association may organize the local Churches into smaller associations.

Church Council

A number of Associations within a larger geographical area will form a Church Council and will also constitute the area of responsibility of the Bishop. The Bishop will preside over the Church Council, but will not have power to suspend any of its decisions.

The Assembly

All the Church Councils of the Church will together form the Assembly\, which will under God be the supreme governing body of the Church. It will have such authority as is necessary to enable it to maintain the life of the Church in loyalty to its Constitution, and to care for institutions or other expressions of the life of the Church which of necessity require an authority wider than that of a Church Council.

APPENDIX-3

North East India Christian Council Affiliated Constituent Units

I. AFFILIATED UNITS

1. Assam Baptist Convention
2. Baptist Church of Mizoram
3. Biateram Presbyterian Church Synod
4. Bodo Evangelical Lutheran Church
5. Cachar Hill Tribe Synod
6. Christ National Church
7. Church of God (Meghalaya & Assam)
8. Church of God (Ecclesia)
9. Church of North India (Diocese of NEI)
10. Council of Baptist Churches in NEI
11. Eastern Evangelical Lutheran Church
12. Evangelical Church of Maraland
13. Evangelical Assembly Church
14. Evangelical Baptist Church
15. Evangelical Baptist Convention
16. Evangelical Baptist Church Manipur
17. Evangelical Free Church of India
18. Garo Baptist Convention
19. Gossner Evangelical Lutheran Church
20. Isua Krista Kohhran, Lairam

21. Karbi Anglong Baptist Convention
22. Khasi-Jaintia Presbyterian Synod
23. Khasi-Jaintia Presbyterian Synod Mihngi
24. Khasi-Jaintia Presbyterian Synod Sepngi
25. Lower Assam Baptist Union
26. Manipur Baptist Convention
27. Manipur Presbyterian Church Synod
28. Mizoram Evangelical Fellowship
29. Mizoram Presbyterian Church Synod
30. Nagaland Baptist Church Council
31. North Bank Baptist Christian Association
32. Northern Evangelical Lutheran Church
33. Ri-Bho Synod
34. The Salvation Army
35. Tripura Baptist Christian Union
36. Zoram Evangelical Fellowship

II. ASSOCIATE MEMBERS

1. Bible Society of India (Shillong Auxiliary)
2. Church's Auxiliary for Social Action
3. Meetei Christian Organization
4. N.E.I Committee of Relief & Development
5. North East India Christian Endeavour
6. Shillong Christian Youth Organization & Conference
7. Students Christian Movement in NEI
8. World Vision of India in NEI
9. Young Men Christian Association[2]

---

[2] North East India Christian Council. Proceedings of the 71st Annual Sessions, Secretary Report of the NEICC, Shillong, at Annual Conference Mokokchng, Nagaland, 14-18 May 2008.

Bibliography

Minutes/Documents/Reports, etc.

Assam Christian Council. Minutes and Proceedings of the Annual Session, 29-31 March, 1940.

Assam Christian Council. Minutes and Proceedings of the 5th Annual Conference, 1942.

Assam Christian Council. Minutes and Proceedings of the 6th Annual Conference, 1943.

Assam Christian Council. Minutes and Proceedings of the 7th Annual Session, January, 1944.

Assam Christian Council. *Minutes and Proceedings of the 8th Annual Conference*, 22-26 August, 1945.

Assam Christian Council. *Minutes and Proceedings of the 9th Annual Conference*, 1946.

Assam Christian Council. *Minutes and Proceedings of the 10th Annual Conference*, 1947.

Assam Christian Council. *Minutes and Proceedings of the 11th Annual Conference*, 1948.

Assam Christian Council. *Minutes and Proceedings of the 12th Annual Conference*, 1949.

Assam Christian Council. *Minutes and Proceedings of the 14th Annual Conference*, 21-26 August, 1951.

Assam Christian Council. *Minutes and Proceedings of the 15th Annual Conference*, 1952.

Assam Christian Council. *Minutes and Proceedings of the 22nd Annual Conference*, 29 April-2 May, 1959.

Assembly of the Presbyterian Church in North East India Golden Jubilee Souvenir 1926-1976. Shillong: Central Ward, 1976.

Council of Baptist Churches in North East India. *Report of the CBCNEI Executive Committee Meeting*, Guwahati, 1988.

Council of Baptist Churches in North East India. *Report of the 57th Annual General Meeting*, Diphu, Assam, April 12-15, 2007.

Council of Baptist Churches in North East India. *Report of the 59th Annual General Meeting*, April 18-20, 2009.

Council of Baptist Churches in North East India. *Report of the 60th Annual General Meeting*, Williamnagar, Meghalaya, April 17, 2010.

Council of Baptist Churches in North East *India. Uniform Practices of Baptist Churches in North East India (CBCNEI).* Published by The Theological Education Committee, CBCNEI, Panbazar, Guwahati, n.d.

Garo Baptist Convention, 52nd CBCNEI Annual Sessions. General Secretary Report 2001-2002, 14-16 February, 2002.

Manipur Baptist Convention, 52nd CBCNEI Annual Sessions. General Secretary Report 2001-2002, 14-16 February, 2002.

Nagaland Baptist Church Council. "A Glimpse of Nagaland Churches." *Nagaland Celebrates Quasqui Centennial.* Kohima, Nagaland: NBCC, 1997.

North East India Christian Council. *The Plan of Church Union and Draft Constitution of the Church of NEI*, Shillong: NEICC, 1970.

North East India Christian Council. *Minutes and Proceedings of the 32nd Annual Meeting*, 19-20 September, 1969.

North East India Christian Council. *Minutes and Proceedings of the Annual Conference*, 6-10 May, 1970.

North East India Christian Council. *Minutes and Proceedings of the 35th Annual Meeting of the Church Union Committee Resolution No. XV: D*, 1972.

North East India Christian Council. *Minutes and Proceedings of the 35th Annual Session*, Cherrapunji, Meghalaya, 10-14 Ma,y 1972.

North East India Christian Council. *Minutes and Proceedings of the 36th Annual Conference*, Kohima, Nagaland, 3-6 May, 1973.

North East India Christian Council. *Minutes and Proceedings of the 38th Annual Conference*, Shillong, 1-4 May, 1975.

North East India Christian Council. *Minutes and Proceedings of the 39th Annual Meeting*, 1976.

North East India Christian Council. *Minutes and Proceedings of the 40th Annual Meeting*, Barapani, 1977.

North East India Christian Council. *Minutes and Proceedings of the Annual Consultation*, Kohima, Nagaland, 6-9 May, 1982.

North East India Christian Council. *Minutes and Proceedings of the Annual Consultation*, Guwahati, 26 April, 1984.

North East India Christian Council. *Minutes and Proceedings of the Annual Consultation*, Laban, Shillong, 9-11 August, 1985.

North East India Christian Council. *Minutes and Proceedings of the 49th Annual Meeting*, Shillong, May, 1986.

North East India Christian Council. *Minutes and Proceedings of the 64th Annual Consultation*, Meghalaya, 20-23 May, 2001.

North East India Christian Council. *Minutes and Proceedings of the 65th Annual Consultation*, Phudmawire Presbyterian Church, Mawlai, 9-12 May, 2002.

North East India Christian Council. *Report and Minutes of the Annual Consultation*, Guwahati, 23-25 January, 2003.

North East India Christian Council. *Report and Minutes of the 66th Annual Consultation*, Aizawl 8-11 May, 2003.

North East India Christian Council. *Reports and Minutes of the 69th Annual Conference*, KJP Synod Mihngi, 11-14 May, 2006.

North East India Christian Council. *Report and Minutes of the 70th Annual Meeting*, Shillong, 9-13 May, 2007.

North East India Christian Council. *Proceedings of the 71st Annual Sessions*, Secretary Report of the NEICC, Mokokchung, Nagaland, 14-18 May, 2008.

Pakyntein E.H. (Convenor), "Reports of the Church Union Committee," *The NEICC Proceedings of 35th Annual Session*, Cherrapunji, Meghalaya, 10-14 May, 1972.

Sesquicentennial Celebration: The 150th Anniversary of the Council of Baptist Churches in North East India. Dimapur, Nagaland, 5-9 February 1986. Guwahati: The Publication Committee CBCNEI Sesquicentennial Celebration, 1986.

Stafford, E. Papers. "*A Brief Report of the Church Union Consultation.*" CBCNEI Office, Guwahati, 1971.

Tennent, J. N. "The Priesthood of Believers." In *Sixth Baptist World Congress: Official Report*. Edited by J. H. Rushbrooke. Atlanta, Ga.: The Baptist World Alliance, 1939.

The Constitution of the Joint Council of the CNI, CSI and MTC. Delhi: ISPCK, 1981.

The Constitution of the Church of North India, (Revised), January, 2006.

Tripura Baptist Christian Union Golden Jubilee Souvenir (1938-1988).

Books

Aier, P. Alongla. *From Darkness to Light*. Kohima, Nagaland: NBCC, 1997.

Aier, Toshi. "Church Union Movement in North East India: A Reflection." In *Perspectives: Current Issues in Theological Thinking*. Edited by Akheto Sume. Aolijen, Mokokchung: Jongshinokdang Trust, CTC, 2002.

Aier, K. I. *The Growth of the Baptist Church in Meghalaya*. Panbazar, Guwahati: CLC, 1978.

Ana, Julio de Santa. "The Ecumenical Movement and the Praxis of Responsibility." In *The Ecumenical Movement at a Crossroad*. Amsterdam: WCC, 2008.

Anton, Hope S. *Living in Oikoumene*. Hongkong: CCA, 2003.

Anderson, Fred, ed. *Baptist Distinctives: A Sourcebook of Basic Baptist Beliefs as Defined by Virginia Baptists of the Past*. Virginia: Baptist Historical Society, 1995.

Aldwinckle, Russel F. *Of Water and the Spirit: A Baptist View of Church Membership*. Canada: The Baptist Federation of Canada, 1964.

Ao, A. Bendangyapang. *History of Christianity in Nagaland: Social Change 1872-1972*. Bangalore: Shalom Ministry Publication, 2004.

Ariarajah, S. Wesly. "The Ecumenical Movement in Asia in the Context of Asian Socio-Political Realities." In *Christian Theology in Asia*. Edited by Sebastian C. H. Kim. UK: Cambridge University Press, 2008.

Barooah, Nerode K. *David Scott in North East India 1802-1831: A Study of British Paternalism*. New Delhi: Munshiram Manoharlal, 1970.

Barpujari, H. K. *Assamese in the Days of the Company 1826-1858*. Guwahati: Lawyers Book Stall, 1963.

__________. *Problems of the Hill Tribes North East Frontier 1822-1844*. Guwahati: Lawyers Book Stall, 1970.

__________. *The American Missionaries and North East India: 1836-1900 AD*. Guwahati: Spectrum Publication, 1986.

Bate, H. N., ed. *Faith and Order: Proceedings of the World Conference Lausanne*. London: Student Christian Movement, 1927.

Becker, C. *History of the Catholic Missions in North East India: 1890-1915*. Shillong: Firma KLM Pvt. Ltd., 1980.

Bhuyan, S. K. *Early British Relation with Assam*. Shillong: Department of Historical and Antiquarian Studies in Assam, 1948.

Birmele, Andre, ed. *Local Ecumenism: How Church Unity is Seen and Practiced by Congregations*. Geneva: WCC, 1984.

Champion, L. G. *Baptist and Unity*. London: A. R. Mowbray & Co. Limited, 1962.

Chakravorty, B. C. *British Relation with the Hills Tribes of Assam Since 1858*. Calcutta: Firma KLM Pvt. Ltd., 1981.

Clark, M. M. *A Corner in India.* Philadelphia: American Baptist Publication Society, 1907.

Downs, Frederick S. *Church Union: Theological and Non-Theological Factors.* Shillong: The Church Union Committee of the NEICC, 1965.

__________. *A Reply to: A Picture of An Organic Church Union.* Panbazar, Guwahati: CLC, 1970.

__________. *The Mighty Works of God.* Panbazar, Guwahati: CLC, 1971.

__________. *Manual of Worship.* Guwahati: CLC, 1975.

__________. *The Wondrous Works of God.* Shillong: Mrs. M.B. Jyrwa, 1980.

__________. *Christianity in North East India: Historical Perspectives.* Delhi: ISPCK, 1983.

__________. *Christianity in NEI.* Delhi: ISPCK, 1983.

__________. *History of Christianity in India: North East India in the Nineteenth and Twentieth Centuries, Vol. V, part 5.* Bangalore: CHAI, 1992.

__________. "Tribal Ecumenism in North East India: The Christian Role in Solidarity Movements." In *Good News For North East India: A theological Reader.* Edited by Renthy Keitzar. Panbazar, Guwahati: CLC, 1995.

__________. "Vision for Tribal Churches in North East India: Historical Perspective." In *Encounter Between Gospel and Tribal Culture.* Edited by A. Wati Longchar. Jorhat, Assam: Tribal Study Centre, ETC, 1999.

__________. *Essay on Christianity in North East India.* Edited by Milton S. Sangma and David R. Syiemlieh. Delhi: Indus Publishing Company, 1994.

Dutta, S. C. *The North East and the Mughals* (1661-1714). Delhi: D.K. Publication, 1984.

Eastwood, Cyril. *The Priesthood of All Believers: An Examination of the Doctrine from the Reformation to the Present* Day. London: The Epworth Press, 1960.

Firth, Cyril Bruce. *An Introduction to India Church History.* Madras: The Christian Literature Society, 1961, reprinted 1992.

Forrester, Duncan B. *Truthful Action: Exploration in Practical Theology.* Edinburgh: T &T, 2000.

Gait, E. *A History of Assam.* Calcutta: Thacker Spink and Co. Ltd., 1905.

Garrett, James Leo. *Baptist Church Discipline.* Nashville: Broadman Press, 1962.

George, K. M. *Church Of South India Negotiation Towards Union 1919-1947.* Kerala: K. M. George, 1997.

__________. *Church of South India Life in Union* 1947-1997. Delhi: ISPCK, 1999.

Gibbs, M. E. *The Anglican Church in India 1600-1970.* Delhi: ISPCK, 1972.

Goswami, B. B. "The Tribes of Assam: A Few Comments on their Social and Cultural Ties with the Non-Tribes." In *Tribal Situations in India.* Edited by S. K. Singh. Simla: Indian Institute of Advance Study, 1972.

Gregories, Paulos Mar. *On Ecumenism.* Edited by Jacob Kurian. Delhi: ISPCK & MGF Kottyam, 2006.

Handy, Robert T. "Baptist." In *A Handbook of Christian Theology.* Cleveland, Ohio: World Publishing Co., 1958.

Henningsen, Bit. *The Church's Contribution for Unity and Welfare in Nagaland.* Kohima: Council of Naga Baptist Churches, 2007.

Hiscox, Edward T. *The Standard Manual for Baptist Churches.* Philadelphia: American Baptist Publication Society, 1903.

__________ . *The New Directory for Baptist Churches.* Valley Forge: Judson Press, 1947.

__________ . *The Baptist Church Directory: A Guide to the Doctrine and Practices of Baptist Churches.* Nashville, Tenn: National Baptist Publishing Board, 1890, revised 1969.

__________ . *Principle and Practice for Baptist Churches.* Grand Rapids, Michigan: Kregel Publication, 1970.

Hminga, Chhangte Lal. *The Life and Witness of the Church in Mizoram.* Mizoram: Literature Committee Baptist Church Mizoram, 1982.

Hobbs, Herschel H. *What Baptists Believe.* Nashville, Tenn: Boardman Press, 1964.

__________. *The People Called Baptists and The Baptist Faith and* Message. Shawnee, Okla.: Oklahoma Baptist University, 1981.

Hooft, W. A. Visser 't., ed. *The First Assembly of the World Council of Churches.* Vol., V. New York: Harber & Brothers, 1949.

__________., "The Word 'Ecumenical'-Its History and Use." In *A History of the Ecumenical Movement, 1517-1948.* Edited by Ruth Rouse and Stephen C. Neill. Philadelphia: Westminster, 1954.

__________. *Has the Ecumenical Movement a Future?* Belfast: Christian Journals Limited, 1974.

Hudson, Winthrop Still and Norman Hill Maring. *A Baptist Manual of Polity and Practice.* Revised. Valley Forge: Judson Press, 1991.

Hudson, Winthrop. ed. *Baptist Concepts of the Church.* Chicago: Judson, 1959.

Imchen, Panger. *Ancient Ao Naga Religion and Culture.* New Delhi: Har-Anan Pub. 1993.

Jones, E. Stanley. *The Reconstruction of the Church-On What Pattern?* (Nashville: Abingdon Press, 1970

Jyrwa, J. Fortis. "Church Union Movement in North East India; A Historical Perspective." In *Church Ministry and Mission: Eassy in Honour of K.I. Aier*. Edited by Renthy Keitzar .Guwahati: CBCNEI, 1988.

__________ . "Church Union Movement in North East India." In *Good News For North East India*. Edited by Renthy Keitzar. Guwahati: CLC, 1995.

Keshishian, Aram. *Conciliar Fellowship: A Common Goal.* Geneva: WCC Publication, 1992.

Kinnamon, Michael. *Truth and Community: Diversity and its Limits in the Ecumenical Movement,* Geneva, WCC, 1988.

Keitzar, Renthy. *Triumph of Faith in Nagaland*. Kohima, Nagaland: Nagaland Baptist Church Council, 1987.

___________. *Church Ministry and Mission: Essay in Honor of K. I. Aier*. Panbazar, Guwahati: CBCNEI, 1988.

___________. "A Study of the North-East India Tribal Christian Theology." In *Good News for North East India: A Theological Reader*. Edited by Renthy Keitzar. Pananzar, Guwahati: CLC, 1995.

___________. *Good News for North East India: A Theological Reader*. Guwahati: CLC, 1995

___________. *In Search of a Relevant Gospel Message*. Guwahati: Christian Literature Centre, 1995.

___________. "Baptist Tamang aser Arogo Yimten Tashi." In *Ao Baptist Arogo Mundang Nungo*. Impur, Literature Department ABAM, 1997.

Killock, James. *Breakthrough for Church Union in North India and Pakistan*. Madras: CLS, 1965.

Koodapuzha, Xavier, ed. *Communion of Churches*. Vadavathor: Oriental Institute of Religious Studies, 1993.

___________ , *Christianity in India*. Kottayam: Oriental Institute of Religious Studies India, 1998.

Lloyd, J. M. *History of Church in Mizoram*. Mizoram: Synod Publication Board, 1991.

Lotha, J. Thungjamo. *Christian Approach to Politics: A Case Study of Nagaland.* Kohima, Nagaland: NBCC, Youth Dept., 1987.

Likok, T. *A Picture of an Organic Church Union*. Impur: ABAM, 1975.

_________ . *Baptist Arogoi Amangbatem*. Mokokchung: Repala & Children, 2000.

Longkumer, Limatula. "Wider Ecumenism and Ecclesiology." In *Ecumenism in India Today*. Edited by James Massey. Bangalore: BTESSC/SATHRI, 2008, 44-56.

Macquaries, John. *Christian Unity and Christian Diversity*. London: SCM, 1975.

Maring, Norman H. and Winthrop S. Hudson. *A Baptist Manual of Polity and Practice*. Valley Forge: Judson Press, 1963.

Massey, James, ed. *Ecumenism in India Today*. Bangalore: BTESSC/SATHRI, 2008.

Morris, John Hugh. *The History of the Welsh Calvinistic Methodist Foreign Mission to the End of the Year 1904*. Calcutta: KLM Pvt. Ltd., 1910.

Muttumana, Mathew. *Christianity in Assam and Inter-Faith Dialogue: A study on the Modern Religious Movements in North East India*. Indor: Satrakasan Sanchar Kendra, 1984.

Naik, J. P and Syed Nurullah, *A Student's History of Education in India*. S.G. Wasani for Macmillan Company of India, 1974.

Quarish, Ferdaen A. *Christianity in the North East Hills of South Asia*. Dhaka: The University Press, 1987.

Ramuny, M. "Historical and Cultural background of North East India from Ancient Time to the Time of Independence." In *Crisis in North East India*. Edited by Adiss Arnold. Madras: Gurukul Publication, 1981.

Rao, O. M. *Baptist Distinctives*. Panpazar, Guwahati: CLC, 1980.

___________. *Christian Unity; Guideline Study Material*. Panbazar, Guwahati: CBCNEI, 1985.

___________. *Focus on North East Indian Christianity*. Delhi: ISPCK, 1994.

Rouse, Ruth and Stephen C. Neill. *A History of the Ecumenical Movement, 1517-1948*. Philadelphia: Westminster, 1954.

Rouse, Ruth, ed. *A History of the Ecumenical Movement 1517-1948*. London: SPCK, 1954.

Routley, Erik. *Congregationalists and Unity*. London: A. R. Mowbray & Co. Limited, 1961.

Saarinen, Risto and Michal Root, ed. *Baptism and the Unity of the Church*. Grand Rapids, Michigan: William B. Eerdmans Publishing Company, 1998.

Sangma, Milton S. and David R. Syiemlieh. *Essays on Christianity in North East India*. New Delhi: Indus Publishing House, 1994.

Sangma, Milton S. "Garo Traditional Beliefs and Christianity." In *The Tribal Situation in India*. Edited by K. S. Singh. Simla: Indian Institute of Advance Study, 1972.

___________. *History of American Baptist Mission North East India (1836-1950)*. Vol. I. New Delhi: Mittal Publications, 1987.

___________. A *History of American Baptist Mission North East India*. Vol. II. New Delhi: Mittal Publications, 1992.

___________ . ed. *Essays on Christianity in North East India: Presented in Memory of Professor V. Venkara Rao*. New Delhi: Indus Publishing House, 1994.

Sahu, Dhirendra Kumar. *United and Uniting: A Story of the Church of North India.* Delhi: ISPCK, 2001.

Sarun, H. K. *Insurgency in North East India: A Study of the Sino-American Role.* New Delhi: Sterling Pub. Pvt. Ltd., 1980.

Shurden, Walter B. *Associationalism Among Baptists in America: 1707*-1807. New York: Arno Press, 1980.

___________. *The Doctrine of the Priesthood of Believers.* Nashville: Convention Press, 1987.

___________. ed. *Proclaiming the Baptist Vision: The Church.* Macon: Smyth and Helwys, 1996.

Snaitang, O. L. *Christianity and Social Change in North East India.* Shillong: Vendrame Institute, 1993.

___________. *A History of Ecumenical Movement: An Introduction.* Bangalore: BTESSC/SATHRI, 2010.

Sundkler, Bengt. *Church of South India: The Movement Towards Union, 1900-1947,* London, Lutterworth, 1954.

Taylor, S. B. *Annual Report of the Chaplaincy of Guwahati, Shillong and Dhupri for the year 1881.* Shillong: The Assam Secretariat Press, 1882.

Thanzauva, K. "Tribal Theological Trends in North East India." In *Good News for North East India: A Theological Reader.* Edited by Renthy Keitzar. Panbazar, Guwahati: CLC, 1995.

___________. *Theology of Community: Tribal Theology in the Making.* Aizawl: Mizo Theological Conference, 1997.

Talibuddin, Ernest W. *The Anglican Church in North-East India (1845-1970): A Missiological Reflection.* Delhi: ISPCK, 2002.

Taylor, James B. *Restricted Communion: or, Baptism an Essential Prerequisite to the Lord's Supper.* Charleston, South Carolina: Southern Baptist Publication Society, 1856.

Thomas, V.V. *Conciliar Ecumenism: The Beginning of the Former CSI-CNI-MTC Joint Council.* Bangalore: BTESS/SATHRI, 2008.

Thong, Joseph S. *Glimpses of Naga Legacy and Culture.* Edited by Phanenmo Kath. Kottayam: Spciety for Naga Students Welfare, Kerala, 1997.

Toshi, N. *Mission to the Nagas.* Impur: Radha Offset Printers, 1995.

Pathil, Kuncheria. *Models in Ecumenical Dialogue.* Bangalore: Dharmaram Publication, 1981.

Paul, Amar Khrishna. *Northeast A-Z General Knowledge.* Panbazar, Guwhati: Good Books Distributors Pub., 2003.

_________. *Ecumenism: Unity and Diversity.* Bangalore: Dharmaram Publication, 2006.

Puthenpurakal, Joseph. *Baptist Mission in Nagaland: A Study in Historical and Ecumenical Perspective*. Calcutta: Firma KLM Private Limited, 1984.

___________. *Impact of Christianity on North East India*. Shillong: Vendrame Institute Publications, 1996.

Puthenpurakal, Joseph. "The Rising Sun: Christianity's Contribution to India's North Eastern Region." In *Indian Christian Directory: For the New Millennium*. Edited by Jose Panthaplamthottiyil. Kottayam, Kerala: Rashtra Deepika Ltd, 2000.

Watson, E. C. *The Baptist* Association. Nashville: Convention Press, 1975.

Whitsitt, William H. *History of Communion Among the Baptists.* New York: J. K. Lees, 1880.

Dictionary and Encyclopedia

Chandran, J. Russell. "Church of South India." *A Dictionary of Asian Christianity*. Edited by Scott W. Sunquist. Grand Rapids, Michigan: William B Eerdmans Publishing Company, 2001, 175-176.

"Conciliarism." *The New Encyclopedia Britannica*. Vol. 3. Edited by Philip W. Goetz. Chicago: Encyclopedia Britannica, Inc., 1815, 515-516.

"Ecumenism." *The New Encyclopedia Britannica*. Vol. 4. Edited by Philip W. Goetz. Chicago: Encyclopedia Britannica, Inc., 1815, 362.

Ladous, Regis. "Spiritual Ecumenism." *Dictionary of the Ecumenical Movement.* Edited by Nicholas Lossky et al. Geneva: WCC Publication, 1991, 948.

Lanne, Emmanuel "Concilirity." *Dictionary of the Ecumenical Movement.* Edited by Nicholas Lossky et al. Geneva: WCC Publication, 1991, 212.

Marty, Martin E. "Ecumenical Movement." *The Encyclopedia Americana International Edition*. Vol. 9. Edited by Grolier. New York: Americana Cooperation, 1996, 623.

McNaspy, C. J. "Coiciliar Theory." *The Encyclopedia Americana International Edition*. Vol . 7. Edited by Grolier. New York: Americana Cooperation, 1996. 504.

Menachery, George. *The St. Thomas Christian Encyclopedia of India*. Vol. 1. Trichur: The St. Thomas Christian Encyclopedia of India, 1982.

Santram, Pritam B. "Church of North India." *A Dictionary of Asian Christianity*. Edited by Scott W. Sunquist. Grand Rapids, Michigan: William B Eerdmans Publishing Company, 2001, 173-175.

Wainwright, Geoffrey. "Federalism." *Dictionary of the Ecumenical Movement.* Edited by Nicholas Lossky et al. Geneva: WCC Publication, 1991, 418.

Journals/Unpublished Papers/Articles, etc.

Apostola, Nicholas K. "How Much Unity? How Much Diversity?" *Greek Orthodox Theological Review*. 50/1-4 (Spring-Winter, 2005): 119-140.

Ariarajah, S. Wesley. "Wider Ecumenism: A Threat or a Promise?" *Ecumenical Review*. 50/3 (July, 1998): 321-329.

Assembly of the Presbyterian Church in North East India. *Golden Jubilee Souvenir 1926-1976* (Central Ward, Shillong: APC, 1976): 1.

Baker, Nathan L. "Baptist Polity and Para-church Organizations." *Baptist History and Heritage*. 14/3 (July, 1979): 62-70.

Barot, Madeleine. "1946: It's Significance for the WCC." *Ecumenical Review*. 39/2 (April, 1987): 216-221.

Behera, A. "Theological Education and Church Union in North East India." *Presbyterian Review*. VIII/32 (Oct-Dec., 2002): 54-67.

Bennett, F. Russell. "The Association in Baptist history." *Baptist History and Heritage*. 17/2 (April, 1982): 1-48.

Broach, Claude U. "Introducing Southern Baptists." *Greek Orthodox Theological Review*. 22/4 (Winter, 1977): 367-375.

Callam, Neville. "Baptists and Church Unity." *Ecumenical Review*. 61/3 (July, 2009): 304-314.

Carpe, William D. "Unity of the Church: Another Model." *Lexington Theological Quarterly*. 11/2 (April, 1976): 49-56.

Chafin, Kenneth. "Communicating Baptist Doctrine in the Local Church." *Baptist History and Heritage*. 13/4 (October, 1978): 8-10.

Chandran, J. R. "Plurality of Religious Faith and Living Community." *National Christian Council Review*. CV1/5 (May, 1986): 284-293.

Clark, Elmer T. "Non-Theological Factors in Religious Diversity." *The Ecumenical Review*. III/2 (January, 1951): 347-356.

"Conciliarity and the Future of the Ecumenical Movement, Commission on Faith and Order, Fouvain 1971." *The Ecumenical Reviews*. 24/1 (January, 1972): 88-91.

Copeland, Edwin Luther. "Ecumenical Movement: Will Southern Baptist ever get with it?" *Perspectives in Religious Studies*. 2/1 (September, 1975): 15-18.

____________. "Ecumenical Movement: will Southern Baptists ever get with it?" *Religious Studies*, 2/1 (Spring, 1975): 15-19.

Conner, Walter Thomas, "Conner, Walter Thomas (1877-1952): The Essentials of Christian Union," *Southwestern Journal of Theology*. 51/1 (Fall, 2008): 24-30.

Crabtree, Arthur B. "Eucharist in Baptist Life and Thought." *Journal of Ecumenical Studies*. 13/2 (Spring, 1976): 296-303.

Crow, Paul A. "Ecumenics as Reflections on Models of Christian Unity." *Ecumenical Review*. 39/4 (October, 1987): 389-403.

Crowe, Frederick E. "Development of Doctrine and the Ecumenical Problem." *Theological Studies*. 23/1 (March, 1962): 27-46.

Day, Peter. "Alternative Model of Church Unity." *Anglican Theological Review*. 2 (Summer, 1973): 42-61.

Dehoney, Wayne. "Southern Baptists and Ecumenism: Options for the Future." *Review & Expositor*. 66/3 (Summer, 1969): 313-320.

Dougherty, Kevin D. and et al., "Religious Diversity in a Conservation Baptist Congregation." *Review of Religious Research*. 50/3 (March, 2009): 321-334.

Downs, F. S. "Early Christian Contacts with North East India." *Indian Church History Review*. V/1 (June, 1971): 69-77.

__________ . "Christianity in Garo Hills." *Indian Church History Review*. 1 (June, 1972): 82.

__________ . "Tribal Ecumenism in North East India: The Christian Role in Solidarity Movements." *Indian Church History Review*. XXIII/1 (June, 1989): 23-38.

Dozo, P. "Hindrance to Church Growth." Manuscript, A Paper Presented at the Church Union Consultation, Shillong, 1985.

Druin, Toby. "The Baptist Standard, Texas Baptists, and Southern Baptists." *Baptist History and Heritage*. 33/3 (August, 1998): 61-70.

Estep, William Roscoe. "The Nature and use of Biblical Authority in Baptist Confessions of Faith, 1610-1963." *Baptist History and Heritage*. 22/4 (October, 1987): 3-16.

Ferguson, Thomas. "That They All May Be One: The Call to Unity Today." *Anglican Theological Review*. 88/3 (Summer, 2006): 457-460.

Florovsky, Georges. "The Doctrine of the Church and the Ecumenical Problem." *Ecumenical Review*. 2/2 (Winter, 1950): 152-161.

Garrett, James Leo. "The Priesthood of All Believers." *Baptist and Reflector* (January 9, 1964): 9.

____________. "Sources of Authority in Baptist Thought." *Baptist History and Heritage*. 13/3 (July, 1978): 41-49.

____________. "Biblical Authority According to Baptist Confessions Of Faith." *Review & Expositor*. 76/1 (Winter, 1979): 43-54.

Gelder, Craig Van. "Defining the Issues Related to Power and Authority in Religious Leadership." *Journal of Religious Leadership*. 6/2 (Fall, 2007): 1-14.

Geevarghese, Coorilos. "Towards and Beyond Edinburgh 2010: A Historical Survey of Ecumenical Missiological Developments since 1910." *International Review of Mission*. 99/1 (April 2010): 6-20.

Gnanadason, Aruna. "New Trends in Ecumenism: Challenges and Possibilities." *Svensk missionstidskrift*. 92/1 (2004): 7-20.

Gros, Jeffrey. "Baptism Today: Understanding, Practice, Ecumenical Implications." *Worship*. 83/3 (May, 2009): 264-266.

Gurney, A. K. "History of the Sibsagor Field." *The Assam Mission of the ABMU* (December 1886): 22-23.

Hadsell, Heidi. "Mission and Ecumenism in the Twenty-first Century." *Theology and Mission*. 28/5 (October, 2001): 473-480.

Handy, Robert T. "American Baptist Polity: What's Happening and Why?" *Baptist History and Heritage*. 12/3 (July, 1976): 176-179.

_____________. "The Baptist Family: A Heritage of Faith." *Review & Expositor*. 84/4 (Fall 1987): 589-598.

Harangkuma, Fanai. "Why are there Many Christian Groups in Mizoram." *Indian Missological Review* (September, 1991): 20-24.

Harmon, Steven R. "Scripture in the Life of the Baptist Churches: Opening for a Differentiated Catholic-Baptist Consensus on Sacred Scripture." *Pro Ecclesia*. 18/2 (Spr., 2009): 187-215.

___________. "Baptist Confessions of Faith and the Patristic Tradition." *Perspectives in Religious Studies*. 29/4 (Winter 2002): 349-358.

Hendricks, William L. "Baptism: a Baptist Perspective." *Southwestern Journal of Theology*. 31/2 (Spr., 1989): 22-33.

Hinson, E. Glenn. "The Baptist World Alliance: Its Identity and Ecumenical Involvement." *The Ecumenical Review*. 46/4 (October, 1994): 406-412.

___________. "Hstorical Patterns of Lay Leadership in Ministry in Local Baptist Churches." *Baptist History and Heritage*. 13/1 (January, 1978): 26-34.

____________. " The Baptist orld Alliance: Its Identity and Ecumenical Involvement." *Ecumenical Review*. 46/4 (October, 1994): 406-412.

Hobbs, Herschel H. "Baptist Faith and Message - Anchored but Free." *Baptist History and Heritage*. 13/3 (July, 1978): 33-40.

Horne, Charles M. "A major Ecumenical Problem: Revelation, Traditions and Church." *Journal of the Evangelical Theological Society*. 12/2 (Spring, 1969): 93-106.

Hudson, Winthrop S. and Scott H. Hendrex. "Non-Doctrinal Factors Affecting Baptist and Lutheran Identity." *American Baptist Quarterly*. I/2 (December, 1982): 129-136.

Imsong, Mayang. "A Better Tomorrow: Hope for the North East India Tribals Suffering in Indo-Naga Conflict." *Journal of Tribal Studies*. VII/1 (January – June, 2003): 232-238.

Jenkins, Daniel. "The Ecumenical Movement and Its Non-Theological Factors." *The Ecumenical Review*. III/2 (January, 1951): 339-356.

Jeyaseelan, L. "Conflict Situation in North-East India: The Church's Response," *Vidyajyoti: Journal of Theological Reflection*. 63/6 (June, 1999): 439-141.

"*Ka Pateng Khristan*. III/ 9 (Shillong: September 1939): 131-132.

Kent, Dan Gentry and Bert B. Dominy, eds. "What Baptists Have Believed." South-*Western Journal of Theology*. 31/2 (Spring, 1989): 12.

Keitzar, Renthy. "Tribal Cultural Ethos and Christianity in NEI." *ETC Journal*. 1/1 (1980): 44-47.

___________. "Tribal Cultural Ethos and Christianity in North East India." *ETC Journal*. II (1988): 45-49.

Kraemer, Hendrik. "The Formation of the World Council and Its Significance for the Relations of the Churches to one Another." *Ecumenical Review*. 1/3 (September, 1949): 260-266.

Kreeft, Peter. "Towards Uniting the Chruch: Is Reunion without Compromise Possible?" *Reformed Journal*, 29/1 (January, 1979): 10-14.

Lalhmangaiha. "A Critical Review of Laban Consultation." *Presbyterian Review*. IX/33 (January-March, 2003): 33-38.

_______________. "NEICC Annual Session 2003." *Presbyterian Review*. IX/34 (April – June, 2003): 21-32.

Lea, Thomas D. "The Priesthood of All Christians According to the New Testament." *Southwestern Journal of Theology*. 30/2 (Spring, 1988): 15-21.

Leyden, Stuart G. "An Appeal for Federal Union: An American Model of Church Union with Ecumenical Horizons." *Journal of Ecumenical Studies*. 20/2 (Spring, 1983): 276-280.

Lorenzen, Thorwald. "Baptists and Ecumenicity; With Special Reference to Baptism." *The Ecumenical Review*. 32/3 (July, 1980): 256-271.

_________ . "Baptism and Church Membership: Some Baptist positions and their Ecumenical Implications." *Journal of Ecumenical Studies*. 18/4 (Fall 1981): 561-574.

Lumpkin, William Latane. "Appraisal of Intent in Baptist Affirmation of Biblical Authority." *Perspectives in Religious Studies*. 1/2 (Fall, 1974): 156-169.

_____________. "The Bible in Early Baptist Confessions of Faith." *Baptist History and Heritage*. 19/3 (July, 1984): 33-41.

May, Lynn E. "Baptist Deacons: A Story of Service." *Baptist History and Heritage*. 25/2 (April, 1990): 3-30.

___________. Role of Associations in Baptist History. *Baptist History and Heritage*. 12/2 (April, 1977): 69-74.

Mayer, Annemarie C. "Language Serving Unity? Linguistic-Hermeneutical Considerations of a Basic Ecumenical Problem." *Pro Ecclesia.* 15/2 (Spring, 2006): 205-222.

McClellan, Albert. "Southern Baptist Roots in Practice and Polity." *Review and Expositor.* LXXV/292 (Spring, 1978): 34-39.

McClendon, James W. "The Concept of Authority: A Baptist View." *Perspectives in Religious Studies.* 16/2 (Summer, 1989): 101-107.

McKibbens, Thomas R. "Our Baptist Heritage in Worship." *Review and Expositor.* 13/1 (January, 1978): 26-34.

Menezes, Rui de. "Insurgency in Northeast: A Christian Response." *Journal of Tribal Studies.* VII/1 (January-June, 2003): 190-202.

Meyer, Harding. "The Ecumenical Dialogues: Situation-Problems-Perspectives." *Pro Ecclesia.* 3/1 (Winter, 1994): 24-35.

Moore, P. H. "History of the Nowgong Field." *The Assam Mission of the ABMU.* (December, 1886): 31.

Morris, C. Eugene. "Unity of Expression, Unity of Purpose." *Catholic Answer,* 25/4 (September/October, 2011): 20-22.

Muana, K. Lung. "North East India and Ecumenical Trends." *Presbyterian Review.* IX/34 (April-June, 2003): 24.

Nagaland Post, 14 November, 1997.

Nanda, Meere. "Postmodernism, Hindu Nationalism and Vedic Science." *Frontline.* 20/26 (December 20, 2003-January 2, 2004): 78-79.

"National Council of Churches events marks 100 years of Ecumenism." *Christian Century.* 127/25 (December, 2010): 17.

Niles, D. T. "Our Search for Unity." *The Ecumenical Review.* III/2 (January, 1951): 357-361.

Nelson, Stanley A. "Reflecting on Baptist Origins: The London Confession of Faith of 1644." *Baptist History and Heritage.* 29/2 (April, 1994): 33-46.

Nelson, John R. "Tradition and Traditions as an Ecumenical Problem. *Theology Today.* 13/2 (July, 1956): 151-165.

Nissiotis, Nikos A. "Towards a New Ecumenical Era." *Ecumenical Review.* 37/3 (July, 1985): 326-335.

Norgren, William A. "Theological Dialogue: A Place in the Future of Ecumenism. *Greek Orthodox Theological Review.* 26/4 (Winter, 1981): 343-351.

"Notes from the Limuru (1970) Conference." *Mid-Stream: an Ecumenical* Journal. IX/2-3, (Winter-Spring, 1971): 13-33.

Patterson, W. Morgan. "The Influence Of Landmarkism Among Baptists." *Baptist History and Heritage.* 10/1 (January, 1975): 44-55.

Patterson, W. Morgan. "Lord's Supper in Baptist history." *Review & Expositor.* 66/1 (Winter, 1969): 25-34.

Patton, Richard D. "Communicating Baptist History in a Local Church." *Baptist History and* Heritage. 12/3 (July, 1977): 175-179.

___________. "Baptists and Regenerate Church Membership: Historical Perspectives and Present Practice." *Baptist History and Heritage.* 13 (January, 1978): 28-32.

Pettigrew, W. "Manipur." *ABMC of the ABFMS.* 1917, 24.

Phan, Peter C. "The World Missionary Conference, Edinburgh 1910: Twenty-first Century." *International Bulletin of Missionary Research.* 34/2 (April, 2010): 105-108.

Phiri, Isabel Apawo. "Church Unity: Claiming a Common Future: Called to be the One Church the Future of Ecumenism, a Protestant Voice." *Ecumenical Review.* 58/1-2 (January-April, 2006): 121-123.

Pierard, Richard V. "The Baptist World Alliance: An Overview of Its History." *Review & Expositor.* 103/4 (Fall, 2006): 707-732.

Pierce, John D. "Of the Baptist faith." *Baptist History and Heritage.* 44/2 (Spring, 2009): 64-70.

Pitts, William L. "The Priesthood of all Christians in the Baptist Heritage." *Southwestern Journal of Theology.* 30/2 (Spr., 1988): 34-45.

"Pluralism and Unity: The Possibility of a Variety of Typologies Within the Same Ecclesial Allegiance." *One in Christ.* VI/3 (1970): 430-451.

Pool, Jeff B. "Christ, Conscience, Canon, Community: Web of Authority in the Baptist Vision." *Perspectives in Religious Studies.* 24/4 (Winter, 1997): 417-445.

Ram, Augustine Ralla. "Organic Church Unity-A Common from India." *The Ecumenical Review.* VIII/3 (April, 1956): 243-248.

Rimmer, Chad. "Prospects for Ecumenism in the 21st Century: Towards an Ecumenical Theology of the Wilderness." *Ecumenical Review.* 60/3 (July, 2008): 254-270.

Rivenburg, S.W. "Historical Sketch of the Angami Naga Mission." *The Assam Mission of the ABMU* (December, 1886): 84-87.

Rust, Eric C. "Authority of the Scripture, the Word of God and the Bible." *Review & Expositor.* 57/1 (January, 1960): 26-57.

Samartha, S. J. "Commitment and Tolerance in a Pluralist Society." *National Christian Council Review.* CV1/2 (February, 1986): 71-78.

Sangma, Milton S. "Advent of the Pioneer Christian Missions in North East India." *India Church History Review.* XXVIII/1 (June, 1994): 9-15.

Saracco, Norberto. "Church Unity: Claiming a Common Future: New possibilities in the Quest for Visible Unity." *Ecumenical Review*, 58/1-2 (January-April, 2006): 127-129.

Sanyu, Visier. "The Nagas in the 1st half of the 20th Century" in *From Darkness to Light* Kohima: NBCC, 1997.

Sellers, Robert P. "A Baptist View of Missions for Postmodernity." *Review & Expositor*. 100/4 (Fall, 2003): 641-684.

Shurden, Walter B. "Church and Association: A Search for Boundaries." *Baptist History and Heritage*. XIV/40 (July, 1979): 23-27.

____________. "The Baptist Identity and The Baptist Manifesto." *Perspectives in Religious Studies*. 25/4 (Winter, 1998): 321-340.

___________. "Spiritual Authority in Baptist life." *Baptist History and Heritage*. 39/1 (Winter, 2004): 6-7.

___________. "The Authority of a Baptist Association." *Baptist History and Heritage*. 40/1 (Winter, 2005): 6-7.

Shullai, Pynhunlang NM. *Colonalism, Christianity and Mission Activities in India: A Postcolonial Perspective* (IJHSSSI, III/V, March 2017): 324-334.

Sills, Kenneth C M. "Church Unity and the Grass Roots." *Source: Anglican Theological Review*, 31/1 (January, 1949): 1-3.

Singh, Gurbachan. "Church Union." *The United Church Review*. 39/9 (November, 1968): 190-196.

Smith, Ken. "The Local Baptist Congregation and the Laity." *Review & Expositor*. 85/4 (Fall, 1988): 645-658.

Snaitang, O. L. "Ecumenism and Hill People's Culture in North East India." *Journal of Tribal Studies*. l/1 (January-June, 1998): 29-52.

__________ . "Development of the Ecumenical Movement in Northeast India." *India Church History Review*. XXXVII/1 (June, 2003): 41-52.

Stancil, Wilburn T. "Recent Patterns and Contemporary Trends in Deacon Life." *Baptist History and Heritage*. 25/2 (April, 1990): 22-30.

Steely, John E. "The Lord's Supper: Theory and Practice Among Baptists." *Southwestern Journal of Theology*. 28/2 (Spring, 1986): 90-93.

Stephens, William H. "The Priesthood of Believers: Baptist Doctrine Study for 1988." *Southwestern Journal of Theology*. 30/2 (Spring, 1988): 3-7.

Stookey, Stephen M. "Baptist and Landmarkism and the Turn Towards Provinvialism: 1851." *Turning Points in Baptist History* (2008): 178-193.

Straton, Hillyer H. "Where is our Authority: A Baptist View." *Anglican Theological Review*. 37/2 (April, 1955): 131-138.

Sundkler, Bengt. "Daring, in Order to Know: The IMC from Edinburgh to New Delhi." *International Review of Mission*. 51/201 (January, 1962): 4-11.

"The Dawn of Baptist Unity." *Christian Century*. 63/24 (June 12, 1946): 742-743.

"The Federal Idea." *Christian Century*. 82/34 (August 25, 1965): 1028-1029.

Thurian, Max. "The Visible Unity of Christians." *The Ecumenical Review*. XIII/3 (April, 1961): 312-334.

Vanlalchhuanawma. "North East India Church Council Marches Towards Peace." *Presbyterian* Review. VIII/30 (April-June, 2002): 2.

____________ . "An Appraisal of Church Union Movement in Northeast India." *Presbyterian Review*. IX/33 (January – March, 2003): 21-32.

Valentine, Foy. "Baptist Polity and Social Pronouncements. "*Baptist History and Heritage*. 14/3 (July, 1979): 52-61.

Vanelderen, Marlin J. "Common Understanding and Vision: Continuing the Discussion." *Ecumenical Review*. 50/3 (July, 1998): 265-404.

World Council of Churches Commission on Faith and Order. "Non-Theological Factors that May Hinder or Accelerate the Church Unity." *Ecumenical Review*. 4/2 (January, 1952): 174-180.

Young, J. Terry. "Baptists and the Priesthood of Believers." *Perspectives in Religious Studies*. 20/2 (Summer, 1993): 131-146.

Webliography

Athyal, Abraham P. "Towards a New Ecumenical Vision," in www.csichurch.com/article/.. ./*communion _of_churches_in_india.htm,1.* (8 January 2012).

"Baptist Believe in Church Autonomy," in www.baptistdistinctive.org. (6 Nov. 2011).

"Baptist Believe in Church Autonomy," Bill of Inalienable Rights, Art.1of the Union Baptist Association, October 8, 1840. www.baptistdistinctive.org (12 November 2011).

Bucher, Richard P. "The Baptists," *in* www.orlutheran.com/html/baptist.html (10 October 2011).

Downs, F. S. "History of the Council of Baptist Churches in North East India," (Since 1836), unpublishedmaterialshttp://www.cbcnei.com/index.php?option=com_content&view=article&id=49&Itemid=69 (21 September 2011).

Christian, John T (vol.1, 1922; Vol. 2, 1926). *A History of the Baptists*. Broadman Press. http://www.reformedreader.org/history/christian/ahob1/ahobp.htm. (24 November 2011).

Goadby, J. Jackson (1871). "Bye-Paths in Baptist History." In http://www.edintone.com/byepaths.html. (25 October 2011).

Lama, Ajoy K. *CBCNEI,* http://cbcnei.com/news-events.htm*CBCNEI,* http://cbcnei.com/news-events.htm (2 November 2011).

Puniyani, R. R. "*The Hindutva Offensive*," in http://www.dalitstan.org/books/offence/offence 2.html. (22 July 2011).

"*Statement of Faith* adopted in June 14, 2000 by Southern Baptist Church," http://www.bible-researcher. com/ baptistfaith.html#family. (23 May 2011).

"The Baptist Faith and Message Adopted by the Southern Baptist Convention," June 14, 2000; http://www.bible-researcher.com/baptistfaith.html#articles (12 January 2012).

"The Communion of Churches in India," in en.wikipedia.org/wiki/Communion_of_Churches_in_India (4 January 2012).

Traffanstedt, Chris. "A Prime on Baptist History: The True Baptist Trail," http://www. reformedreader.org /history/ pbh.htm (19 January 2012).

Vedder, H. C.. "A Short History of the Baptists." *The Reformed Reader*. http://www.reformedreader.org/history/vedder/ch14.htm. (22 January 2012).

Weber, N. (1907). "Baptists," *The Catholic Encyclopedia*. New York: Robert Appleton Company. Retrieved September 30, 2009 from New Advent: http://www.newadvent.org/cathen/02278a.htm (12 January 2012).

Interviews

Aier, K.I. Former CBCNEI, Secretary, Interview, 8 June 2010.

Aier, Toshi, Lecturer, CTC, Aolijen. Interview, 4 July 2011.

Ao, Luin. Ex-Pastor, Ao Baptist Church Mokokchung Town, Nagaland. Interview, 14 May 2010.

Jamir, Lima. Pastor. Kumlong Baptist Church, Nagaland. Interview, 4 June 2010.

Lanunechet. Church Elder, Mangmetong Baptist Church. Interview, 23 June 2010.

Longchar, Kari. Director, Peace Affairs, NBCC, Kohima, Nagaland. Interview, 3 June 2010.

Merennungsang. Ass. Pastor Youth, Alempang Baptist Church. Interview, 27 June 2011.

Ralte, Vanlalnghaka. Lecturer, Aizawl Theological College, Mizoram. Interview, 6 June 2010.

Sentimenla. Ass. Pastro Youth, NCRC, Kohima. Interview, 23 May 2011.

Toshi, N. Former Mission Secretary, Ao Baptist Church Association, Impur, Nagaland. Interview, 5 May 2010.

Walling, C. Walu, Former Literature Secretary, ABAM, Impur, 13 June 2010.